HUMAN RIGHTS
FACT OR FANCY?

HUMAN RIGHTS
FACT OR FANCY?

HENRY B. VEATCH

Louisiana State University Press
Baton Rouge and London

Designer: Christopher Wilcox
Typeface: Baskerville
Typesetter: Moran Colorgraphic
Printer: Thomson-Shore, Inc.
Binder: John Dekker & Sons, Inc.

Library of Congress Cataloging in Publication Data

Veatch, Henry Babcock.
    Human rights.

    Bibliography: p.
    Includes index.
    1. Civil rights.   2. Law and ethics.   3. Natural law.
I. Title.
K3240.4.V42   1985   340'.112   85-6980
ISBN 0-8071-1238-0

To my dear friend, Rocco Porreco, as well as to all my other friends and former colleagues at Georgetown University, to whom I owe so much, and whom I can never thank enough for their stimulus and their companionship.

CONTENTS

ACKNOWLEDGMENTS

For assistance in writing this book, I must first make acknowledgment to the Libertarians, for without their assistance this book would never have been written. But who are the Libertarians? I am not myself a Libertarian, nor is it easy to say just what or who they are, the notion being hardly a univocal one. But at least Libertarians are agreed in their championship of the rights of individuals and in their determination to find a proper philosophical justification for such rights. And so it was that I found myself the grateful beneficiary of two foundations of a more or less Libertarian persuasion, the Liberty Fund of Indianapolis and its program director, Kenneth Templeton, and the Institute for Humane Studies in Menlo Park, California, and its president, Leonard Liggio. By providing generous summer grants and funding for several conferences on moral and legal philosophy, these foundations provided me not only with much-needed opportunities for study and research, but also for contacts and interchanges, particularly with younger scholars from such diverse fields as law, philosophy, history, and economics.

A few from whom I received much stimulus and help are Richard Epstein, David Forte, John Gray, Gilbert Harman, Loren Lamasky, Eric Mack, Wallace Matson, Fred Miller, Joseph Peden, Roger Pilon, Robert Pugsley, Stanley Rosen, Murray Rothbard, Leon Trakman, and, most particularly, my friends Douglas Den Uyl and Douglas Rasmussen. In addition, many scholars, both Libertarians and others, were kind enough to read earlier drafts of my manuscript and to make invaluable comments and criticisms, particularly with respect to the vexed issues of natural rights and the common good. Besides, I received a wealth of critical suggestion from such philosophically disparate readers as John R. Carter, Lee Friedman, Michael Robins, Jeremy Shearmur, the Reverend James Stromberg, Stuart Warner, and George Winnes.

I am also grateful to the Center for Thomistic Studies at the University of St. Thomas in Houston, Texas. There in the fall of 1982, I was offered an opportunity to present a graduate seminar on the material covered in this book. Not only did I have the benefit of the students' questions and reactions, but also I enjoyed and profited from discussions with colleagues on the faculty at the center—the Reverend Victor Brezick and Professors Joseph Boyle and Patrick Lee.

My faithful typist, Mary S. Dyer, deserves my never-ending thanks for having undergone the tortures of the damned on my account, not just because of my atrocious handwriting, but even more because of my constant expectation that material that I had handed her today would be completed no later than yesterday.

I also wish to acknowledge the authors and publishers who have kindly given me permission to quote from their books and articles. The following deserve particular notice:

Oxford University Press, for permission to quote a passage from *The Works of Aristotle Translated into English*, Vol. II, *Physica*, translated by R. P. Hardie and R. K. Gaye, first edition 1930.

Harvard University Press, for permission to quote a passage from Aristotle's *Nicomachean Ethics*, translated by H. Rackham, Loeb Classical Library, Vol. XIX; and for permission to quote from *From a Logical Point of View*, by Willard Van Orman Quine (Cambridge, Mass., 1953).

The University of Chicago Press, for permission to quote from Leo Strauss, *Natural Right and History* (Chicago, 1953).

Harper & Row, Publishers, Inc., for permission to quote from *Morality: An Introduction to Ethics*, by Bernard Williams, copyright © 1972 by Bernard Williams; and for permission to quote from *The Autonomy of Reason: A Commentary on Kant's "Groundwork of the Metaphysic of Morals"* by Robert Paul Wolff, copyright © 1973 by Robert Paul Wolff.

Times Literary Supplement and John Gray, for permission to quote from Gray's article, "The System of Ruins," *Times Literary Supplement*, December 30, 1983.

Macmillan Publishing Co., Inc., for permission to quote from *Jane Austen*, by Douglas Bush (New York, 1975).

The editors of *The Thomist* for permission to quote from an article by Germain Grisez, entitled "A New Formulation of a Natural-Law Argument against Contraception," XXX, 1966.

The editor of the *American Journal of Jurisprudence*, for permission to quote from an article by Dennis Peter Maio, entitled "*Politeia* and Adjudication in Fourth Century B.C. Athens," XXVIII, 1983.

Rowman and Littlefield, for permission to quote from Fred D. Miller, Jr., "The Natural Right to Private Property," in *The Libertarian Reader*, edited by Tibor R. Machan (Totowa, N.J., 1982), 278.

HUMAN RIGHTS
FACT OR FANCY?

CHAPTER I

THE LAW IN SEARCH OF AN ETHICS

The Inescapability of Ethical Questions in the Law

Surely, it is to be hoped that every American knows that no one may be "deprived of life, liberty, or property without due process of law." But why not? What is wrong with depriving people of life, liberty, or property without due process of law? The obvious answer, of course, is that such conduct is "wrong" because it is forbidden by the Fifth and Fourteenth Amendments to the Constitution, and as such would be contrary to the fundamental law, at least as this law applies within the jurisdiction of the United States. Nor is it to be denied that such an answer is entirely proper and sufficient, at least so long as one remains within the confines and context of a particular legal system, say, that of the United States of America.

Still, we all sense that as an answer to the question as to why a certain mode of action or behavior should be wrong, the mere fact of its being contrary to law leaves something to be desired. True, in this particular instance one might go through the steps that are so carefully outlined by H. L. A. Hart[1] in an effort to determine whether one is dealing with a fully developed system of law in the proper sense. Thus there would first be "the primary rules of law"—in this case the multitude of rules detailing the individual's rights in matters of life, liberty, and property and specifying the penalties for the violation of such rules. And if someone should ask whether such rules are valid rules of law, one could then move to those "secondary rules of law," which one finds within the legal system of the United States—in this case rules that Hart calls "rules of recognition," which specify the criteria for determining whether any of the purported primary rules really are valid rules of

1. H. L. A. Hart, *The Concept of Law* (Oxford, 1961), esp. chap. V.

1

law. And certainly, when it comes to rights of life, liberty, and property within the United States, the rules of recognition are provided for within the Constitution—both the rights to life, liberty, and property themselves and the ways the several primary rules of law implementing these rights must be enacted if they are to be recognized as valid rules. Accordingly, there is no question that rights to life, liberty, and property meet the test of valid law within the legal system of the United States. Additionally, any violation of these rights may be pronounced "wrong" in terms of the prevailing system of positive law in the United States.

Being "wrong" in this purely legal sense, though, is clearly not the only sense of being wrong, for there is also the moral or ethical sense. And although it has often been fashionable for lawyers and even judges to insist that as "men of the law" their concern is only with the law and not with ethics, still as human beings there can be no denying that all of us, lawyers no less than ordinary citizens, find it difficult, if not almost impossible, to avoid having to recognize the propriety and even the overriding importance of questions concerning whether things that are wrong in the sense of being contrary to law may not also be wrong in the sense of being contrary to what Aristotle might have called "a natural justice." And let us suppose that being contrary to natural justice may be taken to mean no more than being contrary to the demands of ethics and morality.

Nor is this necessarily all there is to the business of questions of law giving rise to questions of ethics. For rather than a mere chance association of ideas leading us to ask whether that which is forbidden legally is also forbidden morally, it could also be that the very idea of legal rights and obligations somehow necessarily generates questions about the corresponding moral rights and obligations. Thus if we suppose that all positive laws may be regarded as but so many rules designed to govern human behavior, do we not also find ourselves led to make a further distinction—and one indeed that Hart has suggested[2]— between rules that are designed simply to force us or oblige us to behave in a certain way, and rules that carry with them what can only be called a proper legal obligation to act in a certain way? Indeed, Hart's illustration of this concept—an illustration harking back to John Austin—is the robber's command, "Your money or your life!" But as Hart

2. *Ibid.*, 79–88.

observes, although such a command might be said to lay down a certain rule that you are to follow—yes, even a rule that under the circumstances you may well be *obliged* to follow—that by no means implies that you have any *obligation* to follow that rule, certainly neither a moral nor a legal obligation. Or again, rules governing the behavior of prisoners in a concentration camp, or some Gulag Archipelago, might well be rules that oblige or compel the prisoners to follow a rigorously prescribed regimen, at once grinding and debasing. But however much these prisoners might be obliged to follow that regimen, it is hardly to be supposed that they are under any obligation to do so—not even a legal obligation in any proper sense.

In contrast, as citizens of the United States, with its Constitution and Bill of Rights, there is no doubt that we are held to be not merely obliged but obligated to respect our fellow citizens' rights to life, liberty, and property. But must not the fact of such legal obligation, or obligation under the law, necessarily give rise to the further question of whether such an obligation is just—that is, whether we are under obligation really and in ethics, and not just legally? In other words, to the extent to which our being bound by law, and by a given legal system, involves more than our being merely forced to conform to certain rules, the very fact that we are thus held to be under a legal obligation implies that such a legal obligation itself must reflect and rest upon a genuine moral obligation—so much so, in fact, that if it can be shown that in the given case there is no moral obligation, then the legal obligation is, if not abrogated, at least seriously discredited.

No sooner, though, is it suggested that questions of ethics thus grow out of, and transcend, questions of mere law than we would appear to have made the transition from considerations of so-called positive law to considerations of natural law. But have we? Hardly. For merely to raise the question of the relevance of morals and ethics to law still falls short of the specific issue of the claims of a so-called natural law with respect to mere positive law. After all, efforts to judge positive law from the standpoint of ethics are not confined merely to philosophers of a so-called natural-law persuasion. On the contrary, a Jeremy Bentham, for example, in flailing away at his bête noire, William Blackstone, was certainly concerned with what the laws of England ought to be, as opposed to what they actually were. And yet the last thing that Bentham would have wanted to be accused of being, or could have justly been accused of being, was a natural-law philosopher. Accordingly, let us first examine some of the various ways in which moral philosophers, other than "natural-law" thinkers in the more precise sense, have claimed to be able to assess individual laws, and even entire legal systems, from what might be called an ethical standpoint.

Recalling our original focus upon such legal prohibitions as those against depriving persons of life, liberty, or property, the relevant ethical question here is simply one of, granted that such conduct is forbidden by law, ought it be thus forbidden? Is there anything wrong with taking a person's life or property or depriving him of his liberty, and if so, what is wrong? Moreover, since the ethical question cannot be answered merely by adducing evidence to show that such conduct is forbidden by law, and is perhaps in addition distinctly frowned upon by the mores of a given community, then just how is the ethical question to be answered, and can it even be said to have an answer? At least superficially, it is apparent that if the ethical question is to have any answer, it must be in terms of something in the nature of what we might loosely call "right reason"—that is, we need to be brought to see (by "the mind's eye," or by "the natural right of reason") that there is something truly or really wrong, or something wrong indeed, or perhaps wrong in fact, about, say, someone's being deprived of his liberty without due process of law. And how might it ever be possible thus to show or to demonstrate any such real wrong?

THE APPEAL TO NATURAL RIGHTS IN JUSTIFICATION OF LEGAL RULES

Let us begin by considering a comparatively popular and perennial way that moral philosophers have used to demonstrate the wrongfulness of certain specified invasions or deprivations of a person's liberty. Surely, we are familiar with the device of appealing to a so-called state of nature, as if in such a state of nature a human being's natural right to liberty had somehow been established; and given the existence of such a natural right, then no subsequent social contract, or any other social or political arrangement of mere human invention or convention, could justifiably deprive the individual of his natural right to liberty—at least so it has been argued. Moreover, as everyone knows, this theory became commonplace in the seventeenth and eighteenth centuries, with such thinkers as Thomas Hobbes, John Locke, and Jean-

Jacques Rousseau. And although this particular variety of state-of-nature and natural-rights theory would seem to have fallen somewhat out of fashion in the nineteenth century and throughout the first half of this century, it has recently been revived, one is almost tempted to say with a vengeance, albeit with rather different varieties of vengeance, depending upon whether it be a John Rawls or a Robert Nozick or a Bruce A. Ackerman or whoever may be doing the avenging.[3]

Very well, abstracting from manifold differences of detail between these different state-of-nature thinkers, if we may so designate them, let us see if we cannot fix upon the salient feature that in all of these various state-of-nature arguments is supposed to make it evident to right reason just how and why it is wrong—morally or ethically—to deprive a person of his liberty. As to the root meaning of "liberty" in this connection, I would wonder if Hobbes may not have sensed what is ultimately at stake when he suggested that the liberty of a human being in the state of nature is simply a liberty to do as he pleases, without any let or hindrance from laws or moral prohibitions or social conventions. To use a later term, though one that is not altogether unilluminating in this connection, why not say that in a Hobbesian state of nature individuals could be conceived as enjoying a complete liberty or, perhaps even better, a complete freedom of enterprise—that is, a liberty simply to do their own thing, however and whatever a given individual might conceive his own thing to be? That is, it would be a freedom of enterprise in the sense that the individual would be subject to no possible let or hindrance from any quarter such as that of any actual or even hypothetical political community, or even of any social institutions. There just would not be any laws, be they moral laws or otherwise, that could in any way be imagined to restrict the freedom of an individual to do whatever he liked. True, there would be all sorts of what might be called purely physical limitations on the power of any individual to work his will on whomever or whatever he might choose

3. Eric Mack, in an illuminating and seminal article, "Locke's Arguments for Natural Rights," *Southwestern Journal of Philosophy*, X (Spring, 1980), 51–60, might be interpreted as taking issue with this assessment of the history of state-of-nature and natural-rights theories. Mack contends that it is not the radically amoral state of nature, as Hobbes represents it to be, that underlies Locke's thinking; and partly as a consequence, Locke may not rightly be accused of any uncritical inference from nature to norms, such as I have accused most natural-rights thinkers, both past and present, of having fallen afoul of.

5

to work it on. But moral or legal limitations there would not be, and accordingly in this sense it could be said to be "all right" for an individual in the state of nature to do whatever he liked.

Still, would it be entirely "all right," or unqualifiedly "all right," for the individual in the state of nature literally to do anything and everything he wanted, up to the limit that he was physically able to carry out his wishes? To this question the answer of Hobbes would presumably be in the affirmative.[4] But not so for all state-of-nature theorists, particularly for those who would wish to find in the state of nature ground for so-called "natural rights." Not only that, but these same advocates of doctrines of natural rights might conceivably argue that the very logic of a notion such as its being all right for an individual to do whatever he liked must inevitably lead to certain restrictions and qualifications upon the notion, which would almost seem to be generated from within the notion itself. For if it is "all right" for me to do as I please, without let or hindrance from the side of either law or morals, must not that in itself somehow imply that I therefore "have a right," directly within the state of nature, to enjoy just such a freedom of enterprise as was earlier described? Yes, if no one may gainsay me this liberty or freedom of action within the state of nature, must this not mean that I therefore have a right to such freedom and liberty? But if I thus have a right to liberty, must that not mean that others have a duty or obligation to respect my natural right? For what does it mean for one person to have a right, if not that others have a corresponding duty or obligation to respect that right?

In other words, the very vesting of a right in any one individual would seem necessarily to imply a restriction upon the rights of others, in the sense that it can no longer be "all right" for these others to do whatever they like, particularly if their doing as they liked should happen to involve their interfering with the right of someone else. Besides, must not the so-called Principle of Universalizability, as the currently fashionable term now is, immediately take over, the very minute one argues that its being all right for an individual to enjoy a certain liberty of action implies that that same individual has a right to such liberty

4. It is true that Hobbes would insist that human beings even in the state of nature are bound by what he would call "the law of nature." Yet I scarcely think that this necessitates any serious qualification of the principal contentions in this paragraph.

and freedom of enterprise? For what is all right for any one individual in the state of nature must be no less all right for each and every other individual in a similar or comparable situation.[5] Must it not therefore be acknowledged that the very logic of the situation of human beings in a state of nature immediately generates an entire context of mutual rights and duties within this same state of nature, rights and duties which we may therefore properly call natural rights and duties?

Accordingly, is it not apparent that the logic of our argument for natural rights and duties has thus transported us into the midst of a full-fledged natural-rights philosophy in the manner of a John Locke, say, but no less so in the manner of a Thomas Jefferson in the Declaration of Independence, or again perhaps of a Robert Nozick in our own day, with his talk of the freedom of the individual in the state of nature being limited by so-called "side constraints." For no sooner is it acknowledged that any one individual in the state of nature has a right to liberty and to a true freedom of enterprise than it immediately follows that all others have a corresponding duty or obligation to respect that liberty. But correspondingly, just as others have an obligation to respect the liberty of the first individual, no less does he have an equal and answering obligation to respect the several liberties of each and every one of these others. Nor is this condition, involving as it does an all-pervasive pattern of mutual rights and duties, confined only to the state of nature. For it is no less than the natural rights and duties of human beings in the state of nature that then come to serve as the norms or standards for the organization of human beings in civil society: the civil rights of men as they come to be recognized in, say, a system of common law, or in, for instance, the Constitution of the United States— these presumably are supposed to be copies or reproductions of the natural rights of men in the state of nature. Positive law, in other words, is thus thought of as being infused with considerations of natural rights. Even more than that, positive law, when scrutinized from a natural-rights perspective, comes to be regarded as standing under judgment,

5. Cf. John Locke, *Second Treatise of Government*, ed. C. B. Macpherson (Indianapolis, 1980), chap. II, "Of the State of Nature," 8–9. It might be said that Locke's citation of Hooker in this passage is to precisely this purpose and effect. It is presumably an anticipation of what so many modern writers on ethics would call the Principle of Universalizability.

so to speak, depending upon whether it manages to measure up to certain objective standards of ethics and of natural justice.

THE FAILURE OF
THE APPEAL TO NATURAL RIGHTS

With this argument, have we not got before us a clear example of how so-called positive law, or the law of civil society, may be recognized as being subject to the judgment of ethics—in this case the ethics associated with the so-called philosophy of natural rights? Still, it is not enough for our purposes merely to cite the example. We need also to see whether the example is warranted in the sense of whether the ethical standards of a natural-rights philosophy, through which one might attempt to assess existing law in terms of what the law ought to be— whether these ethical standards are truly objective and whether they really do commend themselves to right reason. And to this question, I am afraid that the answer now must be resoundingly negative. There does not seem to be any proper or reliable evidence that any of the so-called natural rights and natural duties, which a natural-rights philosophy must insist upon, are anywhere to be found in nature. After all, just recall: how was it that the natural-rights philosopher attempted to show that, as individuals, we really do have rights, and more particularly with reference to the present discussion, rights to liberty? Apparently—at least to judge from my own earlier representation of the matter—the natural-rights philosopher sought to argue from the fact that in a state of nature it has to be adjudged *all right* for an individual to do as he pleases that it therefore follows that that individual *has a right* to such a liberty, or such a comparatively unrestricted freedom of enterprise. But is this not a patent non sequitur? True, it may be conceded that there is indeed a sense in which in the hypothetical state of nature it is all right for an individual to do whatever he chooses, simply for the reason that in the state of nature—at least as Hobbes conceived it—there are no laws to forbid such action. But so also, would it not be possible to maintain that in a state of nature it is all right for water to seek its own level? That is, there are no moral or legal prohibitions against its doing so. Yet from the fact that, in a completely nonmoral sense of "all right," it is *all right* for water to seek its own level, it certainly does not follow that water thus *has a right* to behave this way. Accordingly, what is sauce for the goose is sauce for the gander: if in nature there is not only no evidence for, there is scarcely any sense to the notion that water has a natural right to seek its own level, then likewise in nature there is neither evidence for, nor sense to, the idea that human beings have a natural right to their liberties and their freedom of enterprise. And of course, the inference from *all right to* to *having a right to* will not bear scrutiny for an instant.

THE APPEAL TO SOCIAL CONTRACT IN JUSTIFICATION OF RIGHT-CLAIMS IN LAW

Very well, supposing that there is apparently no way in which natural-rights philosophers can generate or conjure up such rights from a mere consideration of a state of nature, still, many of the thinkers who are addicted to the idea of a state of nature, be it as a mere hypothesis or otherwise, may be found to be not entirely without resource when it comes to trying to get ethics into the picture. True, one has to give up any idea of moral rights and duties being natural; but why not think of them as arising through social contract or compact? Thus Hobbes argued that by entering into the social contract, human beings in effect vest all power in the sovereign; and having done this, they are then under obligation to obey the sovereign. Not that such an obligation may be regarded as in any way strictly natural. No, it is no more than a contractual obligation. And certainly—so it is argued—a person has a moral obligation to honor one's contracts. And similarly, albeit *mutatis mutandis*, as regards Rawls (or at least on one interpretation of Rawls),[6] one has no natural duty or obligation to respect the two principles of justice; but one does have a moral obligation, in virtue of one's hypothetical, and yet nonetheless effectual, agreement, as it were, from behind "the veil of ignorance" to honor these principles of justice.

Much the same question, however, returns to plague us that we found plaguing us as regards natural rights. The earlier form of the

6. Reference might here be made to the interpretation, or perhaps construction, that Ronald Dworkin would place on Rawls's view. As Dworkin understands it, "the abstract right to equal concern and respect" is a right which Dworkin feels is to be found in the deep structure of Rawls's theory. Hence such a right may not be regarded as one that receives its justification solely on grounds of its having been agreed upon in some hypothetical social contract (Ronald Dworkin, *Taking Rights Seriously* [Cambridge, Mass., 1977], 181).

question was whether it is possible to find a footing for ethical considerations by appealing to natural rights or duties? And now the question is whether any mere entering into a contract, be it either hypothetically or actually, ever really commits us, or binds us morally, to observe that contract. More specifically, with respect to our concern over individual liberty, supposing that in the state of nature we have a natural freedom of enterprise, does our entering into a social compact, in which we agree to respect this same liberty in others, in any way bind us morally to do so? Surely, it would seem not. For remember that we are dealing with a more or less Hobbesian state of nature, which is radically and totally amoral: that water should seek its own level we can certainly concede to be natural; but it clearly is neither right nor wrong, neither good nor bad. In other words, a Hobbesian state of nature—and presumably a Rawlsian or a Nozickian or Dworkinian state of nature as well—has to be nothing if not the nature of modern natural science. And nature from the point of view of modern science must be admitted to be wholly and completely amoral.

Very well, then, if in nature and in reality, we human beings have no duties or obligations of any kind, how can it possibly be supposed that we then come to acquire such duties merely by social contract or convention—as if human beings were somehow able to create rights and duties, much as God creates the world, literally out of nothing? Or put it the other way around: granted that we do acquire rights and duties by some social convention, then it can be said to be only by social convention that we are morally bound in any way, or are under ethical obligations of any kind. This is not to say, of course, that moral rights and obligations being mere creatures of social contract and convention, we are therefore at liberty to disregard them, whenever we wish, and with complete impunity. Far from it, for the society will probably have the power to enforce its conventions and to punish violations of those conventions. Hence it could well be to our interest or advantage—one might argue—to abide by our obligations under the social contract; but what might at one time be in our interest to do, we can certainly not be said to be in any deeper sense morally or ethically bound to do should it later turn out not to be in our interest to do so. In other words, if I have agreed by social contract to respect the liberties of others, then presumably I need have not the slightest moral compunction about violating such liberties, assuming that I take it in my head to do so and that I am confident I can get away with doing so.

The Resources of Contemporary Ethics as a Justification for Human Rights and Duties

Once again, are we not right back at square 1, at least with regard to our original undertaking of trying to determine whether there might be any legitimate ethical stance from which one would be in a position to judge the law as it is in terms of the law as it ought to be? Certainly, with respect to our investigation thus far, and specifically as regards the Fifth and Fourteenth Amendment guarantees of life, liberty, and property—particularly the guarantee of liberty—there does not seem to be any proper ethical or moral ground in terms of which such legal guarantees of individual liberty could ever be justified, or their repudiation condemned—not by any appeal to supposed natural rights, and not by any appeal to supposed moral obligations, as these might be determined by some form of social contract.

Why, though, should we not now abruptly change course? For is there not something decidedly old-fashioned, not to say almost counterintuitive, about trying to find a basis for human rights by resorting to appeals to natural rights or the device of the social contract? True, each of these doctrines has recently enjoyed a curious, and seemingly almost an anachronistic, revival at the hands of people such as Rawls and Nozick. And yet why pay heed to these new-found fashions that have suddenly come out in praise of what everyone had reckoned to be both antiquated and long discredited doctrines, dating back to the seventeenth and eighteenth centuries? Indeed, up until a scant twenty years or so ago, it would seem that nobody talked much about justifying human rights in terms either of natural rights or of social compact. Instead, the field of ethics appeared to be pretty well divided between so-called "teleologists" (or perhaps Utilitarians) on the one hand and so-called "deontologists" (or perhaps Kantians) on the other.

Accordingly, human rights to life, liberty, and property, for example, tended often to be justified on what might be considered general Utilitarian grounds—as if a respect for the rights of man were an obligation incumbent upon human beings, presumably for no other reason than that in the long run such a respect would surely make for the greater happiness of the greater number. Or as an alternative, on deontological grounds, it was argued that a respect for life, liberty, and property was to be regarded simply as a categorical duty, incumbent upon everyone and recognizable simply by man's practical reason. And why, on this latter view, ought one thus to respect the life, liberty, and property of others? Certainly not because such conduct would necessarily be to one's ultimate advantage, or even to the advantage of mankind as a whole. No, one ought, simply because one ought—at least such was the rigorism that seemed to be demanded by a Kantian ethical deontology.

Supposing such to be the currently fashionable ways of trying to justify human rights, as well as our corresponding duties and obligations to respect such rights, still, considered as means of moral justification, can these regnant theories of ethical teleology or ethical deontology fare any better than did those earlier views, which, as we saw, involved appeals to natural rights or social contract? Unfortunately, and by way of anticipation, we fear it needs to be flatly declared that neither the Utilitarians nor the Kantians would seem able to do any better than did the contractarians or the natural-rights theorists at providing an adequate foundation and justification for human rights and duties. Nevertheless, to develop these criticisms and to make them properly telling philosophically, we must first attempt to characterize more fully and adequately just what one is to understand by a so-called ethical teleology, on the one hand, as contrasted with an ethical deontology, on the other.

Have no fears, though. For the last thing I would either propose to do, or would be competent to do, would be to engage in a learned and tortuous review of the likes of David Hume, John Stuart Mill, and Henry Sidgwick, and even trickling down to R. M. Hare and David Lyons of the present day—all of this on the one hand; and on the other hand, a no less interminable rehearsal of the views of Immanuel Kant and of his later English followers such as H. A. Prichard and W. D. Ross, and coming on down to the likes of Warner Wick and William Frankena and Alan Donagan *et al.* in this country today. No, I propose instead to strip down both ethical teleology and ethical deontology to their bare bones, as it were, and then to characterize them in terms of a somewhat homely, not to say even homespun, language. For why cannot one say that an ethical teleology is nothing but a "desire-ethic," and an ethical deontology nothing but a "duty-ethic," or perhaps an "ought-ethic"? In the one, the ultimate determining factor as to what men should do, and how they may best order their lives, is simply the factor of what their desires and their likings and their interests happen to be. In the other, what as human beings we may want to do or like to do ultimately is thought to have no bearing on what as human moral agents we ought to do or have a duty to do. No, in a deontological ethics, "oughts" are simply the ultimate and irreducible factor in the moral life; nor is there any way in which such "oughts" and duties may ever be thought to be derived from what may be taken to be to an individual's, or to mankind's, greatest interest or ultimate advantage.

Moreover, while we are still engaged in this somewhat overall characterization of a teleological ethic in contrast to a deontological one, and vice versa, it might not be amiss to note, in passing, one fundamental respect in which these two types of ethics are alike. It might be said that both of them represent attempts to found an ethics without having to make appeals to any "goods" or "bads" in reality, or to any "rights" or "wrongs," "oughts" or "ought nots," as these might be supposed to exist in the real world, or *in rerum natura*.

To be sure, in subsequent discussions, we shall have occasion to discuss further how what I earlier referred to as being a natural-rights ethics, and what I shall later call a natural-law ethics, both attempt to find a basis and grounding for moral norms directly in nature—as if there were actually a basis in fact and in nature for human rights and human duties. Clearly, though, in this day and age and among people who are at all "with it" either philosophically or scientifically, it strikes anyone and everyone as being nothing if not absurd to suppose that "oughts" and "ought-nots," "goods" and "bads," rights and wrongs, and so on can ever be found or discovered in nature, or simply read off the face of nature like so many scientific findings. No, for surely we recognize nowadays that nature, as it presents itself to the modern scientist, is nothing if not totally value-blind, as well as morally blind.

Very well, but if men may no longer look to the facts of nature and of reality for guidance in matters of morals and ethics, why then would it not seem plausible simply not to worry about what is right or what is wrong, as this may be prescribed for us by nature? No, if there are no moral requirements set for us by nature and in fact, then why does it not make sense for us but to occupy ourselves with getting the most we can out of life—that is, with gratifying our interests and desires so far

13

as possible and not worrying about whether to do so is really right or really wrong, particularly if there are no such things as real rights and real wrongs, or natural rights and natural wrongs, with an ontological status in reality, that we might be able to be guided by? And with this, what do we not come out with if not a theory of ethics that has all the marks of what I have been calling a desire-ethic or, if you will, a mere interest theory of ethics? That is, our goal in life becomes nothing more nor less than the gratification of as many of our human wants, needs, interests, and desires as possible, and without our having to pay the slightest heed to the question of whether such a course of action is prescribed for us by nature.

Nor is it possible to make a rejoinder at this point that surely our human interests, needs, and desires must be regarded as natural phenomena; and that therefore in trying to maximize whatever it is that is in our human interest, and to minimize whatever is contrary to that interest, we are not so much going contrary to the requirements of nature as acting in accordance with the dictates of nature? The answer is that, of course, our human desires and inclinations are unquestionably natural phenomena; and yet there is nothing anywhere in nature—at least not in nature as it is understood by the natural scientist—that tells us that it is morally right for us to pursue whatever our natural impulses and desires impel us to pursue and strive for.

Likewise, and no less than with a desire-ethic, a duty-ethic in the Kantian sense is in no wise held to be based upon nature. Quite the contrary; Kant would insist that it is not by any study of the facts of nature that we human beings can ever hope to learn what our moral obligations as human beings are and how as human beings we ought to conduct ourselves. Instead, it is simply by the exercise of our practical reason (as Kant conceived this to be) that we should be able to determine that it is wrong, for example, to violate the life, liberty, or property of our fellow human beings, or that we are obligated—to take another and specifically Kantian example—never to treat human beings merely as means and not as ends.

Moreover, the way in which our practical reason is supposed thus to be able to discern the moral imperatives that are incumbent upon us as human beings is not through any scrutiny of the so-called facts of nature. For in Kant's eyes, facts of nature belong to the world of mere phenomena, and in the phenomenal world one can find no evidence for moral duties and obligations. For these, Kant thought, one must reckon with the noumenal world and not with the merely phenomenal world. The only trouble is that the noumenal world is incapable of being known by human beings, at least in any articulated fashion. And so, Kant seems to argue, the only way that human beings can come to recognize that they are subject to certain moral duties and obligations is that whenever a person seeks to disregard or repudiate his subjection to genuine moral demands, as contrasted with the demands of his mere interests and desires, he inevitably finds himself caught up in all sorts of contradictions and practical inconsistencies. In other words, it is almost as if for Kant considerations of mere logical consistency or inconsistency bring home to a person that he is subject to moral obligations, and not any considerations about the way the world is, or about what nature may be reckoned as requiring of us, and so forth.

For example, as Kant would insist, for a person to treat another human being "merely as a means and not as an end" must inevitably implicate that person in serious practical inconsistencies. Indeed, were some tough-minded amoralist to insist that he cannot see why he should not have the right to rob, enslave, maim, kill, or otherwise exploit his fellow human beings, the very logic of his position would presumably force him to recognize that if as a human being he had a right to treat his fellows in any way he might please, then they for their part must have no less a right to treat him in any way they please. And with that, the shoe would indeed seem to be on the other foot. For our would-be despiser of morality is simply "hoist with his own petard"—and it would appear that by logic alone he is thus hoisted. For what is it that our moral tough guy has done if not simply try to play fast and loose with the simple truth—and indeed it is tantamount to a logical truth—that what is sauce for the goose is sauce for the gander.

In other words, from all of this it begins to be clear how the partisan of a duty-ethic, no less than the partisan of a desire-ethic, thinks he can dispense with any appeals to the facts of nature in support of his deontological ethics. Unlike the ethical teleologist, he does not hold that moral obligations like rights and duties are binding upon us merely because if we disregard them it will make for the greater disadvantage and suffering in the long run either of ourselves or of mankind as a whole. Instead, the deontologist simply insists that our moral duties and obligations cannot be evaded or avoided without our falling into logical contradiction and inconsistency.

Can Either a Desire-ethic or a Duty-ethic Be Defended?

Granted that an ethical teleology and an ethical deontology, so-called, have the respective philosophical characters that I have thus loosely attributed to them, why not return to the proposal that I made at the beginning of this chapter? This was the proposal that we try to see whether either an ethical teleology or an ethical deontology in the contemporary sense might possibly be able to do what we earlier found that neither a natural rights theory of ethics nor a contractarian theory of ethics was able to do, that is, to provide a proper basis and foundation for our supposed human rights and duties. Or to characterize our undertaking a bit differently: is either an ethical teleology or an ethical deontology able to show that moral norms and standards can ever be grounded in anything that in any proper sense might be called "right reason"?

Moreover, to try to find a properly responsive answer to this question, I propose to proceed more or less dialectically. For I think it in no way unfair to say that in the history of modern ethics, the course of moral philosophy has never run smoothly. Either the deontologists are busy muddying the waters of the teleologists, or the teleologists in turn are roiling the springs of the deontologists—and so on, back and forth, seemingly almost ad infinitum, if not also ad nauseam.

Why do we not start off by recognizing that the teleologists seem to have at least one initial advantage in their dialectical interchange with the deontologists? When it comes to a question of justifying anything like moral "oughts," rights, duties, and the like, the teleologists, or partisans of a desire-ethic, do appear to have the jump on the deontologists. For is it not true that with respect to any and every moral judgment of whatever kind—"You ought to do thus and so"; "I have a right to this, that, or the other"; "It is only right that one should pay one's debts and speak the truth"; "Honor thy father and thy mother"; and so on—is not the question "Why?" always and in principle pertinent? "Why do you say that I ought to do this?"; "On what grounds do you claim to have such a right?"; or "Why do I have a duty to honor my mother and my father?"

To all such "why-questions" as they bear on moral duties and obligations, the teleologist can offer a ready and largely unequivocal answer: "You ought to because it is to your advantage to do so; or if not to your own personal advantage, then at least to mankind's advantage, or to the advantage of the greater number of human beings." In other words, in a desire-ethic, "oughts" and obligations are held to be always and in principle relative to and conditional upon what our human desires, ends, and purposes happen to be.

Nor is it hard to find any number of ready illustrations in even some very trivial examples drawn from outside the moral sphere. Thus suppose that I want to get to San Francisco from New York, and in as short a time as possible, would it not be appropriate to say that I *ought* to go by air? Or again, in the case of all of the various arts and techniques, does not one recognize that the way a particular job ought to be done will depend on the end that the particular art or skill is directed toward achieving? Thus surely, there are still a few of us oldsters left who remember those homely remedies and cures for illnesses such as "Starve a fever and stuff a cold." That is, if you want to get over your cold, you ought to eat heartily; or if you want to get over your fever, you had better starve yourself. And so it goes, even for the most sophisticated of human arts, skills, and technologies: given that such and such is the end or goal to be achieved by the art or technology, the "right" way to go about doing the job, or what the practitioners of the art "ought" to do, is thus and so.

But, then, why should it not be a like case with moral "oughts" and duties as it is with nonmoral ones? For no sooner does one ask the question "Why?" with respect to any alleged duty that is supposedly incumbent upon one—"Why do you say that I am duty bound to act thus and so?", or "Why am I under an obligation to do this rather than that?"—than the answer seems always to be the same, at least in principle. For no matter how stringent the moral obligation may be, the only proper answer that one would appear able to give to the relevant "why-question" would presumably have to relate to the benefits and advantages that will accrue—either to oneself or to mankind—as a result of honoring such obligations. Yes, take even the Ten Commandments, if you will, and specifically the Fifth Commandment: "Honor thy father and thy mother." Why? The reason is given directly in the text of Exodus 12:12: Thou shouldst honor thy mother and thy father, in order that "thy days may be long in the land which the Lord thy God giveth thee."

And so it is that the ethical teleologist comes to lay down as a veritable principle of his desire-ethic that any and all "oughts" and duties can be justified only in terms of their serving our human interests or desires or purposes: "Why ought I to do thus and so?" Surely, there is no other way of answering this "why-question" than by recognizing that only by doing thus and so, or by proceeding in this particular way rather than some other, can I ever hope to attain certain posited ends or goals or purposes. And so it would seem at first glance that the great resource of a desire-ethic as against a duty-ethic is that in the final analysis duties are all conditional upon desires. It is these, in other words, that are the ultimates in ethics; and that also indeed is why ethical teleologists are called teleologists, because they hold that any and all moral obligations and requirements must be justified ultimately in terms of some human end or *telos*.

No sooner, though, do the teleologists talk in this vein than the ire and indignation of the deontologists would seem to know no bounds. Yes, it is as if one could already see rising before one the dread ghost of an Immanuel Kant, who doubtless never smiled either in life or in death, and from whose lips, in death no less than in life, the words, "Duty! duty! duty!" appear ever to have issued forth in stern and monotonous regularity. Nor is it hard to recognize the source of this disapproval which Kant and his followers among the deontologists would level at the partisans of a desire-ethic. For is it not incredible that in what the ethical teleologists claim is an entirely legitimate moral philosophy, they dare to advance, as being no less than a principle of their ethics, the contention that there are no moral duties or obligations, except those that are entirely conditional upon what our human interests, desires, and purposes happen to be? For how can anyone claim to be a moralist, and at the same time blithely announce that moral obligations are binding upon us only so long as we want them to be?

Did I not note in the earlier discussion of a contractarian morality that the fatal weakness attaching to any such theory of law, or of ethics, or of politics, was that no sooner do we, or any other individuals, enter into social contracts or compacts, and agree to be bound by the terms of the agreement simply on the grounds that we consider it to be in our own best interest to do so, than the inevitable consequence must be that

18

no sooner do the interests of any one of us undergo a change, such that we no longer esteem it to be to our interest to abide by the contract, than immediately our obligations under the contract become null and void? And what kind of a morality is it that remains binding upon us only so long as we want it to be binding?

Yet is not this the character and consequence of any desire-ethic? Duties are made entirely contingent upon our human desires and upon whether we reckon it to be to our advantage to be bound by such duties. And yet surely—at least so the deontologists argue—in any morals or ethics that properly deserves the name, it must be the other way around: all of our human desires, purposes, objectives, and inclinations stand under judgment, so to speak, in the face of what our moral sense or moral consciousness tells us our duties are.

Nor need the deontologists stop even here. For seemingly, they do not merely have to maintain that it is counterintuitive for our moral obligations to be dependent solely upon interests and desires. In addition, they can round on their opponents among the teleologists by pointing out that when you come right down to it, there is no discernible necessary or rational connection, be it in fact or in logic, between my liking to do something or my enjoying it and its being right that I should do it or its being the something that I ought to do. In other words, the transition from "I want to" to "Therefore, I am entitled to" simply does not commend itself to right reason. How, then, can the teleologists and the partisans of a desire-ethic ever presume to make mere human likings, preferences, and desires the ultimate factor in ethics? So far from being ultimate, the mere fact that a human individual, or mankind as a whole, may have certain likings and preferences provides not the slightest evidence that such is what that individual, or those individuals, ought to do, or that it is what it is right for them to do.

In fact, Kant would even go so far as to say that the mere fact of a human being's desiring or liking something is neither a necessary nor a sufficient condition of that thing's being what the person in question ought to do or that it is right for him to do. Yes, and St. Thomas Aquinas as well, who in many ways is at the opposite pole from Kant in matters of ethics, to say nothing of being so in matters of philosophy generally, would certainly go along with Kant in insisting that the mere fact of a human desire for a thing, although there is a sense in which it might perhaps be a necessary condition of such a thing's being right for that

19

person to do, could still never as such be a sufficient consideration of the rightness of such action.[7] But of this, more later.

In the meantime, where does this leave the poor teleologists, battered as they are by these devastating attacks from the deontologists? Alas, it would seem that they are left in complete disarray—yes, even driven from the field, leaving the ethical deontologists, with the ever-dour Kant at their head, ready to parade down the streets of modern moral philosophy in a veritable Roman triumph.

Not so fast, though. For the deontologists, directly in their criticisms of ethical teleology, would appear to have overlooked one simple but crucial item in the situation. They were undoubtedly right to insist that mere human desires and purposes, considered solely as such and without qualification, can scarcely provide an adequate foundation for a morals or an ethics: the mere fact that I want something—or even that all men want it—is hardly ground for supposing that it is therefore right (morally right) that I should have it, or that the thing should be done.

Unhappily, though, in their eagerness to press home their point that mere human desires and purposes can never provide a sufficient ground for moral duties and obligations, the overzealous deontologists suddenly find themselves in the embarrassing position of having overlooked an initial consideration from which this entire discussion took its rise. This was the consideration that any and all moral judgments—judgments as to good and evil, right and wrong, what ought to be and ought not to be, and so on—would seem never to be self-evident. Instead, the question "Why?" is always relevant with respect to them: "Why ought I to love my neighbor?"; "Why is it wrong for me to deprive a fellow citizen of life, liberty, or property?" Moreover, what proves to be especially embarrassing about these ever-relevant "why-questions" with respect to moral judgments—at least embarrassing to the deontologists—is that there would seem to be no way of answering such questions save by appealing to human ends, purposes, or desires. Have we not already had occasion to note how a question as to why one ought to do thus and so would appear invariably to call for an answer

7. This is in the sense in which for Aquinas "good" or *bonum* can be understood only with reference to "desire" or *appetitus*. Cf. *De Veritate*, Qu. 1, Art. 1, and Qu. 21 and 22.

in terms of some human purpose or benefit which such an "ought-action" would seem to serve?[8]

This, though, cannot but put the ethical deontologists in a most troublesome predicament. For having devoted all their efforts to showing that no mere appeal to human ends, purposes, or desires can ever warrant an inference to the existence of any moral "ought" or obligation, they now suddenly discover that the tables are turned and that, lacking at least some appeal to human desires or purposes, all moral "oughts" or imperatives suddenly turn out to be without apparent warrant or justification.

Yes, dear reader, to bring the matter close to home, why not ask yourself directly: "How can anyone presume to tell me that I am under obligation, or am duty bound, to do thus and so, if at the same time my moral preceptor is unable to tell me why or on what grounds I am so obligated? Instead, he simply brushes my demand for reasons aside by sternly telling me that I ought just because I ought, and that's an end of the matter." Surely, there could be no tactic that would appear to be more high-handed than this. And yet is it not the tactic that the deontologist must ultimately resort to? And what possible resource can the deontologists claim to have at hand when they are brought up short by such a challenge?

But however desperate might be the plight of the deontologists, when they have to show that their categorical imperatives and duties are not utterly arbitrary and without foundation, one would never guess at such desperation from reading them. And so why not consider some of the ways the deontologists have resorted to in an effort to show that their categorical "oughts" are justified and without having to make any appeal to human interests, ends, or purposes?

Why not begin with the example of Kant himself? Recalling one of his more celebrated pronouncements, and simplifying it somewhat, on what grounds does Kant insist that it is always wrong to make a lying promise—that is, a promise I have no intention of ever keeping? Of course, we do not need to be reminded that Kant continually inveighs against the notion that a lying promise might conceivably be justified upon occasion if it can be shown that sufficient human benefit might

---

8. Cf. the pronouncement of St. Thomas Aquinas, *Summa Theologiae*, I–II, Qu. 99, Art. 1: *Quod autem aliquid debeat fieri, hoc pervenit ex necessitate alicuius finis.*

possibly accrue from such action. No, never! says Kant. But why not? Why must it always be wrong to make a lying promise, whatever the consequences? I have already remarked that Kant's apparent resource in trying to meet such a challenge would seem to be to contend that the man who makes a promise with no intention of keeping it cannot but implicate himself in serious practical inconsistencies by such action. But how?

Presumably, Kant's answer would be somewhat along lines like the following. No sooner—Kant seems to be saying in effect—do I make the claim that it is only right that in certain circumstances I make a lying promise, particularly when I see that it would be to my advantage to do so, than my judgment as to the rightness of such an action would have to be reckoned as universalizable, this being the character of any judgment to the effect of an action's being either right or wrong. Accordingly, my judgment being universalizable, must I not then acknowledge that not just I but any and every other human being is no less entitled to make a lying promise—yes, even ought to do so, if he has his wits about him? But—so Kant's argument runs—this must surely involve me in an inconsistency: for no sooner would I thus advocate that anyone and everyone should make a practice of making deceitful promises, when he thinks it to his advantage to do so, and the very institution of promising would be completely undermined. And yet my original intent was not to subvert the institution of promising but simply to exploit it to my own ends. And so, Kant argues, my attempted justification of making lying promises must inevitably land me in an inconsistency—at least in an inconsistency with my own express intent and purpose in making the lying promise in the first place.

And yet does it? For surely, I can say that, supposing the institution of promising does come to be weakened, if not seriously undermined, through my insistence upon anyone and everyone's right to make a lying promise, is that not something I might judge that I could perfectly well live with? For admitting that I can no more trust the promises of others than they can trust mine, so what? I am still willing to run the risk of playing the fake promising game, and playing it against other fake promisers, and winning it on my own terms. And surely, there is no inconsistency here. Nor would it seem that Kant's other examples of how a violation of moral duties is bound to lead one into inconsistency would fare any better than the example of the lying promise. Quite the contrary; there would seem to be no reason why the moral imperatives of Kantian philosophy could not all be simply denied, without the slightest risk of any logical or even practical inconsistency, such as Kant would seem to have supposed.

Moving beyond Kant, however, and coming to the more immediately contemporary situation, I think it no misrepresentation to say that there would appear to be scarcely any deontologists of the present day who have not abandoned Kant's tactic of arguing that for one ever to violate a categorical duty or obligation must involve one in contradiction and practical inconsistency. Instead, the fashion nowadays among deontologists would seem to be to claim that the truth of moral imperatives is guaranteed by "intuition"—as if, in our capacity as rational animals, we are able simply to "intuit" what our obligations and responsibilities are.

Note that I have here set the word "intuition" in quotes, and for two reasons: first, because of late years it has come to take on the status almost of a technical term for designating the way in which human moral agents can come to recognize what their moral responsibilities are; and second, because, at least superficially, it would seem to be little better than an ad hoc, and hence highly dubious, device, whereby we conjure up a seemingly mysterious faculty of moral insight, simply to assure ourselves that as human beings we can and do have a genuine knowledge of moral principles. And yet, unfortunately, why might not such a supposed intuition be the resource of just about any prejudiced or even fanatical Tom, Dick, or Harry, whenever the occasion might serve him to make appeal to it? Presumably, all he would need to do would be to invoke his moral "intuition" in support of what might be no better than blind moral prejudices: "The Germans should be respected as a master race"; "All property is theft"; "Health care is a human right and no longer a privilege limited to those who can afford it"; "Abortion is murder"; "Some human beings are natural slaves"; and so on. This is not to say, of course, that such moral judgments, however horrendous or commendable they might prove to be, might not conceivably be either defended or rebutted by evidence and argument. And yet suppose that instead of adducing either evidence or argument, one simply took one's stand on one's intuition: "I simply have an intuition that my judgment is true." Would not such a procedure give every appearance of rendering moral judgments nothing if not arbitrary in the extreme?

Surely, though, it would appear scarcely to be supposed that among

23

sophisticated contemporary moral philosophers those who appeal to intuition are being arbitrary and dogmatic when they do so. On the contrary; both Rawls and Donagan, for example, have attempted to provide explanations and defenses of what they would hold to be considered appeals to our moral intuitions in support of our moral judgments. The only trouble is that such justifications as have thus been given for the reliability of our moral intuitions, for all of their subtlety and sophistication, have not always carried conviction—at least not with everyone.

Accordingly, why do we not take a couple of salient examples of recent moral judgments, or imperatives, that have been claimed to be vouchsafed to us simply in terms of our moral intuitions, and see if a good case can be made for the reliability of such supposed moral intuitions as guarantors of moral obligations? For example, Alan Donagan has, with great perceptiveness, adapted to his purposes Kant's second formulation of the categorical imperative. Dissociating this idea more sharply than Kant ever did from the first formulation of the Kantian imperative, Donagan enunciates the principle of the imperative as being intuitively evident: "So act as to treat human nature, whether in your own person or in that of another, always as an end and never merely as a means." And for purposes of convenience and economy, Donagan abbreviates this simply to "Respect human nature."[9]

As a second, and somewhat cognate, example, let us take Ronald Dworkin's formulation of a categorical imperative—an imperative that Dworkin thinks underlies the entire Rawlsian apparatus of "the initial agreement," "the veil of ignorance," "the two principles of justice," *et al.* Dworkin enunciates his principle: "We may say that individuals have a right to equal concern and respect in the design and administration of the political institutions that govern them." Or following Dworkin's discussion on a subsequent page, we might express the principle as if it were a fuller version and amplification of Donagan's: "Human beings, being moral persons and not mere animals, have a right to equal concern and respect."[10]

On what grounds is a judgment such as this last one to be accepted as being true and binding upon us, *viz.*, that human beings have a right to an equal concern and respect? No doubt, most of us might be willing

9. Alan Donagan, *The Theory of Morality* (Chicago, 1977), chap. 2.2, esp. pp. 65–66.
10. Dworkin, *Taking Rights Seriously*, 180–81.

to testify that we do, indeed, have a "feeling"—almost a gut reaction—that human beings do have a claim to equal concern and respect and that men may thus justifiably insist upon this as their right. Still, is a mere feeling all that a moral intuition may be said to amount to? Surely, this cannot be all there is to it, for however much you and I and ever so many others may feel bound to acknowledge that our fellow human beings are all entitled to an equal concern and respect, it is not hard to imagine someone, who, to all intents and purposes, is perfectly rational and responsible, and yet frankly avers: "But I just don't see why I am under any obligation to show no less concern for my distant neighbor, whom I scarcely know, than I do for members of my own family. Besides, I happen to know for a fact that this same neighbor is a pompous ass and has been guilty of some notably sharp practices. How, then, can it be maintained that such a person is entitled to a respect from me that is equal to the love and respect that I have for my family, my friends, and those whom I admire most?"

Suppose that a Dworkin or a Donagan were to try to rebut such a challenge to one of their moral first principles? Could they say much more than that the truth of their principle of equal concern and respect for all is confirmed simply by their intuition, and that ends the matter? Surely, this response does seem arbitrary, to say the least. Perhaps, though, Donagan and Dworkin might have resorted to a device used by more traditional philosophers—for example, St. Thomas Aquinas—when called upon to justify the first principles of their ethics. For Aquinas would be the first to acknowledge that in ethics, just as in any other branch of philosophy, there must be certain first principles that are ultimate and indemonstrable. As Aquinas puts it, "Just as every judgment of speculative reason springs from a natural cognition of first principles, so likewise every judgment of practical reasons proceeds from certain principles that are naturally known."[11]

What, though, does Aquinas mean by expressions like "natural cognition" or "naturally known"? Could he mean principles that are simply "intuited"? Hardly, for Aquinas would understand a principle that is "naturally known" to be one that is self-evident, or evident just in itself—*per se notum*. And the notion of a self-evident principle has a precise technical meaning in the context of traditional Aristotelian logic. There a self-evident principle means a principle that does not admit of

11. St. Thomas Aquinas, *Summa Theologiae*, I–II, Qu. 100, Art. 1.

being made evident through the device of a proper middle or mediating term in a syllogism. In fact, as examples of such evident practical principles—though it must be admitted that, so far as we know, these are not examples that Aquinas himself ever adduces anywhere—we might cite each of those principles that I invoked earlier, the one to embarrass the teleologists, and the other to embarrass the deontologists. Put baldly, the principle that was used against the teleologists was that the mere fact that someone desires something can never, as such, be a ground for saying that it is therefore only right that he should have what he desires. Likewise, we could put baldly the other principle that I invoked to embarrass the deontologists: no judgment of duty or obligation, but what it demands a justifying reason; and no justifying reason can ever be given for an obligatory action, unless it be in terms of some end or purpose which such an action serves.

Very well, I suggest that both of these principles, which I would say are fundamental to moral philosophy, can never admit of demonstration through outside evidence. That is, there is no middle term by which it might be demonstrated that mere human interests and desires as such can ever be taken as evidence of what it is morally right for human beings to do. Nor again could one possibly come up with a middle term that could mediate between the notion of moral obligation and the notion of human ends and purposes, in such a way as to demonstrate that there can be no other ground of moral obligation, save insofar as the putatively obligatory action can be shown to contribute to our human purposes or ends. Instead, the only way in which principles such as these may be evidenced is through their being seen to be evident simply in and through themselves. In other words, they are either self-evident or not evident at all.

Very well, then, let us return once again to that moral principle which Dworkin has enunciated, and which he presumably would say is warranted simply in terms of his moral intuition—the principle that all men are entitled to an equal concern and respect. Would Dworkin then say—or would Donagan or any other contemporary moral philosopher say—that such moral principles as they claim to intuit are ever self-evident, in the precise technical sense that I have just explained and illustrated? Presumably, the answer must be "No."

For one thing, the principle that Dworkin puts forward could scarcely claim to be self-evident in any strict sense, simply for the reason that, as we have already seen, it can so easily be challenged. To

Dworkin, and indeed to many of the rest of us as well, it might seem evident, at least superficially, that any and every human being is entitled to an equal concern and respect; and yet it is not hard to imagine that to others such a principle would be anything but evident. Any principle that is properly self-evident is one the opposite of which is inconceivable. Accordingly, the mere fact that it can be doubted that human beings are necessarily entitled to an equal concern and respect indicates that whatever may be our moral intuitions respecting the truth of such a principle, those intuitions are not to be construed as ever revealing the actual self-evidence of any such principle.

Besides, there are even more general considerations of a largely logical nature that would no doubt militate against any contemporary analytical philosopher ever availing himself of a notion of self-evidence in support of his principles.[12] For one thing, far too much water has flowed under the logical bridge in the last seventy-five years or so, largely as a result of developments in the newer so-called mathematical logic, ever to permit a contemporary philosopher to fall back on a notion like that of self-evidence, such as is associated with the older Aristotelian logic. Thus in the lower functional calculus of modern logic, the relation of subject to predicate in propositions is scarcely even conceived in such a way any more as to permit of so-called essential predications in the older sense. But self-evident truths are such truths as those in which the predicate is recognized as pertaining to the very essence of the subject.

For another thing, also, even to the extent to which in modern logic it may still be permissible to conceive of propositions in which the very notion of the predicate term is to be thought of as being contained within the notion of the subject, such propositions are almost certain to be relegated to the class of truths which Kant would have called analytic, as opposed to synthetic truths. But analytic truths, as Kant insisted, can never be truths about the world, but rather only logical truths or linguistic truths. Nevertheless, in contrast to such so-called analytic truths which have played such a role in the context of modern logic, such supposed self-evident truths as were acknowledged by traditional logic were all held to be truths of fact, or truths about the world. And

---

12. A number of these logical considerations which follow in the text, and which are still far from being accepted as noncontroversial, are all points which I have gone into in some detail in an earlier book, *Two Logics: The Conflict Between Classical and Neo-analytic Philosophy* (Evanston, 1969), esp. chaps. I–IV.

so for all of these reasons, it would seem that the possibility is excluded for modern moral philosophers ever to construe their truths of intuition as being truths that are self-evident in the traditional sense.

Very well, but if the truths of modern moral philosophy—at least as conceived by the deontologists—are guaranteed not in the sense that such truths are self-evident, being instead merely "intuited," then how can one guard oneself against the accusation that such truths cannot show themselves to be other than purely arbitrary? Alas, I do not think that they can be defended against this charge. Besides, the decisive consideration that in the final analysis serves to expose the arbitrariness of all modern deontological principles in ethics is that the ultimate principles of any deontological ethics cannot be other than principles assertive of our human moral duties and obligations. But duties and obligations, as we have seen—yes, we have even seen it to be so in terms of no less than a self-evident principle—can never be literally categorical principles, as Kant and the deontologists would have them be. No, for any assertion of a duty or obligation rightly generates the inescapable question of "Why?" And there can be no other possible answer to a "why-question" in such a context, save through an appeal to human ends and purposes.

And with that response, is not any and every type of deontological ethics thereby undone? For the underlying contention of any deontological ethics is that appeals from moral duties and obligations to human ends, purposes, and objectives are to be ruled out in principle. But unhappily, they cannot be ruled out either in principle, or in logic, or in any other way: drive the devil (in this case our human ends, purposes, and desires) out the door, and he comes right back in through the window. Nor is there any way that the deontologist can ensure the ultimacy of his deontological principles by his would-be appeals to intuition. For in this connection intuition turns out to be little more than a desperate remedy for an irremediable situation.

A FURTHER WORD ON UTILITARIANISM

Need anything more be said respecting the two leading varieties of ethical theory that currently dominate the moral-philosophical scene in the English-speaking world—teleological theories on the one hand and deontological theories on the other? For has not each theory been shown to have played itself out and now to be at its wits' end, when it comes to finding any proper justification for itself in terms of right reason? The teleologists are unable to show how a mere pursuit of our human interests and desires can ever provide a proper basis for anything like moral rights and obligations. And the deontologists, though they seem to have no difficulty in confidently propounding moral imperatives, nevertheless fail to show how such imperatives can ever ultimately have any proper justification or commend themselves in any way to right reason. And what does all of this signify, if not that neither teleology nor deontology can ever manage to provide a sound moral or ethical basis for law, to say nothing of that usual panoply of rights and duties that in Western culture, at least, we are accustomed to having spelled out for us in any reputable legal system.

Why, then, in the concluding sections of this chapter am I proposing to devote more specific attention to that commonest of all forms of ethical teleology, Utilitarianism, as well as to a curious variant on the more usual Utilitarian varieties of desire-ethics—those that have come to be designated as Ethical Egoism or Rational Individualism? The reason is that as soon as it is scrutinized closely, Utilitarianism may be seen to compound the characteristic weakness that attaches to any and every teleological ethic or desire-ethic—compounding the weakness by two further and very revealing weaknesses that attach more specifically to Utilitarianism. In contrast, if one takes the trouble to look at the ethical position that in recent years has come to be known as Ethical Egoism or Rational Individualism, one discovers that this is a position that manages to evade the two fatal flaws of Utilitarianism; but in doing so, it unhappily only tends to confirm and to accentuate that more radical weakness that afflicts any desire-ethic. It is just the weakness, *viz.*, that a desire-ethic ultimately turns out to be an emperor with no clothes: it cannot claim to be an ethics at all.

First, though, let us examine Utilitarianism. Surely, we are all aware of how in very recent years, and particularly since the publication of Rawls's book, Utilitarianism, or Ethical Consequentialism as it is sometimes called, has fallen into bad odor, and particularly when it comes to a defense of individual rights and personal liberties. For suppose a situation to arise—so this now standard criticism of Utilitarianism runs—in which the general welfare of the community, or the greatest happiness of the greatest number, might conceivably be furthered or increased by the sacrifice of the liberty, or the well-being, or even the life of a single individual, or, say, of a minority of individuals, will not the consistent Utilitarian or Consequentialist have to admit that thus sacrificing the life, liberty, or property of such individuals might be, not just the ineluctable consequence, but even the moral obligation, of anyone's adhering strictly to Utilitarian principles?

Nevertheless, telling as this line of criticism is with respect to classical Utilitarianism, it still does not get at what, I would suggest, is an even more fundamental weakness in Utilitarianism. No, for considered as the leading candidate for the role of an adequate and true-blue ethical teleology, Utilitarianism, be it surreptitiously or perhaps unconsciously, lets itself in for a very embarrassing compromise with deontology. Utilitarianism turns out to be nothing if not a somewhat squinting type of desire-ethic: while pretending to be undeviating in its commitment to teleology, and to our mere pleasures, interests, and desires as being the ultimate determinants in matters of morals and ethics, it nevertheless, at the same time, squints badly in the direction of a deontology or duty-ethic. At the outset and in its initial stage, a Utilitarian theory tends to sound unexceptionably teleological. For what is supposed to guide the individual in his choices on such a theory? Initially the answer is unequivocal: "Nothing but a consideration for one's own interests and one's own ends and purposes." Or if one's Utilitarianism is construed in hedonistic terms, one might put it that the individual is to be guided in anything and everything that he does by considerations solely of what will give him the most pleasure.

Suddenly, though, at this point, and quite inexplicably, the Utilitarian shifts his ground, insisting that the end or *telos* that serves as the ultimate standard of determination in Utilitarianism is not by any means to be identified simply with the individual's own personal good or happiness, but rather with the greatest happiness or the greatest good of the greatest number. And yet surely, this is odd, for the two certainly are not the same. For while I clearly want my own good and my own happiness, and in this sense I can readily recognize them as being in accord with my own end or *telos* or goal, I do not see how or why other people's happiness, or the greatest happiness of the greatest number, should necessarily be my goal. In fact, suppose I simply affirm that the well-being of my fellowmen is not anything I desire or concern myself with. True, had I been endowed by my Creator with a generous quantity of "sentiments of benevolence," as they once were called, then it could well be that the welfare of others might be among the things that

I myself might just happen to desire and thus try to bring about. But in fact, let us suppose that I turn out to be one of those more unfortunate creatures who is lacking in any such endowment of benevolence, and that therefore the happiness or well-being of others is not anything that I either want or have the least concern for. How, then, can the Utilitarian say that my end is not just my own happiness but the greatest happiness of the greatest number, when it is not?

Of course, if the Utilitarian were to rejoin by saying that even if the greatest happiness of the greatest number were not in fact my end, it ought to be—that would be nothing if not a disastrous betrayal of Utilitarianism's own professed teleological principles. For the hallmark of any teleological ethic, as I have noted, is its contention that duties can never finally take precedence over desires and interests. In other words, to be consistent with any properly teleological ethics—or at least any of those we have considered thus far—one has to recognize that the only reason one can ever be said to be under any obligation to choose or to act in a certain way would ultimately have to be because such a choice, or such a course of action, would be in one's own interest—that is, conformable to one's end or *telos* or purpose. But in the instant case, the well-being of others is not anything that I consider to be in my interest; it is not a part of my end or purpose in any way, shape, or form. Accordingly, if the Utilitarian wishes to insist that even if the greatest happiness of the greatest number is not my goal, it ought to be, then that is to compromise the professed teleological stance of Utilitarianism irreparably.

Everyone is familiar with the ploy that Utilitarians have long tended to resort to when confronted with such a difficulty. Thus John Stuart Mill, for example, has sometimes been interpreted as having sought to argue that if it is the individual's own happiness that is the good of each individual taken singly, then the general happiness of mankind must be the end or goal of all human beings collectively.[13] But this particular argument of Mill's, if it really was his argument, must be reckoned as being, if not incomprehensible, then a downright non sequitur. And indeed, wishing to avoid such a fallacy, subsequent thinkers in the Utilitarian tradition have succeeded in developing a supposedly tight argument to show that "moral and value predicates are such that if they belong to an action or object, they also belong to any other action or

13. John Stuart Mill, *Utilitarianism* (London, 1910), chap. IV, p. 33.

object that has the same properties."[14] This has come to be known as the Principle of Universalizability, and many Utilitarians have seemed to think that it can be employed to effect the sort of conclusion that we found Mill seeking to establish in the passage referred to above, and yet not really succeeding in establishing. The argument runs: if I judge my own happiness to be something that is right or good, and therefore something that I am justified in pursuing, then I am committed to judging that other people's happiness, being like mine in all relevant respects, must be no less right or good than my own. By employing such an argument, present-day Utilitarians are convinced that, without having to appeal to natural rights or social contracts or anything of the sort, they can nonetheless show that, by mere logical or linguistic considerations alone, one can be brought to admit that one is under obligation (moral obligation) to respect, and to help bring about, the happiness or well-being of others no less than his own.

And yet clearly this will never do. One cannot by a linguistic or logical legerdemain with the Principle of Universalizability manage to convert a purely egoistic concern with one's own happiness and advantage into a purportedly altruistic concern with the greatest happiness of the greatest number. Moreover, one can pretty well pinpoint where the fallacy here arises. For recall our earlier formulation of the Utilitarian argument, as it seeks to invoke to its own ends the Principle of Universalizability. The individual is said to argue: "If I judge my own pleasure or happiness as being something that it is only right that I should pursue, then I am committed to recognizing that, other people's happiness being like mine in all relevant respects, it is no less right—that is, morally right—that they should pursue their happiness than that I pursue mine." Fine. In this conditional proposition, the consequent indeed does follow from the antecedent. And yet the trouble lies not in the matter of logical consequence but rather in the antecedent. For how and on what grounds can I ever maintain that merely because I want to do something, or find it to be to my interest or advantage to do it, it therefore follows that it is only right or morally justifiable that I do it? This is a non sequitur if there ever was one!

Indeed, may we not say that at this point the Utilitarian manages most egregiously to beg that very question that we have earlier found to be the stumbling block for any and all varieties of desire-ethic? For

14. William Frankena, *Ethics* (2nd ed., Englewood Cliffs, N.J., 1973), 25.

32

how can one possibly conjure up out of mere human interests, desires, likings, tendencies, or what not, anything that may be said to be of proper moral import? Quite the contrary; we have but to reiterate that same self-evident truth that I repeatedly enunciated in connection with the earlier discussions of a desire-ethic: the mere fact that I, or anyone else, should happen to desire or to want something in no wise entails that I ought to have it or that it is right that I have it or pursue it. Moreover, may we not say that the squinting character of any Utilitarian ethics immediately stands exposed for all to see: the Utilitarian simply tries to parlay his original insistence upon the ultimacy, in any teleological ethics, of our human interests and desires, into a supposedly bona fide deontology, in which it is insisted that we have a moral obligation to respect the interests and desires of others, even though these may not be what we ourselves desire at all. And with that conclusion, should we not, as Mark Twain might say, simply "draw the curtain" on Utilitarianism?

Ethical Egoism as a Libertarian Philosophy of Rational Individualism

Even if Utilitarianism is written off as a moral philosophy that is beyond redemption, it still is not the only desire-ethic, or ethical teleology, that is conceivable. In recent years there has been a revival of Ethical Egoism, or Rational Individualism, as it is sometimes called. Charles King has undertaken to defend a moral philosophy of Ethical Egoism along avowedly Libertarian lines.[15] Moreover, as I have already intimated, although a moral philosophy of this sort is unmistakably a desire-ethic, it nevertheless successfully obviates the two fatal weaknesses that attach to any Utilitarian desire-ethic. For one thing, an Ethical Egoism of this type cannot be accused of ever sacrificing individual rights to the goal of the greatest good of the greatest number; and for another, a Rational Individualism or Egoism of this sort never

15. J. Charles King, "Rational Individualism," available only in typescript. For a lucid summary of King's views, see J. Charles King, "Moral Theory and the Social Order," in *The Libertarian Reader*, ed. Tibor R. Machan (Totowa, N.J., 1982), 16–36. King's work is an illuminating example of a Libertarian ethic of rational individualism or egoism, but it is not the only form that a Libertarian ethic might take. On the contrary, "Libertarianism" is far from being a univocal term, and as such it tends to embrace many variants in matters of moral philosophy.

compromises its steady commitment to a desire-ethic by smuggling categorical duties or moral obligations into the picture. The only trouble is, as we shall soon see, when all is said and done, can one say that an Ethical Egoism such as this can claim to be an ethics at all?

Still, we are getting ahead of ourselves. Instead, why not begin our examination of Ethical Egoism by simply noting that in its capacity as such a moral egoism or individualism, this ethical theory is unequivocal in its insistence that it is not the happiness or well-being of all, or even of most, that is the end or goal in such an ethics, but rather the happiness or well-being simply of the individual himself. That is, when as an individual I ask myself why I ought to do thus and so, or ought to act in this way or that, the only possible answer that can be given to such an ought-question has to be in terms of what my own end or goal is, or, to put it a bit more baldly, in terms of what it is that I want myself. Accordingly, let us call such a theory of ethics not just an interest theory but more precisely a self-interest theory of morals and ethics. And no sooner do we so describe it than its immediate and obvious advantages over rival ethical teleologies of a more or less Utilitarian sort become at once patent and obvious. Not only does such an ethics of Rational Individualism succeed in being a consistent teleology in a way in which Utilitarianism obviously did not, but also and along the same lines, one has no trouble in recognizing that from the standpoint of such an ethics there is never any problem of one's being able to understand how there can be reasons—good and sufficient reasons—in justification of such duties and obligations as in such an ethics it is maintained that we do indeed have. For ultimately the grounds of our duties and obligations are simply our own personal ends and objectives. To put it crudely, one might say that such an ethics of Rational Individualism might take as its slogan "No duties save in terms of our own personal ends," or "No one ever has a duty to do anything other than what he wants to do."

Let us move directly to consider some of the details of this present-day Libertarian development of the ethics of Rational Egoism or Rational Individualism. Certainly as we read them, such Libertarians seem sometimes to take as their point of departure the hypothesis of a more or less Hobbesian state of nature. For in such a state of nature, it is held that one may clearly recognize the human individual as being completely free, at least in the sense that, as noted earlier, there is no legal or moral let or hindrance to the individual's doing his own thing, or enjoying a complete freedom of individual enterprise. Moreover, it is just such freedom or liberty in this sense that the Libertarian moralist may be thought primarily to focus upon and to hold most dear. Does the Libertarian then go on to claim that it is only "right" that as an individual he should thus be free to do his own thing and to live as he pleases? No, for there is no need, nor is there any justification, for the Ethical Egoist to introduce any moral rights or wrongs into the picture. Thus rather than ever claiming that it is in any sense "right" (*i.e.*, morally right) that he be free, the Egoist need only maintain that "naturally" (*i.e.*, in the hypothetical state of nature) he is free as a matter of fact. Not only that, but he will doubtless also go on to insist that this "natural" freedom of action, which he cherishes so deeply, is something that he is determined to keep for himself and to hold onto at all costs. Yes, he will even fight for it, and die for it, if need be; not as a matter of right, be it noted, but always simply on the ground that he likes his freedom and wants to keep it.

But, then, what if other human beings move in to restrict this natural freedom of the individual, or even perhaps deprive him of it altogether? Once again, the Rational Egoist, if he is consistent, cannot say that there is anything "wrong" with others thus infringing upon his liberty. At the same time, because the Libertarian Egoist is determined to fight for and defend his liberty, he may succeed in making it highly inexpedient for his neighbor thus to try to violate his liberties. But although he may be able to make it inexpedient or unwise for his fellow citizens to interfere with him, he still cannot maintain that there is anything "wrong" in such interference, or that his neighbors have any duty or obligation to observe any "side constraints" on their own behavior with respect to him. Given such considerations, one can see how the Libertarian is then able to explain and account for, and even in a somewhat weakened sense, to justify a transition from a state of nature in which each individual is entirely on his own to a state of civil society in which the individual is perforce caught up in various common enterprises with his fellows. For rather than uncritically assuming that a state of nature in which each individual is completely free to do just as he likes must necessarily lead to a Hobbesian war of all against all, the Libertarian could insist instead that, rather than fighting each other, the liberty-loving egoists of the state of nature might well make up their minds that mutual accommodation between individuals would surely be preferable and better than mutual strife and internecine warfare.

After all, the Libertarian reasons, it may be presumed that he is not the only one who loves liberty; on the contrary, most, if not all, of his fellow human beings must surely love their liberties no less than he. Not only that, but they, as well as he, can readily come to understand that so long as individuals are under constant threats of force or fraud or violence from their neighbors, neither they nor their neighbors can very well enjoy their freedoms and their liberties in any way or in any measure that could be considered to be at all satisfactory. And so it is that what I have already designated as being a mutual accommodation between individuals—whether by tacit agreement or by formal contract or however—is something that patently recommends itself to each and all alike. Accordingly, mutual protective associations, and perhaps minimal states, yes, maybe even full-fledged states, may come to be born, the underlying principle in all of these being the restriction, and the hope of the eventual elimination, of all force, fraud, and violence on the part of individuals toward one another. By such means, naturally free individuals can hope thus to come to live in peace and harmony with one another to such a degree as to permit a maximum enjoyment on the part of each of such liberties as can be preserved from the state of nature and as are compatible with the maintenance of at least a minimal social order.

The Sheer Consistency of the Principal Argument for Rational Egoism

This summary account of such an ethics of Egoism or Rational Individualism suffices to show that as an ethical position it is consistent. At no point and at no place is there any squinting in the direction of deontology. For remaining true to the radical roots of any proper desire-ethic, such an Ethical Egoism will have no truck with "oughts," duties, or obligations, save only such as are entirely conditional upon what the Rational Individualist himself considers that he wants or desires. "Oh," but you will say, "has it not emerged directly from the account of the matter given above that Rational Egoists and Individualists are very much given to entering into agreements with their fellow human beings, agreements that may well attain to the status of social contracts or compacts no less? And given that a Rational Individualist does thus enter into a social contract—a contract that presumably would involve the establishment of an entire legal system designed to outlaw all force, fraud, violence, *et al.*—will it not then be the case that such a Rational

36

Individualist will be bound by the terms of that contract, regardless of whether in a given instance he finds it to be to his interest or liking to abide by that contract?"

But no, the Libertarian moralist need never admit—provided he is careful in how he states his case—that such a social contract ever binds him to act contrary to what he sees it to be in his own interest to do. No, for as a Libertarian who is at the same time a Rational Individualist, he will be the first to recognize that there are many things that, in a non-moral sense, one "ought" to do or will be obliged to do, if one is ever to attain the ends and goals that one has set for oneself. Thus in a social context, it is not hard for any individual to see that at least one goal or objective that cannot be other than very dear to him is what old Hobbes called "peace." And peace, or "the peace," means social order, and social order means the elimination of force, fraud, and violence. Accordingly, as a Rational Egoist, although I can recognize that there are many occasions when I might think it to my advantage, say, to defraud my neighbor or my fellow citizen, or to do him violence, in some way or other, a moment's reflection will tell me that it is not really to my advantage thus to practice force or fraud or violence against someone, simply because that is likely to "disturb the peace."

Once again, be it noted that in the context thus described, there would be nothing that would be "wrong," in the sense of morally wrong, in my defrauding my neighbor. No, it is just that I recognize that in the circumstances it would be the wrong thing to do, merely in the sense of its being an unwise or inexpedient thing for me to do under the circumstances. And so likewise, if it is objected that the consequences of any such Libertarian or Egoistic ethics are bound to be nothing if not disastrous, if it is nothing but this sort of ethics that underlies the maintenance of social order within the community as a whole, then the answer to this objection is readily forthcoming; and yet it attains its full force only after some dialectical interplay. After all, if an individual is in no wise bound to observe any commitments or obligations, save only insofar as and to the extent that he wants to observe them, then social order will become impossible—or at least so it will be said. Even this horrified reaction to this particular Libertarian position, however, need not phase the really determined Libertarian, or Rational Individualist. For he has only to observe that of course the individual is no longer bound by any commitment or obligation, if he no longer considers it to be expedient to abide by any such earlier agreements. But that will only mean that for the maintenance of any proper social order, it will be necessary to keep individuals continually in mind of the fact that it is expedient for them to observe their contracts and obligations. And one of the more obvious reasons why presumably it is thus expedient for individuals to keep their promises is that if they do not, they will be punished or otherwise come to grief. In other words, if the consequences to individuals of their not heeding their contractual duties and obligations are serious enough, this would surely operate as a powerful persuader, making individuals see that such duties and obligations as they may have thought it no longer in their interest to abide by are very much in their interest to abide by.

Returning once again to our perennial example of our obligations as American citizens under the Fifth and Fourteenth Amendments not to deprive our fellow citizens of life, liberty, or property without due process of law, if one were now to ask the Libertarian moralist, "But why and by what right am I thus prevented from depriving someone of his life, liberty, or property?" the answer would need to be: "Ultimately the only reason for your not doing such things is that you don't want to do such things to a fellow citizen, and the reason that you don't want to treat him that way is that you recognize that it would not be wise, or expedient, or to *your* advantage to treat him that way." To all of which we might imagine someone's frustrated rejoinder: "Oh, but such a program for ethics and law in society never will work. It is much too bland! If the only deterrent to individuals perpetrating the very worst crimes against their neighbors is only that it is not in their interest to do so, then that will surely spell a quick end to all law and order, not to mention all morals and ethics!" To which the answer surely is, "Bland it may well be, but at least it is consistent." Nor can it be said to be guilty of any Utilitarian squint in which it is pretended on the one hand that in any desire-ethic it is only on the basis of our desires that our duties may be determined, and then, on the other hand, it is suddenly asserted that our supposed duties in the matter of altruism are such as to take precedence over our personal interests and desires after all.

Does the Application of the Principle of Universalizability Shatter That Consistency?

Wait a minute, though, for there is still a serious lacuna in our case for an ethics of Rational Individualism as being able to provide a sound

38

rationale for human rights and duties, as well as an apparatus of justification for such guarantees of personal liberty as might be enunciated, say, in the Bill of Rights of the U.S. Constitution, or, indeed, in the entire tradition of so-called common law rights. That lacuna is our failure thus far to deal adequately with that one standard line of criticism that it has long been fashionable to level against any and all forms of so-called egoism in ethics. It is precisely this line of criticism that could be singularly telling, supposing that it could be sustained, against the Rational Individualism that is often associated with present-day Libertarians. This is the criticism that turns on that so-called Principle of Universalizability that I earlier mentioned. It is a criticism to which in recent times G. E. Moore might be said to have given a particular currency. But of course, the basic line of thought that Moore availed himself of in his "refutation of egoism" could doubtless be traced back to Kant.

Still, however much such refutations of egoism may have been the stock in trade of both latter-day teleologists and deontologists in ethics, it is not a "refutation" that need touch any Rational Egoist who is sufficiently careful and informed as to keep his logical and linguistic skirts clean. Nor is it a refutation that I have not already considered and weighed in the balance and found wanting. For it was just such a refutation of egoism in terms of the so-called Principle of Universalizability that in the preceding section I found the Utilitarians to be ever trying to invoke to prove that in any desire-ethic, one is necessarily bound to reckon not only with one's own interests, desires, pleasures, purposes, and so on, but also to reckon with the interests of others—that is, with the greatest happiness of the greatest number. Accordingly, having already seen that such a line of argument will not work to uphold a position of Utilitarianism, we have now but to see how it will equally fail to work in undermining a position like that of Rational Egoism or Individualism.

Indeed, to see how the Principle of Universalizability is supposed to work as a refutation of such a Rational Egoism, let us project ourselves imaginatively into the situation that the Rational Egoist recognizes himself as being in, and then let us proceed more or less dialectically in an attempted assessment and appraisal of that situation. Thus as a Rational Egoist, suppose that I simply ask myself directly what some of the things are that I value most in life and that mean more to me than anything else. And suppose that I respond by saying that I tend to cherish my personal liberty above all else. Again, by personal liberty, let it be understood that I mean a condition of my very being or existence that will enable me to exercise continually that very freedom of enterprise that I have already alluded to repeatedly. It is this, let us say, that I do not merely cherish and hold dear in any superficial sense, but rather as something that I would most assuredly be willing to fight for, and even die for, if need be.

But why? it may be asked. Why would I be willing to go to such lengths to secure and to defend my personal liberty? In answer, suppose that I simply try to hew to the line of the Rational Egoist. My reasons, I would say, for wanting to defend my own liberty are purely selfish. For surely, my personal liberty is not anything that I can be said to be determined to keep for anyone else's sake, or out of any regard for a sense of duty, or even out of any fancied notion that it is somehow mine by right. No, the simple fact is that I want to be free because that is my preference, and that ends the matter.

Right here, though, is the point at which one might imagine some sophisticated, latter-day wielder of the Principle of Universalizability moving in on the scene and attempting to show that my attempted justification of personal liberty on purely selfish grounds entails a manifest inconsistency. For surely, as a Rational Egoist, when I am challenged to give a reason for my passionate love of liberty, I can scarcely say that the reason that I would be willing even to die for my liberties is just that I would. After all, such a reason is tantamount to no reason at all. And yet surely, as one who claims to be a Rational Egoist, or Rational Individualist, I must be prepared to give some reason for my commitment and devotion to liberty. Moreover, such reasons must be reasons, not in the sense of possible causal forces, psychological or physiological or sociological, that happen to operate upon me and that might be thought to influence my behavior; no, they need to be justifying reasons for my determined devotion to and pursuit of liberty. Immediately, though, would not the very logic of any such presumed logical justification somehow compel me as a Rational Egoist to maintain that the reason I so value my personal liberty is because it is of unquestionable worth and value to a human being: it is something that is good in itself, and thus is of value not just for me but for any human being—"the pearl of great price," if you will.

No sooner, though, does the force of the dialectic bring me to acknowledge this much than my very egoism would thereby appear to be effectively undermined. For was not my original claim that my love of personal liberty was entirely selfish? It was something that I wanted simply for myself, and for no other reason than that I tended to be drawn to and to cherish it on personal grounds alone. But now—so the universalizability argument runs—have I not been brought to acknowledge that my reason for my devotion to liberty is not just that I happen to like it, but rather because I see it to be of genuine worth and value? And yet how can anything that is reckoned to be of worth and value—that is, to be good—for one person not be reckoned also to be of worth and value universally, and for anyone and everyone alike?

Indeed, in this connection, defenders of the Universalizability Principle have argued that value judgments may be compared strictly to certain factual judgments. Thus if I say that X is square, or that it is made of iron, I cannot possibly mean that it is square, or made of iron, only for me. No, I must mean that X is square, or that it is made of iron, really and in fact; and that therefore these are facts that anyone and everyone must recognize simply because they are true. It is true that I might be mistaken in my judgment either that X is square, or that it is made of iron; and then, of course, I might be brought to admit that when I made my original judgment, X must have only seemed to be so to me but was not really so. Still, this does not affect the meaning and import of my judgment when originally I made it; and that was that X was square and was made of iron and that it was so, and not just for me but also for anyone and everyone who might fairly consider the evidence. And so also with judgments of worth or value: the so-called Rational Egoist cannot possibly maintain that the things so judged are of worth or value only for him; no, if his judgment is true, those things must be reckoned to be of worth and value for anyone and everyone given similar circumstances.

Would it not seem that as a Rational Egoist I can no longer maintain that my concern with my own personal liberty is no more than a purely private and personal concern? On the contrary, by my own admission I have been brought to recognize that liberty is a true good, and hence something that must be reckoned a good, not just for myself but for any and every human being alike. Indeed, the only way any egoist, who at the same time would be a Rational Egoist, could ever justify or give a reason for his own pursuit of personal liberty would be by recognizing that such liberty was of genuine worth and value: it was just this concession that was needed to provide the Egoist with a basis for justifying his conduct, in that he can now maintain that his own liberty is something that it is only right that he should pursue. But if it is right that he should pursue such a goal, then the implication must be that this very rightness and justifiability of his conduct and behavior must be recognized by anyone and everyone else. Not only that, but having thus been brought to claim that he has a right to his own liberty and freedom of enterprise, he must then for his part—by the logic of the universalizability of all moral and ethical terms and notions—acknowledge others to have an equal right to freedom and liberty of action no less than he. In other words, so far from being any longer able to maintain that he need occupy himself only with his own private concerns and purely personal tastes and interests, the Rational Egoist would now seem to have been brought to the place at which he cannot but acknowledge himself to be caught up in an entire order of interlocking rights and duties with respect to other human beings, and they with respect to him. And what does this do to his pretended egoism, as well as to his earlier insistence that in his own conduct and behavior as a Rational Egoist he did not need to concern himself in any way with duties toward others, or, for that matter, even with any fancied rights of his own, which others would have a duty to honor and respect?

But Does Not the Principle of Universalizability Turn Out to Be Inapplicable?

It would seem, then, that the entire edifice of an ethics of Rational Egoism, or of rational self-interest, comes tumbling down like a house of cards, and all because of the applicability of the Principle of Universalizability. And yet does it? Is it true that any and all forms of an uncompromising ethics of Rational Egoism or Rational Individualism must find themselves to be undone, once contemporary moral philosophers have got through wielding their favorite ax in the form of the Principle of Universalizability? Hardly. Indeed, as I have already intimated, it would seem that all the Ethical Egoist needs to do is to be a bit more careful in the language he uses in formulating his position, and immediately the criticism in terms of the supposed universalizability of ethical terms and expressions will be seen to be happily and totally irrelevant.

For just consider: the universalizability argument depends for its cogency upon little more than a simple and obvious distinction that recent linguistic philosophers have been particularly keen to seize upon and to point up. This is the distinction between what we might call mere "desire"-words, or words of mere liking and preference on the one hand, and what might be called moral words or "value"-words on the other. Indeed, it is this distinction that becomes singularly illuminating, so far as the Principle of Universalizability is concerned. Thus if I say, for example, that I like X, or that I find X pleasing, there is no way in which such a judgment can be considered to be universalizable: the mere fact that I like X, or find it to my taste, in no way implies that anyone else necessarily has to like it or find it to his taste. In contrast, if I say "X is good," or "is of worth and value," or "is right" or "wrong," or "is what I ought to do," then each and every one of these judgments is inevitably and inescapably universalizable: that it is right for me to act in such and such a way under certain circumstances implies, by the logic of a moral word like "right," that such conduct is no less right for any and every other human being under similar circumstances. Likewise, to say that the character of a certain person is good—that he is a good man, let us say—inevitably implies that any and every other person of a like character must be adjudged to be good as well.

But now note that this difference in what might be called the logical grammar or linguistic behavior of "desire"-words, on the one hand, and moral or "value"-words, on the other, is a distinction which the Ethical Egoist can perfectly well admit. Indeed, once he does admit it, he can then turn it directly to his own advantage by using it neatly to circumvent the Principle of Universalizability. Nevertheless, to see how this can be done, we need to consider still another distinction or, perhaps better, ambiguity in word usage, which is of particular pertinence in the present connection. This time the distinction is attributable not to our latter-day linguistic and analytical philosophers but rather to Plato; and it is a distinction that bears directly on the meaning and use of the word "good." Recalling the question Socrates raised in the *Euthyphro:* [16] are we to call things good because they are beloved of the gods, or are they beloved of the gods because they are good? In other words, there would seem to be no denying that sometimes we use the word "good" simply to signify that we like something. "I think beer is good"— does this mean anything more than that I like beer? The so-called goodness or value of a thing, in such instances, means simply that we

16. Plato, *Euthyphro*, 10 a.

like it. On the other hand, and in other connections, we frequently judge things to be good—a good man, or a good painting, or a good cause. But this time our judgment that something is good does not mean merely that we like it; rather, it means that the man, or the painting, or the cause is something that we ought to like, or ought to value, whether we actually do or not, and that, for the very reason that the man or the painting or the cause is held to be really good or objectively good, and hence good not merely relative to our liking it, or finding it to be to our taste.

Very well, why may not the Ethical Egoist, availing himself now of what might thus be called the *Euthyphro* test, simply take the position that whenever he uses the word "good," he uses it only in the sense in which things are said to be good because they are desired, and not in the sense in which things are said to be desired because they are good? Moreover, having thus determined upon his particular way of using the word "good," and for that matter all other value-words as well, why may not the Ethical Egoist then round on his critics and point out that the Principle of Universalizability is applicable only when "good" is used in the sense of values that determine our desires, rather than in the sense of values that are determined by our desires? Indeed, the only reason that our imagined Rational Egoist seemed to be worsted in the dialectical game that we went through earlier was that he let himself be trapped into admitting that his own personal liberty was a good for him and was of value to him, not simply on the ground that he liked it, but rather on the ground that it was something that was supposedly somehow objectively good, and therefore that ought to be liked and desired, whether it was actually so or not. But for the Rational Egoist to admit that his personal liberty was of value to him in this latter sense could only mean that it would have to be no less of value to any and all other human beings as well. And having conceded this much, the egoist would then have to acknowledge that no sooner did he thereby allow himself to be drawn into trying to justify or to defend his own pursuit of liberty, on the ground that it is something that is right for him to pursue, than the Universalizability argument would immediately become applicable, and the poor egoist would be undone: if it is right for the egoist to pursue his personal liberty, then it is no less right for any and every other human being to do so as well; and if others therefore have a duty to respect that which it is only right for the egoist to seek for himself, it is no less a duty for the egoist to respect the same right in everyone else as well.

But no, the egoist does not have to be drawn into this dialectic of the Universalizability argument. All he has to do is to be consistent in his determination to use "good" in one sense of the *Euthyphro* test and not in the other. For him "good" is to be understood as meaning no more than that something is to his (the egoist's) taste and liking. And if he is challenged to explain or justify why he should thus pursue what he likes or desires, he need only refuse to be drawn into that trap. For is it not perfectly obvious why a person should do what he wants to do, or should follow his own tastes and likings, or seek after his own ends? Why need one ever feel called upon to give any further reason in such cases? Is it not reason enough that a person should be doing what he does, or should be leading the life that he is leading, simply because that is what he wants to be doing? Accordingly, by taking such a position, and by being consistent about it, the Rational Egoist can thus obviate the applicability, so far as he is concerned, of that dreaded Principle of Universalizability.

The Final Undoing of Rational Egoism: It Is Not an Ethics at all

Does not this last argument restore the ethics of Rational Egoism or Rational Self-Interest to grace and favor? The widespread assumption of contemporary moral philosophers that any egoistic ethics cannot avoid inconsistency, once the Principle of Universalizability is applied to it, may now be seen to be largely unwarranted: the Principle of Universalizability, though entirely valid as a formal principle of language or logic, is nevertheless not a principle that is applicable in the case of such systems of egoistic ethics as can claim to be carefully conceived and crafted. Moreover, once an ethics of Rational Self-Interest is thus found to be perfectly self-consistent, we need then but remind ourselves that presumably it is only an ethics of this nature that can rightly claim to be properly teleological. And if our earlier analyses are correct, there would seem to be no other way in which either legal or moral obligations can ever hope to find a proper basis and justification, save in terms of an ethical teleology. For if any legal system is largely an affair of various specified rights and duties, the rights being always understood in terms of the corresponding duties to respect those rights, then the question becomes practically inescapable as to just why, and how, and with what justice, a given individual, or set of individuals, may be held to be obligated to perform, or to refrain from performing, certain actions. But when such a question is put to the mine-run of our latter-day ethical deontologists, they seem sadly to flunk the test. For they seem unable to conceive of duties as being in the final analysis anything other than prior to human ends and desires, as if always what as human beings we may want to do, or purpose to do, must give way before considerations as to what it is right for us to do, or what we ought to do. But this unfortunately consigns moral "oughts" (and indirectly legal "oughts" as well) to a condition of sticking up like so many sore thumbs, and without any ultimate rhyme or reason. Why, for example, ought I to respect the life, liberty, and property of my neighbor? The notions that I am naturally obligated to do this, or contractually obligated, or even linguistically obligated do not seem to have any telling evidence to support them. And so we find ourselves brought back to the idea that ultimately the only basis on which it can be said that anyone ought to do thus and so is because it is only by doing thus and so that he can ever hope to achieve some purpose or objective which he has set for himself. Here is a way of providing a reason, or a rational justification, for what, in a given case, it is said that we ought to do; besides, it is a reason which is at once intelligible and cogent.

From this, then, must not our one conclusion be that, insofar as we think of the law as being in search of an ethic, the one and only type of ethics that can end such a search is a more or less Libertarian ethic of Rational Individualism or Rational Self-Interest? Not quite. For we have seen how a Libertarian ethic, although it may be entirely self-consistent, still might prove to be unworkable. Who can ever honestly believe that human beings can, by and large, be persuaded, either by reason or by threats, to recognize that it is in their own interest to respect the rights of others to life, liberty, property, and all the rest; and that, seeing that such moral and law-abiding behavior is in their own interest, they will then act accordingly? All of this seems, alas, highly unlikely.

Still, waiving this point as to what we might call the feasibility of a Libertarian ethic, or ethic of Rational Individualism, there is an even more serious difficulty that would appear to defeat this ethics. It is the difficulty that an ethics that is erected entirely upon considerations of rational self-interest is not really an ethics at all. Consider: it may be all very well for a defender of an ethics of Rational Individualism to claim that his is the only consistent desire-ethic, in that it allows itself never to involve rights and duties, save such as may be derived solely from considerations of the individual's own self-interest. And yet just what rights and duties are those that are derivable only from considerations of self-interest?

Thus for one thing, although it is true that if I desire X, or if X is my end, then if *a*, *b*, and *c* are necessary means to attaining that end, there is a sense in which it may be said that it is only "right" that I do *a*, *b*, and *c*, or that I "ought" to do *a*, *b*, and *c*. And yet clearly, must it not be said that what I thus ought to do in this latter sense is an admittedly nonmoral "ought"? In fact, it is no different from such "oughts" as are relevant in the various arts and crafts. That is, they are "oughts" only in the sense in which the various how-to-do-it rules in the several arts and crafts specify what ought to be done if one is to ply one's art or craft well. Thus when I am fishing, if I want to cast my bait out in such a way as to make it come down at a certain spot not too distant from the shore, then I ought to hold the rod in such and such a way, and thumb the reel so much and no more, and so on. These, however, are clearly not moral "oughts," but only what might be called the "oughts" that go with a particular skill or craft.

Likewise, as noted earlier, it is all very well for the Libertarian moralist to say that he would be the first to respect the rights of his fellow citizens to life, liberty, and property, and yet that he does this out of no more than considerations of his own self-interest. And yet what is this, if not to admit that others do not have such rights after all, it being only to the extent that the Rational Individualist finds it to his advantage to pretend that they have them and to act as if they had them. The Libertarian or Rational Individualist needs to go even further and acknowledge that he cannot claim to have any real rights of his own, as against his fellow citizens. No, for he must acknowledge that his own rights are contingent upon others' feeling it to be to their advantage to concede him such rights; but given that it should cease to be to their advantage to respect his life or his liberty or his property, and even the Libertarian must admit that his own right-claims must cease forthwith. And what rights are those that are contingent merely upon the whims of others?

Finally, even those means that the Rational Egoist successfully resorts to in beating back efforts to refute his egoism by appeals to the Principle of Universalizability, in turn, serve to discredit the claims that the Egoist makes that his position is properly moral or ethical. Thus as we have seen, if the Egoist claims that his personal freedom and liberty, for example, are things that he cherishes most highly, and that he would never want to surrender, it is important that he here invoke the *Euthyphro* test and that he make it abundantly clear that he considers his freedom and liberty good only in the sense that he happens to value or cherish them, and not in the sense that he values and cherishes them because he recognizes them to be good—that is, truly good or objectively good. Nevertheless, the minute he interprets goodness and value in this way, immediately those things which he holds to be good or to be of value lose all moral import. Why? Is not the reason traceable to that same radical weakness that we earlier found to be characteristic of any and every desire-ethic? The mere fact that I desire something, or like it, or want it, is no ground for supposing that I am morally entitled to it, or that I ought to have it, or that it is only right that I should have it. In other words, to try to get mileage for morals or ethics out of the mere fact that human beings have certain interests or desires or purposes is very like trying to get blood out of a turnip.

And with that, the fatal weakness of any supposed ethics of Rational Egoism or Rational Self-Interest is spelled out in starkest detail: there is no way that it can claim to be an ethics.

CHAPTER II

NATURAL LAW AS THE ANSWER TO THE LAW'S QUEST FOR AN ETHICS

NATURAL LAW: A DESPERATE REMEDY FOR A DESPERATE SITUATION?

From my first chapter it should have become clear that one has no choice but to write off practically the whole of contemporary ethics as being largely bankrupt. Indeed, none of the regnant ethical theories that dominate the present philosophical scene, at least in the English-speaking world—neither teleology nor deontology, neither a desire-ethic nor a duty-ethic, neither Utilitarianism nor Kantianism—would seem competent to provide an adequate basis or foundation for human rights claims or for any moral or ethical principles.

Nor must it be thought that I am alone in having reached so sweeping, not to say devastating, a conclusion with respect to present-day theories of ethics. In his recent book, *After Virtue*, Alasdair Mac-Intyre has bluntly concluded that contemporary Analytical Philosophy, as it has come to be called, has so signally failed to provide any adequate basis or grounding for ethics that it now has no other option but to close up shop and counsel its adherents among present-day moral, legal, and political philosophers that they might as well be reconciled in the future to going either the way of Aristotle or of Nietzsche.[1]

Why Aristotle or Nietzsche? And what is the sense of MacIntyre's pronouncement that contemporary ethics has no choice but to go either the way of Aristotle or of Nietzsche? Of course, our immediate and ready suggestion is that the way of Aristotle is tantamount to the way of natural law. And the way of natural law, in turn, boils down to an insistence that the only way a proper basis and grounding can ever be

---

1. Alasdair MacIntyre, *After Virtue: A Study in Moral Theory* (Notre Dame, Ind., 1981), esp. chap. 9.

found for ethics is in reality and in the facts of nature. But what is this, if not to say that moral laws need to be seen as no more and no less than natural laws, discoverable in the very facts of nature?

To continue in the same vein, I would ask what else has been responsible for the collapse of modern ethics if not the attempt that has consistently been made either to confine ethics to an exclusive concern with trying to figure out how as human beings we may best satisfy our manifold interests and desires—even though there seems not to be the slightest evidence that what men desire or find it to be to their advantage to do is necessarily the right thing for them to do; or, as an alternative, to restrict ethics to a concern with so many categorical "dos" and "don'ts," which apparently have no warrant for being binding upon us, unless it be the pathetically slim warrant that we somehow intuit them to be binding. Why, then, worry any longer about the different forms of ethics, which, whatever rhyme or reason they might seem to have on the surface, nevertheless turn out to be without basis or foundation? And so, exit modern ethics. In its place, why not retrieve the simple truth that for any ethics, no less than for any other branch of human knowledge, the one and only basis must be in the facts of nature and of reality? This, indeed, is what a return to the way of Aristotle, or, as we might prefer to call it, the way of natural law, would amount to. "The stone which the builders rejected should now become the head of the corner." (Matt. 21:42).

And now, in turn, what may we understand by that alternative to the way of Aristotle—at least as proposed by MacIntyre—viz., the way of Nietzsche? Can this be anything other than our simply saying to ourselves: "If moral and ethical judgments may never be based on fact, and cannot even claim to be in any sense properly cognitive judgments, or judgments that reflect knowledge, then why not recognize that the practice of morals and ethics can amount to little more than an exercise of the will to power? After all, if there can be no reasons ultimately for our recommendations of what men ought or ought not to do, or of what it is right for them to do, what else is behind such recommendations except our will that these recommendations be heeded, as well as our determination to force them to be heeded? In other words, such a way in ethics is none other than the way of the will to power."[2]

2. The term "the way of Nietzsche" is MacIntyre's. But I make no claim that my exposition of the implications of this so-called way of Nietzsche is necessarily faithful to the specific teachings of Nietzsche.

Why not pause a minute to illustrate more graphically and concretely what some of the implications might be of our deciding to make
ethics depend on nothing more than an exercise of the will to power?
Thus consider the following passage from Thucydides, Book III:

When troubles had once begun in the cities, those who followed carried the revolutionary spirit further and further, and determined to
outdo the report of all who had preceded them by the ingenuity of their
enterprises and the atrocity of their revenges. The meaning of words had
no longer the same relation to things, but was changed by them as they
thought proper. Reckless daring was held to be loyal courage; prudent
delay was the excuse of a coward; moderation was the disguise of un-
manly weakness; to know everything was to do nothing. Frantic energy
was the true quality of a man. A conspirator who wanted to be safe was
a recreant in disguise. The lover of violence was always trusted, and his
opponent suspected. He who succeeded in a plot was deemed knowing,
but a still greater master in craft was he who detected one. On the other
hand, he who plotted from the first to have nothing to do with plots was
a breaker up of parties and a poltroon who was afraid of the enemy. In
a word, he who could outstrip another in a bad action was applauded,
and so was he who encouraged to evil one who had no idea of it. The tie
of party was stronger than the tie of blood, because a partisan was more
ready to dare without asking why. (For party associations are not based
upon any established law, nor do they seek the public good; they are
formed in defiance of the laws and from self-interest.) The seal of good
faith was not divine law, but fellowship in crime. If an enemy when he
was in the ascendant offered fair words, the opposite party received them
not in a generous spirit, but by a jealous watchfulness of his actions. Re-
venge was dearer than self-preservation. Any agreements sworn to by either party, when they could do nothing else, were binding as long as both
were powerless. But he who on a favourable opportunity first took courage, and struck at his enemy when he saw him off his guard, had greater
pleasure in a perfidious than he would have had in an open act of re-
venge; he congratulated himself that he had taken the safer course, and
also that he had overreached his enemy and gained the prize of superior
ability. In general the dishonest more easily gain credit for cleverness than
the simple for goodness; men take a pride in the one, but are ashamed
of the other.

The cause of all these evils was the love of power, originating in ava-
rice and ambition, and the party-spirit which is engendered by them when
men are fairly embarked in a contest. For the leaders on either side used
specious names, the one party professing to uphold the constitutional

equality of the many, the other the wisdom of an aristocracy, while they made the public interests, to which in name they were devoted, in reality their prize. Striving in every way to overcome each other, they committed the most monstrous crimes; yet even these were surpassed by the magnitude of their revenges which they pursued to the very utmost, neither party observing any definite limits either of justice or public expediency, but both alike making the caprice of the moment their law. Either by the help of an unrighteous sentence, or grasping power with the strong hand, they were eager to satiate the impatience of party-spirit. Neither faction cared for religion; but any fair pretence which succeeded in effecting some odious purpose was greatly lauded. And the citizens who were of neither party fell a prey to both; either they were disliked because they held aloof, or men were jealous of their surviving.[3]

Now for all of its power, and for all of the gruesome and unsettling picture it paints, what Thucydides here depicts is still not an entirely just and adequate representation of either the resources or the full import of the way of the will to power. For it is as though Thucydides were saying that when men become obsessed with the love of power, they are driven to little else than, as the Greeks would say, "making the worse appear the better part," as if black could be made white or good could be made evil, or right made wrong. And equally, of course, the other way as well: for under the conditions of "the troubles once they had begun in the cities," the white was no less made to appear black, and the right wrong, and the good evil.

But the real import of a situation in human affairs, when men give themselves over to guidance from a mere will to power is that the wrong and the right, the good and the evil, the black and the white, become but so many fictions or appearances, so many ways of looking at things, which the power of men creates and then foists upon the face of reality. And thus it is that might does not merely make right; rather, it makes both right and wrong; and not just right and wrong but the entire color and character of being and reality—these are all functions of what our human will to power would make or compel the facts to be. "Nothing is good and evil," you say, "but thinking makes it so." And in a will-to-power philosophy it is not just thinking that makes things appear to be so but the power to enforce our thoughts upon things and then to compel these things to be the way we want them to be—that is the decisive import of a will-to-power philosophy.

3. *Thucydides*, trans. Benjamin Jowett (2 vols., Oxford, 1900), Vol. I, Bk. III, pp. 242–44.

Moreover, even though Thucydides seems not to sense the full import of a will-to-power philosophy, he nevertheless succeeds in putting his finger on one of the key instruments in any exercise of man's will to power. It is the instrument of language: "The meaning of words had no longer the same relation to things, but was changed by them as they thought proper." Thucydides might thus be said to anticipate the Orwellian implications of a Nietzschean will-to-power philosophy. For surely, if human beings are able (*i.e.*, have the power) to make words mean whatever we want them to mean, and without having to pay the slightest heed or regard to what the facts may be (or what truth or reality may be), then the facts themselves will turn out to be no more than what our language represents them to be or forces them to be. And so far from our thoughts and our language having ever ultimately to conform to the way the world is, or the way things are, it must rather be that the facts themselves—even being itself—must conform to the way our language and our thoughts would have them be. Nor is there, then, any stopping short of those grisly phenomena which George Orwell depicts under the heading of "Newspeak," or in which, as Orwell recounts it, the very telling and writing of history—even simply telling the truth—turns out to be a gigantic enterprise of causing that which did not happen actually to have happened or of making that which is not true, true. Such, indeed, would be the import of opting for the alternative of the way of Nietzsche, or the way of the will to power.

The Stumbling-Block to the Way of Aristotle

So much for a characterization of the two alternatives MacIntyre suggests as being possible ways out of the desperate straits which present-day moral philosophers find themselves in—the way of Aristotle and the way of Nietzsche. Which way shall we ourselves take? MacIntyre, of course, leaves little doubt that he would prefer the way of Aristotle to the way of Nietzsche. And so would I. True, we shall need later on to advert once more to the way of Nietzsche and try to mount a somewhat more proper critique of it, not just a horrified reaction. For the present, though, let us turn our attention to a more full-dress explanation and defense of what MacIntyre calls the way of Aristotle, and what I might prefer to call the way of natural law.

At the outset, I should offer a firm disclaimer: I would not want it to be thought that my own contentions in regard to natural law are designed simply to parallel those of MacIntyre in regard to Aristotle. And I say this out of concern not just for MacIntyre's reputation but for my own as well. MacIntyre will develop and defend his Aristotelianism in his way and I in mine.

So far as natural law is concerned, we are all no doubt aware that there once existed an ancient and honorable tradition of natural-law teachings, stemming from Aristotle, developed by the Scholastic philosophers, notably St. Thomas Aquinas, and extending well down into modern times. This Aristotelian natural-law tradition, if we may so term it, comprised both a well-thought-out set of moral principles and an assemblage of legal and political doctrines, fitting into an elaborately articulated set of philosophical teachings. In our own days, however, natural-law doctrines are distinctly out of fashion—and they have been out of fashion ever since the seventeenth century. For I have already remarked several times that ever since the advent of modern science, it has tended to be supposed that morals and ethics could not be based on facts of nature. Instead, both ethical teleology and ethical deontology need to be interpreted as representing different attempts by modern moral philosophers to base their ethics on foundations other than those of the real world and the *natura rerum*. And as I have suggested, this might well have been the reason why almost the entire enterprise of modern moral philosophy has been such a resounding failure. Why, then, might it not be well to try to recover for moral philosophy a basis in natural law? Again, "The stone which the builders rejected," and so on.

Still, is not the trouble that this particular stone which the builders rejected—that of a natural law within the domain of morals and ethics—was rejected for good reason and that there seems to be no way in the present day to restore that stone, much less to make it the head of the corner? Consider the question: how is natural law to be thought of as providing at once a foundation and a norm with respect to positive law? Is it as if there either were, or could be, "a natural law," actually existing somehow, somewhere, in reality, which might for this reason be thought able to exercise a normative, and perhaps a corrective, and maybe even an attractive, function with respect to positive laws, as these exist in various human societies? This idea sounds Platonic, you might say; or, worse yet, "medieval". And indeed, it doubtless is medieval in that it was St. Thomas Aquinas who in the thirteenth century provided a largely definitive formulation of the doctrine of the *jus naturale* and *lex naturalis.* "The only trouble is," you will say, "we live in the twentieth century, not in the thirteenth. What possible significance can the idea of a natural law have for us today, unless it be merely one of antiquarian curiosity?"

Besides, one cannot very well use a term like "natural law," without there being immediately brought to mind the very similar term but quite different notion of "law of nature." And to the extent to which it is still fashionable today to use an expression such as "the laws of nature," we surely mean "scientific laws." But who is not perfectly well aware that "nature," or "the world of nature," or "the natural order," are all terms used to designate what everyone nowadays recognizes to be the modern scientists' area of investigation? Clearly, though, "nature" in any of these senses differs, one is tempted to say, *toto caelo* from "nature" in Aristotle's sense, and accordingly from any such *natura* as Aquinas may have had in mind when he talked about "natural law." With reference to our discussions in Chapter I, is it not significant that almost the last thing that even those modern thinkers who are concerned with trying to find a basis or justification in ethics for positive law would do would be to suppose that the morality with which they would wish positive law to become imbued could ever reflect a supposed natural or real morality in nature itself? That would seem nothing if not downright ridiculous.

Nor is it mere prejudice that has set the minds of modern moral philosophers so irrevocably against the notion that moral facts or moral laws could ever be discoverable in the natural world. The late John Mackie has put his finger on what it is that is not just radically wrong but practically inconceivable about the idea of treating moral laws as if they were natural laws. For as Mackie avers, any and every attempt within the discipline of ethics to treat moral and ethical principles as if they were objective, and hence discoverable directly in fact and in nature, has to face up to and deal with "the argument from queerness."[4] For, Mackie thinks, is it anything other than queer or odd to suppose that right and wrong could exist in nature, as if they were discoverable as verifiable facts of nature? Indeed, if this is what a natural-law ethical stance must entail, then in today's world the doctrine sounds not so much queer as downright crazy. And so we find ourselves brought face

4. J. L. Mackie, *Ethics: Inventing Right and Wrong* (Harmondsworth, 1977), 39–42.

to face with the question: as contemporary defenders of natural law, how can we possibly rebut this argument from queerness?

A Proposed Changed Understanding of Nature

Addressing this question, I must admit that for the present and in this current chapter, I will try to advance a temporary and half-baked defense in support of the view that despite all current prejudices to the contrary, there is a truly moral dimension to nature after all. For to make good on any such answer to the argument from queerness, I would need radically to reexamine those two fundamental and rival conceptions of nature—the Aristotelian or teleological account on the one hand, and the modern scientific, or what I would like to insist is a largely Cartesian, conception of nature on the other. Nor will it be enough merely to examine these two conceptions of nature—the teleological versus the nonteleological. It also is necessary to advance both evidence and argument to show that the Aristotelian or teleological account of nature is still defensible and thus not to be discarded out of hand.

But to bring off such a refutation of the argument from queerness—and particularly one along the lines just suggested—is a major undertaking, and one that will take some doing. That is why it is a job that must be deferred until my final chapter. For the present, I beg my readers' indulgence and offer a few considerations that might serve to render a teleological account, if not of the whole of nature, then maybe of human nature, at least initially plausible. After all, the very essence of any natural-law ethics is that there should be a veritable natural end, or natural perfection, or natural *telos*, of human life, discernible empirically and directly in the facts of nature. Given such a natural end, it should then be possible to determine what relevant natural laws a human being must observe, if he is ever to attain his natural end. And with that it would seem that the question that now confronts us is whether there could ever conceivably be a natural end in nature, and more specifically whether there could ever be such an end or *telos*, so far as human life is concerned; and if so, what is it?

Thus our work is surely cut out for us! First, then, reiterating one point that I have already made, the word "nature" is not always unambiguous. Not only is the term used in the modern scientific sense, but also we occasionally find it used in such a way as would require that it be understood in a sense that underlies an expression like that of "natural law." And to justify this latter usage I must confess to be under no illusions as to how tempting it has often been for modern defenders of natural law, especially in the Thomistic tradition, simply to try to set the clock back and to pretend to discard out of hand the modern scientific notion of nature in favor of a nature conceived on a more ancient model. But such temptations we must try to resist.

At the same time, there are features of the more ancient concept of nature which are by no means outmoded or irrelevant or even dispensable, to our present-day scientific understanding of nature. Thus we still continue to speak upon occasion of nature, in the sense of "the natures of things," as contrasted with nature as a whole or the overall order of nature. Thus one might say that it pertains to the nature of gold to be soluble in *aqua regia*; and yet is this true for every element, or is it true in the same way? Or again, so long as we are sticking to mere common-sense examples, we might return to our old favorite once again: it is the nature of water to seek its own level; but it is not true of iron. And so, too, with respect to almost any object that one can name in the natural world: are they not all subject to their characteristic actions and reactions, or characteristic behaviors, depending upon their specific natures? After all, the actions or reactions one expects from a tadpole are not the same as those one expects from a pine tree; and the life cycle of a deciduous tree is markedly different from that of a conifer. And hydrogen is unlike oxygen, and oxygen unlike manganese— they are not the same elements, which, again, is but to say that they have different natures.

This does not mean, of course, that in a sophisticated formulation of scientific theory, be it chemistry, biology, or geology, the scientist will necessarily be inclined to use so loose and imprecise a notion as "the natures of things." And yet merely because such a notion might not appear in the scientist's final, formalized account of his science, it is not a notion that he would dispense with entirely, certainly not in everyday use. In addition, he would no doubt say that for all of their imprecision, to talk about "the nature of lead," or "the nature of an oak leaf," or "the nature of a gas" is not wrong or mistaken. Indeed, considering the imprecision of such expressions, their continued use presumably signifies no more than that they cannot be reduced entirely to quantitative equivalents. And this is hardly ground for even the scientists to consider them wholly dispensable and therefore not true.

And now for still another step. Granted that objects in the natural world have the natures that they do, may we not also think of these natures as being causes in a sense? That is, they serve as an explanation of the differing modes of action and reaction of different objects. Why does water seek its own level but iron does not? Is it not because it is in the nature of water to behave in this way? Or again, why does a seed in the ground germinate and sprout, whereas a pebble does not? May we not say that a pebble is not capable of growth and development in the manner of a plant?

Letting this, then, suffice as a preliminary, and we might hope an initially plausible, characterization of "nature" as it needs to be understood in the context of a notion such as "natural law," ought we not now to say something about the notion of "law" as it functions in that same expression? Again, this can only be preliminary to my fuller treatment in the next section. But for the moment, may we not simply remark that just as we find ourselves speaking of the natures of objects and of these natures as being in a sense the causes and reasons why those objects behave as they do, do we not also talk about the laws that govern the behavior of the objects that have such and such natures? For if the nature of water, for example, determines the behavior of water in seeking its own level, why may we not speak of this as being a law of nature, or more specifically as a law of the nature of water, *viz.*, that it seeks its own level? In fact, "Water seeks its own level" is nothing if not a law of nature, even if a somewhat crude one; and certainly, as a law of nature, it is more specifically a law of the nature of water.

Laws of Nature as Rules of Action

But wait. Before we allow ourselves to be drawn further into a consideration of how "nature," in the sense in which we now understand that term, may be thought of as being subject to law, and of how in consequence terms like "natural law" or "law of nature" may best be understood, perhaps we ought first to consider what the more general notion of "law" may be taken to mean. Not that we want to leap into any formal and final definition of law as such, or of law in general. Instead, let us start with a comparatively uncontroversial characterization of law and then work into some of the more controversial implications of this characterization, attempting as we go along to dispel these controversies *seriatim* as they arise. To begin with, it is not uncommon to understand a law as being a rule, and perhaps more specifically, a rule of action or behavior. Such an initial characterization of law is common alike to St. Thomas Aquinas and to H. L. A. Hart—and that certainly covers a wide spectrum of difference.[5] Moreover, a further connotation of the notion of rule—as, for example, in my earlier reference to so-called how-to-do-it rules in the various arts and technologies—is that as a rule of action a law must at the same time be a norm or standard of action as well. It is in this sense that taking a law to be a rule, it would seem that the notion of a law could hardly be taken simply as reporting mere regularity of action or behavior that happens to occur. No, a law would also seem to be a recognizable ordering or regulating of that action, indicating how it should be done or ought to be performed.

Immediately, though, having said this much, we shall surely find ourselves met with both suspicion and protest. For no sooner is it made apparent that a definite normative element is reputedly built into any notion of law considered as a rule of action than the further and still more questionable element of a *telos* or end or purpose would seem equally indissociable from any notion of law as a rule of action. How otherwise could one possibly make sense of the idea of a law's being a norm or standard of the way something ought to be done, save by reference to the end to be accomplished by the action? Surely, this is undeniably the case with how-to-do-it rules in the arts. For what other ground could there be for someone's specifying a rule to be followed, as a way that an action should be performed, be it in butchering or bakering or candlestick making, than in terms of the relevant end that is in view—the meat to be offered for sale, or the loaf of bread to be put on the table, or the candle to burn in the candlestick? In other words, any law, conceived as a rule of action, necessarily presupposes some end toward which the action is aimed.

But what must this do if not discredit the entire conception of law that I am here proposing? Oh, it might be all right, someone might say, to think of so-called human laws, or man-made laws, as perhaps having a normative character; and perhaps one might even concede them to have the character of directing our human actions toward various ends.

5. For the characterization of law in St. Thomas Aquinas, see *Summa Theologiae*, I–II, Qu. 90, Art. 1: *Dicendum quod lex quaedam regula est et mensura actuum secundum quam inducitur aliquis ad agendum vel ab agendo retrahitur*. For the characterization in H. L. A. Hart, see *The Concept of Law* (Oxford, 1961), esp. chap. V.

Certainly, one can make a plausible case for the various laws and rules of skill in connection with the different arts and technologies having this characteristic. And so also one might perhaps say the same with respect to moral laws, provided that these moral laws are construed as little more than presumed how-to-do-it rules for the living of our lives. But when one moves from human laws to what we are in the habit of calling laws of nature, one can hardly say that these laws are normative with respect to the changes that occur in nature; and certainly one cannot say that such laws actually direct the changes in entities in nature that are subject to these laws to their proper ends. To make such a presumption would be to lapse back into that same antiquated notion of nature and of a supposed natural teleology which we are ever being reminded it is the business of an updated theory of natural law to try to avoid.

And yet might the danger here be more exaggerated than real? For in our earlier discussion of "nature," and of "nature" taken in a sense that is not excluded from modern natural science, we found that the so-called natures of objects in large measure explain the behavior of those objects. Also, insofar as the natures of objects determine their behavior, one can say that their behavior is determined by the law, or laws, of their natures. And so it is then not amiss to say that laws of nature in this sense have an ordering, or even a governing, function with respect to the behavior of such objects. More specifically, why do we not for the moment concentrate on so-called living things, or things that are subject to growth and development? Immediately, we are led to think of and speak of such a thing's natural growth or development—a development that is determined by the thing's nature, or by the law of its nature. And from here the next step can only be to acknowledge that the notion of such a natural growth or development implies the further notion of an endpoint or point of completion of that natural growth or development, which is the natural end of that thing's development. True, "natural end" here certainly need not, and should not, connote conscious purpose; and yet it does connote the idea of a fulfillment or perfection. Otherwise, one could not speak of a development having taken place.

We may take a crude example—say, the development of a human embryo. The example may not be crude, but our amateurish treatment may be. Still, have not biologists been wont to talk about laws governing such a development—say, the law of ontogeny recapitulating phylogeny; and may not one determine what the regular stages are in the development—each stage being preparatory to the next until the process comes to term and the child is ready to be born? And with such laws of development, is it not possible also to determine when something in the process goes wrong, that is, when disease or disturbances from the outside, for example, operate to upset the process? The process is then said to have been interfered with or inhibited so as to keep it from attaining its natural end. And when one speaks and thinks in this way, is not one attributing to the laws that govern the development of the embryo an unmistakably normative and, in this sense, a regulative function?

It is true that to talk about an ordering or regulative function of laws would seem, at least linguistically, to imply the existence of an "orderer" or a "regulator" with an end or purpose consciously in mind. And yet this notion surely will not do when one makes the transition from what one might call human laws to natural laws. For human rules and laws, when they exist, seem to bespeak the existence of human agents who apply the rules in view of ends and who may thus be regarded as the agents of such purposive actions, which the rules might be said to serve as the standard and measure of. In contrast, in the changes that go on in nature, even the developmental changes, it is neither obvious nor relevant to concern oneself with the agents of such natural changes. And of course, it is not only obvious but misplaced and even wrongheaded to suppose that such natural agents must have conscious ends and purposes as do human agents. But still, merely because it may not always be possible clearly and unequivocally to determine the agencies that may be at work in effecting changes in the natural world, and merely because the end or term or completion of such a process of development in the world of nature is not a conscious purpose, does not mean that there are no ends in nature in any sense of the word, or that there are no processes directed toward ends. In fact, we have already noted that in any developmental change in nature, even when no human agents are involved, the notion of a development entails the notion of a relevant end or completion of the process. Accordingly, returning again to the notion of "law," it would surely seem that although the term may not be strictly univocal, as used in a human context and in the context of nature as a whole, there is still a sufficient community or analogy of meaning to make the use of the one word "law" at once significant and indispensable. For in the areas alike of human nature and of nature generally, a law is nothing if not a rule or measure that determines the requisite process of development if a certain end state is to be attained.

One could possibly do no better even today than to fall back on that singularly illuminating, if somewhat fulsome, characterization of law given by Richard Hooker in the sixteenth century: "All things that are have some operation not violent or casual. Neither does anything ever begin to exercise the same without some foreconceived end for which it worketh. And the end which it worketh for is not obtained, unless the work be also fit to obtain it by. For unto every end every operation will not serve. That which doth assign unto each thing the kind, that which doth moderate the force and power, that which doth appoint the form and measure of working, the same we term a law."[6] At first reading, this passage may strike us as but so much sonorous Tudor prose. But reflect upon it a bit, and it can be seen to tick off with a singular precision all of the various elements that need to be taken account of in any understanding of law as being a rule or norm or standard governing both human actions and natural processes. We still cannot pretend to have shown that all changes in nature must necessarily obey laws in this sense. And yet that at least many of the changes in nature are what I earlier characterized as being developmental changes there can be no doubt; and these changes are surely all ordered, manifesting laws in the sense described. Moreover, for our present purposes, to concede this much is sufficient to enable us to get under way with our further account not just of law but of natural law specifically. Later, of course, we will need again to return to a more adequate demonstration of how and why it needs to be recognized that presumably all of the changes that take place in nature, be they with reference to human agents or not, must display that character of being lawful in the sense Hooker describes.

Moral Laws, Laws of Skill, and Laws of Nature

But a new and almost opposed problem promptly confronts us. For having been at pains to show that a multitude and diversity of changes, alike in nature generally and in human nature, can be regarded as manifesting and exhibiting and being obedient to law in the sense de-

6. Richard Hooker, *The Laws of Ecclesiastical Polity*, Bk. I, chap. 2, any edition.

fined, we now have to consider some of the salient differences between these different laws, particularly if we are ever eventually to understand the differences between natural law and positive law. Thus as examples of law—all of them in Hooker's sense—I noted that there are laws of nature, that there are moral laws, and that there are also how-to-do-it rules in the various arts, skills, and techniques. Surely, these cannot all be held to be "natural" laws—at least not all of them equally and in the same sense. But what is the difference?

First, let us consider a bit more carefully the character of the rules of skill, or how-to-do-it rules, that are to be found in the various arts and technologies. Here indeed we might do well to fall back on the distinction that Aristotle drew between "art" and "nature." And of course, this distinction turns on the difference between things that may be said to come to be, or processes that take place, by nature, and those that come to be, or take place, by art. A house or a statue, for instance, is clearly a product of art, whereas the wood of the building or the marble of the statue is a product of nature. Or again, a horse or a human being is not produced by human art, as is a harness for the horse or clothes for the person. True, the horse or the person may fall sick and be restored to health, and such a restoration to health might come about as a result of natural causes or of treatment and medication by a physician—in which cases it would seem that the same end or result could be brought about by either nature or art.

Indeed, the closer one considers the line to be drawn between a natural process and an artificial one, the more it seems that that line is anything but easily drawn. The physician who heals the patient by his art or skill does not do so without relying upon nature or the laws of nature. On the contrary, that is why we say he must be a "physician," or one who knows about *physis* or "nature," if he is to ply his art with a proper skill or knowledge. And for that matter, not only the physician but any artist or technician or man of skill, be he an engineer, a pilot, a farmer, a tailor, or a butcher or baker or candlestickmaker, must have a thorough knowledge of and familiarity with the various relevant natural forces and conditions and circumstances that are prevalent in the area in which he claims to be able to exercise his art. For art or skill or technique is a knowledge of how to use and exploit natural forces and natural conditions so as to accomplish one's particular end as artist or expert. That is why Aristotle tends to reiterate that art imitates nature in the sense that the artist or expert or man of skill seeks to proceed in the way nature would have proceeded, if the particular end in view, which the artist wishes to achieve, were to have been achieved by natural processes.[7]

Given this close and deliberate approximation of all artistic processes to natural processes, what is the difference between the production of something by nature and by art? Surely, the final and ultimately decisive difference between the two can be determined only by whether the end or goal of the process is an end which nature has set for herself, or whether the end or goal is one that has been set up by human beings or by the artist himself. To recur to our earlier example of the development of the human embryo, if the process goes along simply by itself, one can say that the end or term was reached by nature through the unfolding of a purely natural process. On the other hand, if the process happened to be impeded by disease or adverse accidents, and a physician were called in to correct the malfunctioning and so help bring the process to completion, then one could say that the end was achieved by art, at least in part. Yet note that, in either case, whether the result is brought about by art or by nature, the notion of law, as I have sought to define it, is equally applicable. For if a law is a rule of action or procedure that needs to be followed if a certain result or end is to be achieved, then clearly natural processes and procedures will take place according to what may be called laws of nature, much as the procedures of artistic production will take place according to what might be called the laws or rules of skill that govern the particular activity of artistic production that is in question.

There are, however, ambiguities in the distinction between man-made laws and laws of nature. Pushing this line of inquiry still further, it becomes an interesting question whether the relevant laws in these two domains of nature and of art may properly be considered "natural laws." Of course, what we have called "laws of nature"—that is, the laws that govern natural processes—are "natural laws" without question. But what about all of the various rules of skill in the different arts and technologies? If, following my definition of "law," we call these rules "laws," may we also call them "natural laws"? At first, it might seem not, considering that in the case of the arts the products are those of art and not of nature. And yet is it not obvious, and have I not been at some

7. *The Works of Aristotle Translated into English*, Vol. II, *Physica*, by R. P. Hardie and R. K. Gaye (Oxford, 1930), Bk. II, chap. 2, 194a, 22.

pains to stress that any and every process of artistic production is both a utilization and exploitation of countless natural forces and processes? That is why the training of any doctor or engineer or architect or any other skilled person must necessarily presuppose a grounding in the sciences of nature such as physics, chemistry, geology, and biology? Perhaps, then, we might answer the question as to whether the laws and rules that make up the different arts and technologies are "natural laws" by saying that although they may not be accurately describable as "laws of nature" because they are the man-made rules of artists and technicians, they are nonetheless "natural laws" because every rule of skill or operation that is devised by the artist or expert has to be based upon, and determined in the light of, laws of nature.

The point is best put by Aristotle himself:

> Further, where a series has a completion, all the preceding steps are for the sake of that. Now surely as in intelligent action, so in nature; and as in nature, so it is in each action, if nothing interferes. Now intelligent action is for the sake of an end; therefore the nature of things also is so. Thus if a house, e.g., had been a thing made by nature, it would have been made in the same way as it is now by art; and if things made by nature were made also by art, they would come to be in the same way as by nature. Each step then in the series is for the sake of the next; and generally art partly completes what nature cannot bring to a finish, and partly imitates her. If, therefore, artificial products are for the sake of an end, so clearly also are natural products. The relation of the later to the earlier terms of the series is the same in both.[8]

What, then, of moral laws and of ethics? For although it may be all very well to distinguish the humanly devised laws of the different arts and technologies from laws of nature in the more fundamental sense, our primary purpose must be to try to determine whether moral laws may be considered natural laws. Already, we have sought to understand moral laws on the analogy of what we have called the how-to-do-it rules, or rules of skill, in the various arts and techniques. Thus just as the rules of the medical art, or of civil engineering, or of farming teach us how to practice medicine well, or how to build a bridge well, or how to plant and harvest crops successfully, so also I have suggested that the laws of ethics and morals might be understood as laws that govern the art of living, or of living well. They teach us how to be human, in other words.

8. *Ibid.*, Bk. II, chap. 8, 199a, 8–9.

But given this similarity, what is the difference between moral laws, considered as the how-to-do-it rules that need to be followed in any successful or fruitful living of our lives as human beings, and those imperatives of skill, or how-to-do-it rules, that need to be followed in the successful accomplishment of the various arts, crafts, and techniques? We have already seen that moral rules and rules of art are alike in that they both involve prescriptions that need to be followed if a given end is to be achieved. They also are alike in that, although both of them consist of sets of rules that are man-made rather than laws of nature in the strict sense, they nonetheless both need to be based upon nature and upon the laws of nature. In other words, it is only insofar as the how-to-do-it rules in either morals or art are based upon and grounded in the relevant laws of nature in the pertinent areas that the man-made rules in either morals or art can ever hope to be the "right" rules or prescriptions, that is, the rules or prescriptions which, if one follows them, will lead to the accomplishment of one's end. Indeed, as noted above, the key to the difference between laws of nature that are natural, and not man-made, and the rules of art and skill that human beings have had to devise for themselves is that in nature the ends to be achieved by natural processes are set by nature, whereas in the arts the ends are set by human beings, with the result that it is up to human beings to determine the ways to achieve their ends.

Still, for all of their likenesses, there must be some differences— even no doubt major differences—between morals and ethics on the one hand and the various arts and techniques on the other. Accordingly, let us at this point throw out the tentative suggestion, which we will need progressively to try to explain and defend as we proceed, that the difference between morals and ethics and the arts is that the end or goal or fulfillment of human life as a whole is not anything that human beings may simply opt for in the light of their particular whims and preferences. No, the true end or goal of a human existence is set and determined by nature, or by man's very nature as a human being, if you will. It is thus a natural end in a literal sense. In contrast, in the various arts and skills and techniques the ends that these skills are aimed at achieving are ones of our own human determining and thus cannot be said to be determined for us by nature.

But does this, then, mean that the moral laws that prescribe the courses men need to follow in attaining their natural ends are like those laws of nature that govern natural processes of growth and development, such as take place in nature generally? Not quite. For as we shall have occasion to consider in much greater detail later, is it not obvious that the only way human beings can attain their natural ends in life is by knowing what these ends are and then deliberately devising the ways and means for their achievement? In contrast, in the world of non-human nature, a tree or a frog, for example, does not first have to understand what its full flowering or development involves for it to determine the courses of action that need to be followed to attain its natural end. Moreover, so far as moral laws being natural laws is concerned, we can perhaps now see more clearly how, even though they are laws that human beings need to determine for themselves, moral rules and laws are nevertheless at the same time natural laws, or at least based on natural laws, which nature prescribes as being necessary to follow if one's natural human end is to be achieved.

Man's Natural End or *Telos* as the Reference Point for Moral Duties and Obligations

But wait. Have we not gotten ahead of ourselves? In our eagerness to exhibit how laws of nature, laws of skill, and moral laws (and also, as we shall see later, civil laws as well) are capable of either approximating or at least being based upon what we have been calling "natural laws," we have failed to provide any proper explanation, not to say justification, of the keystone of this entire overarching concept of natural law. Clearly, that keystone consists precisely of that puzzling, not to say for many highly questionable, notion of "natural ends." It is easy to understand what we mean by ends in the case of the various arts and technologies. But these are, of course, not natural ends. Also, it might be—though this is certainly more dubious—that we have managed to give at least a minimal plausibility to the notion of natural ends in the case of natural processes—the development of an embryo, the growth of a tree, the development and eventual flourishing of fish or fowl or good red herring. But what in heaven's name did I mean when I casually and confidently spoke of a "natural end" in the case of human beings? For how can one suppose, much less maintain, that as human beings we must recognize there to be a single goal, or standard of perfection, toward which our lives are oriented and which, if we do not achieve it or attain it, our lives can be said to have fallen short or perhaps even to have been downright failures? Indeed, if we cannot make good on this notion of a natural end in human life, then we certainly cannot make good on any notion of an ethics of natural law; and if no ethics of natural law, then no ethics at all, considering our earlier accounts of the collapse and bankruptcy of both deontological and teleological ethical theories; and if no ethics, then no basis for any claims for justice, so far as either civil law or common law is concerned; and if no basis for justice, then certainly no basis for civil rights and personal liberties. In short, disaster.

The Idea of a Natural Human Perfection
or Flourishing

Proceeding directly to the question of the natural end or goal of human life—whether there really is such a thing and if so, what it is—we need first to consider two difficulties, either one of which would appear to render the idea of a natural end either impossible or intolerable. This time, let us again call J. L. Mackie to witness. Recall how, in his *Ethics*, he enunciated what he labeled the "argument from queerness"—an argument which, he insisted, militated decisively against any natural-law ethics. For how could it be supposed, Mackie asks, that there really are such queer entities as "oughts," or duties, or rights, or even ends, or teleological structures existing in nature and the natural world?[9]

To this argument from queerness, however, I have presumably now given at least a partial answer, and I shall attempt to give an even more definitive answer in my concluding chapter. For the present, though, the point is that all one really needs to do is to shake oneself free from that rigid stereotype of nature that has come to be widely and uncritically accepted in many circles today; and almost at once it becomes apparent that there is nothing queer about the idea that a natural flourishing, or a natural excellence, is appropriate to various species in nature. Rather, nothing would seem more natural than that there should be countless instances in nature of what might be called the natural flourishing of things and thus of the attainment by things of their natural ends or perfections.

Nor is that all, for what is the natural end or natural perfection of

9. Mackie, *Ethics*, 38–42.

anything in nature, be it man or bird or beast, if not the good of that thing? St. Thomas Aquinas would define the good of a thing as being that thing's own proper end or perfection. For how else may we understand "good" or *bonum*, save as the good of something? And what is the good of a thing if not its full being, or its fulfillment or perfection, toward which it is ordered by nature or by its own nature.[10] An acorn is ordered toward becoming a full-grown oak tree, a tadpole toward becoming a frog, or a human infant toward being a mature adult. In each of these cases, the familiar Aristotelian distinction between potentiality and actuality is what is relevant: an acorn has the potentiality to become an oak, or a tadpole a frog, or an infant an adult. Moreover, the potentialities and capacities of one entity are not those of another—the potentialities of the acorn are not those of the tadpole, and those of the tadpole are not those of the human infant. And in each of these cases, as well as in countless others throughout the whole of nature, the actuality of the entity in question—the actuality that corresponds to the entity's potentialities—is to be understood as simply that which it is able to be but often is not yet. And what else is it that an entity might be, or could have a capacity or potentiality to be, if not that which by nature it ought to be, in the sense of that which is its very perfection or fulfillment and therefore its end or *telos* or good?[11]

Besides, is there not still another feature or note that needs to be inserted into this picture of the equivalence of the good of an entity with its own proper actuality, its end or *telos*, its perfection or what it ought to be (though, of course, not necessarily in a moral sense)? And this further note is that of desiring, wanting, striving for, tending to-

10. *Cf.* St. Thomas Aquinas, *De Veritate*, Qu. 21, Art. 2: *Cum ratio boni in hoc consistat quod aliquid sit perfectivum alterius per modum finis. Cf.* also *Summa Theologiae*, I, Qu. 5, Art. 1, *passim*. When Aquinas uses the expression *ratio boni*, he is really advancing what might loosely be called a definition of *bonum* or "good." True, for Aquinas, *bonum* or "good" is a transcendental and cannot be defined in the ordinary sense of *per genus et differentiam*, inasmuch as a transcendental cannot be limited to any genus. That Aquinas would appear to be offering a definition of "good" is likely to arouse the suspicions of most moral philosophers in the English-speaking world today who have been brought up in the analytic tradition of G. E. Moore. For Moore, it would seem, continues to excite a certain uncritical veneration because of his insistence that "good" is indefinable. I hope, however, that I have finally scotched this snake of the "indefinability of goodness." *Cf.* Henry Veatch, *For an Ontology of Morals: A Critique of Contemporary Ethical Theory* (Evanston, 1971), chap. II.
11. I am not claiming, in this connection, that the "ought" is here a moral "ought."

ward, all of these understood in a broadly analogous sense. For surely, it is correct to say that any substance that is thus naturally ordered to its own good or *telos* therefore "desires" its own good. And conversely, the proper goodness or perfection of an entity can rightly be understood as that which it may be said naturally to desire and to which it is thus naturally ordered to become and be.[12]

No sooner, though, does one thus understand the good of an entity as being that which it naturally desires or tends toward, and therefore as being that which it is only right that it should be, or ought to be, than one can also begin to see the sense and import of what Aquinas puts forward as being the first principle of practical reason. For such a principle is understood as being the specific *telos* or good of a human being. Accordingly, the principle is that good or *bonum* is to be done and to be pursued (*faciendum et persequendum est*), and evil is to be avoided.[13] What does this mean, and what is its import, if not that the good of a human being is no more and no less than what any human being ought to be—and this time with the "ought" being conceived in a properly moral sense? From this, then, it follows that the primary duty and obligation of any human being is to bend his every effort toward becoming what he ought to be—that is, toward attaining his natural end and natural perfection. And so it is that when it is said that we all ought to seek the good, that means that we all ought to seek that which we are naturally disposed toward, as toward our end, and that which we therefore naturally desire and are thus ordered to, insofar as we are human.

Have we not, then, in large measure alleviated that "queerness" which Mackie says we cannot help feeling as soon as we start talking about values, duties, and obligations—even moral obligations—as if they were a part of the order of nature? They certainly are a part of nature if in nature there are distinctions between the natural potencies

12. *Cf.* St. Thomas Aquinas, *Summa Theologiae*, I, Qu. 5, Art. 1: *Unumquodque est appetibile secundum quod est perfectum, nam omnia appetunt suam perfectionem.* Also, *ibid.*, *ad 1ᵐ: Sed bonum dicit rationem perfecti quod est appetibile, et per consequens dicit rationem ultimi.*

13. This is St. Thomas Aquinas's celebrated "first principle of practical reason" that is discussed at length and with great perceptiveness by Germain Grisez in "The First Principle of Practical Reason: A Commentary on the *Summa Theologiae*, 1–2, Question 94, Article 2," *Natural Law Forum*, X (1965), 168–201; reprinted in abbreviated form in Anthony Kenny, ed., *Aquinas: A Collection of Critical Essays* (Garden City, N. Y., 1969), 340–82.

of things and their acts; or if in nature there are natural ends which are the goods of those things of which and for which they are the natural ends; or if finally, with respect to human nature, there is a natural human good or a natural end, which it is "meet, right, and our bounden duty" as human beings to seek after and try to attain. And with that, why need Mackie's argument from queerness trouble us any further?

No sooner, though, is Mackie's argument from queerness thus disquieted, if not dispelled, than Mackie immediately follows with a second argument, directed at the notion that there could ever be a natural end or a natural good of human life, which it is the duty and responsibility of every human individual to pursue.[14] This is what Mackie calls the "argument from relativity." For is it not patent and obvious to everyone that the ends or goals which men have set for themselves have been as varied and various as the cultures and civilizations in which men have lived? Nor are the ends and goals of men relative only to the several cultures or societies to which human beings have belonged. They are no less relative to all of the varied and various tastes and preferences which men have manifested as individuals. Of course, when it comes to oak trees, or raccoons, or smallmouth bass, one can no doubt say that for each such species one can pretty well determine within broad outlines what the standard of perfection is, or what a truly developed and flourishing condition for each of these species—and indeed for each of the individual members of these several species as well—must consist of. But surely, for human beings this could never be.

At once, though, does it not seem strange that Mackie, following a common pattern among intellectuals of the present day, could be so confident that it is impossible for human beings ever to have made, or ever to make, reliable judgments or judgments based on sound evidence, about their human good or that as individuals any one of us has ever managed to achieve in life what we ought to have achieved? On the contrary, do we not make such judgments every day, which we believe are firmly based in experience?

Most of our contemporaries, once they have achieved what they would consider to be a certain level of sophistication, would probably say that even if there were a naturally grounded standard of perfection for the living of our lives, such an end or standard could not possibly be determined in any manner other than *a priori*. It is as though

14. Mackie, *Ethics*, 36–38.

we have to intuit what our human perfection consists of, it not being possible to discover *a posteriori*, and in the facts, what our human excellence or perfection amounts to. No, of course not, we shall be told, for a norm or standard of human achievement (and therefore of human shortcoming or failure as well) is not ever discoverable in the facts because it is applicable to the facts from the outside, as it were.

But wait. Surely, there is something amiss about this notion of standards of excellence and lack of excellence, of perfection and imperfection, being never discoverable in experience. On the contrary, is it not by experience that we come to learn what a truly healthy or flourishing condition of a fish, or of a live oak, or of an angleworm, must consist of? Likewise, moving to the more or less analogous situation in regard to matters of human art or skill, it is surely only through experience that we come to learn how to be a good surgeon, as distinct from one not so good, or a good fisherman rather than a poor one, or a good architect, or a good cook, or a good bowler, or a good computer programmer, or whatever.

This is not to say that there may not be disputes and differences of opinion in the determination of artistic excellence or skill. And yet just because there may be differences of opinion about whether someone is a good surgeon, or a good accountant, or a good general, or whatever, it by no means follows that there is no difference between the skilled physician and the quack, or between an accountant who has mastered the art and a tyro, or between a general who knows how to win battles and one who is incompetent. Nor does it follow that we come by a knowledge of such differences between truly skilled performances and those not so skilled only *a priori* or in virtue of direct intuition or illumination. Quite the contrary; we become proficient in making such judgments of expertness, or discernments of excellence, only through experience. The point is that we do indeed learn from experience how to tell whether someone is good at what he is doing or whether he knows what he is about.

Very well, but suppose now that we make the transition from the notion of being a good surgeon, or a good accountant, or a good general, to that of being a good human being. Is it possible to say that there are objective standards of what we might call a properly moral excellence, no less than there are of artistic excellence or skill? Surely there are. Nor would it seem that our standards of achievement and excellence in being human are any less based on experience than are standards of excellence in the various skills and techniques.

For example, we may consider our ordinary everyday ideas of human flourishing and well-being. There is no denying that we all have such ideas, however uncritical they may sometimes be. Accordingly, would not all of us recognize that although many of our notions of human flourishing are conceived analogously to the flourishing that we ascribe to plants and to animals throughout the rest of nature, still there is something markedly different and distinctive about the perfection or flourishing that human beings are capable of? For in the human case a great deal more is recognized as being involved than mere attainment of physical health or biological well-being. Thus do we not all know from experience people who could be said to be in perfect health—excellent physical specimens, in fact—and yet who do not amount to much as human beings? Such a one, we might say, is a "sad sack" as a person, or maybe even a damned fool.

For an illustration, let us recall Jane Austen's character of Sir Walter Elliott in *Persuasion*:

> Sir Walter Elliott of Kellynch Hall, in Somersetshire, was a man who, for his own amusement, never took up any book but the Baronetage; there he found occupation for an idle hour and consolation in a distressed one. . . .
>
> Vanity was the beginning and end of Sir Walter Elliott's character: vanity of person and of situation. He had been remarkably handsome in his youth, and at fifty-four was still a very fine man. Few women could think more of their personal appearance than he did, nor could the valet of any new made lord be more delighted with the place he held in society. He considered the blessings of beauty as inferior only to the blessing of a baronetcy; and the Sir Walter Elliott who united these gifts, was the constant object of his warmest respect and devotion.[15]

From this account, can anyone doubt that the trouble with poor Sir Walter was that he had never gotten the message of what Alexander Pope once called "that secret to each fool that he's an ass!" And incidentally, must it not also be acknowledged that our being able to "see" the shortcomings of someone like Sir Walter Elliott is nothing if not a matter of experience? Is it not like the judgments which skilled prac-

15. *The Novels and Letters of Jane Austen*, ed. R. Brimley Johnson (12 vols.; New York, 1906), *Persuasion*, X, 1–3.

titioners of a given art or skill might make when they realize that one of their number is not very good—that he is, say, no better than a bumbling plumber as a practitioner, rather than a skilled surgeon.[16]

But let us return to the judgments we tend to make in the sphere of human living and human flourishing, as opposed to the expert judgments that are made in the various skills or crafts. Suppose that in the more general human context we find ourselves up against someone who is not a mere fool or ass. Rather, might it not be a case of our recognizing that the person with whom we are dealing was not lacking in intelligence and ability but, for one reason or another, had squandered or abused his talents or had directed them toward mistaken ends? Thus it surely is a reality that the likes, say, of an Alcibiades, or possibly an Aaron Burr, or a Richard Nixon have not infrequently surfaced in the course of the world's history. Or what about a Hamlet or a Macbeth? Such "bad actors," if we might so call them, have often "strutted and fretted their hour upon the stage." And as for the rest of us more ordinary mortals, who have been sitting in the audience during such world stage performances, would it ever for an instant be questioned that, as witnesses of such performances, we were indeed able to recognize, simply in virtue of our own experience with the world, that here indeed were examples of singularly gifted human individuals, who nevertheless had made the wrong choices, or wasted their talents, or injudiciously, and possibly early on, had made a wrong turning?

For instance, consider John Dryden's deft portrait of the earl of Shaftesbury:

> Of these the false Achitophel was first;
> A name to all succeeding ages curst:
> For close designs and crooked counsels fit,
> Sagacious, bold, and turbulent of wit,
> Restless, unfix'd in principles and place,
> In pow'r unpleased, impatient of disgrace;

16. Throughout this chapter, I shall stress the analogy between the various arts and skills on the one hand, and what might be termed the art of living—that is, knowing how to live well, or how to live as a human being ought to live, on the other. Nevertheless, there is no more than analogy, and never any identity, between what Aristotle would call the "practical sciences" (morals, ethics, politics) and what he would call the "productive sciences." For Aristotle's way of distinguishing between these two analogous forms of knowledge, see *Nicomachean Ethics*, Bk. VI, esp. chaps. 4 and 5. For a more popular and contemporary way of making the same distinction, see my *Rational Man* (Bloomington, Ind., 1962), chap. 4.

A fiery soul, which working out its way,
Fretted the pigmy body to decay:
And o'er-informed the tenement of clay.
A daring pilot in extremity;
Pleas'd with the danger when the waves went high,
He sought the storms; but, for a calm unfit,
Would steer too near the sands, to boast his wit.
Great wits are sure to madness near allied,
And their partitions do their bounds divide;
Else why should he, with wealth and honor blest,
Refuse his age the needful hours of rest?
Punish a body which he could not please,
Bankrupt of life, yet prodigal of ease? . . .
In friendship false, implacable in hate,
Resolv'd to ruin or to rule the State.[17]

Perhaps as still another example, one might consider the unsettling account which Henry Adams gives of General Ulysses S. Grant:

Badeau took Adams to the White House one evening and introduced him to President and Mrs. Grant. First and last, he saw a dozen Presidents at the White House, and the most famous were by no means the most agreeable, but he found Grant the most curious subject of study among them all. About no one did opinions differ so widely. Adams had no opinion, or occasion to make one. A single word with Grant satisfied him that, for his own good, the fewer words he risked the better. Thus far in life he had met with but one man of the same intellectual or unintellectual type—Garibaldi. Of the two, Garibaldi seemed to him a trifle the more intellectual, but, in both, the intellect counted for nothing; only the energy counted. The type was pre-intellectual, archaic, and would have seemed so even to the cave-dwellers. Adam, according to legend, was such a man.

In time one came to recognize the type in other men, with differences and variations, as normal; men whose energies were the greater, the less they wasted on thought; men who sprang from the soil to power; apt to be distrustful of themselves and of others; shy; jealous; sometimes vindictive; more or less dull in outward appearance; always needing stimulants, but for whom action was the highest stimulant—the instinct of fight. Such men were forces of nature, energies of the prime, like the *Pteraspis*, but they made short work of scholars. They had commanded

17. *The Best of Dryden*, ed. Lewis I. Bredvold (New York, n.d.), *Absalom and Achitophel*, 139–40, ll. 235–59.

thousands of such and saw no more in them than in others. The fact was certain; it crushed argument and intellect at once.[18]

Again, suppose that we shift our stage, this time even more radically, and consider the character of Socrates as depicted in the *Apology* or in other of the early Dialogues of Plato. In Socrates we find someone who devoted his life not to becoming rich or to maintaining his social position or to engaging in politics, business, or generalship but to the pursuit of knowledge. Yet it was not knowledge in the accustomed modern sense, but rather a self-knowledge, or perhaps a self-understanding. Likewise, in Socrates there was not the slightest trace of snobbishness or pomposity or self-complacency, such as were characteristic of a Sir Walter Elliott, or even, in a somewhat different way, of Socrates' sometime rival, the famous Sophist Protagoras, or indeed of many of our self-satisfied intellectuals and academics in the present day. And of course, in Socrates there was none of that apathy or indifference or even hostility to what might be called the intellectual life that so impressed Adams about General Grant.

We all know the examples of moral (and physical) courage that Socrates set for his fellow Athenians on more than one occasion. Recall how he defied punishment and death at the hands of the Thirty Tyrants because he quietly yet steadfastly refused to be a party to the crime against Leon the Salamanian. And of course, we know that he finally suffered death at the hands of the Athenian democracy, a government that was at the opposite extreme from the oligarchy of the Thirty. And for what reason did he suffer death? Was it not ultimately because he resolutely refused to give over his own devotion to the pursuit of self-knowledge or to cease and desist from trying to get his fellow citizens to be honest with themselves, constantly reminding, now this person, and now that, that the unexamined life which they were living was not worth living?[19]

What, then, is it, if not our experience with the likes of a Socrates or a Sir Walter Elliott, or the earl of Shaftesbury or Alcibiades, or, to vary the examples, of the somewhat zany character of Von Humboldt Fleisher in Saul Bellow's novel *Humboldt's Gift*, or the sensitive, refined, and principled Viscount Falkland as depicted in Clarendon's *History of*

18. *The Education of Henry Adams* (Boston, 1918), 264–65.
19. *Plato: With an English Translation*, I, *Euthyphro, Apology, Crito, Phaedo, Phaedrus*, trans. Harold North Fowler (London, 1914), *Apology*, 38A.

the Rebellion that brings us to an ever greater perceptiveness and appreciation of how indeed some men and women approximate what a human being truly can be and ought to be, while others fall sadly short of the goal, and, in their unfortunate behavior and characters, tend to exemplify the extent to which we poor mortals can become the sorry victims of our own follies, ambitions, greed, smugness, pettiness, willful eccentricity, laziness, and heaven knows what else?

Aristotle's Criteria of Human Perfection or Well-Being

But these are enough examples. It now is time to consider the criteria that enable us to determine what man's natural end is—or, in other words, what the perfection of human life or human happiness or well-being really consists of. And here I propose to follow the lead of Aristotle. Recall the opening of the *Nicomachean Ethics*: "Every art and every investigation, and likewise every practical pursuit and undertaking, seems to aim at some good: hence it has been well said that the good is that at which all things aim. . . . As there are numerous pursuits and arts and sciences, it follows that their ends are correspondingly numerous: for instance, the end of the science of medicine is health, that of the art of ship building a vessel, that of strategy victory, that of [domestic economy] wealth." Aristotle then moves to the obvious conclusion:

> If therefore among the ends at which our actions aim there be one which we wish for its own sake, while we wish others only for the sake of this . . . it is clear that this one ultimate End must be the Good, and indeed the Supreme Good. Will not then a knowledge of this Supreme Good be also of great practical importance for the conduct of life? Will it not better enable us to attain what is fitting, like archers having a target to aim at? If this be so, we ought to make an attempt to determine at all events in outline what exactly the Supreme Good is, and of which of the theoretical or practical sciences it is the object.[20]

We may now return to the Good which is the object of our search, and try to find out exactly what it can be. For good appears to be one thing in one pursuit or art and another in another: it is different in medicine from what it is in strategy, and so on with the rest of the arts. What def-

---

20. Aristotle, *The Nicomachean Ethics*, trans. H. Rackham (Rev. ed.; Cambridge, Mass., 1934), Bk. I, 1094A, 1–10, 19–27.

inition of the Good then will hold true in all the arts? Perhaps we may define it as that for the sake of which everything else is done. This applies to something different in each different art—to health in the case of medicine, to victory in that of strategy, to a house in architecture, and to something else in each of the other arts: But in every pursuit or undertaking it describes the end of that pursuit or undertaking, since in all of them it is for the sake of the end that everything else is done. Hence if there be something which is the end of all things done by human action, this will be the practicable Good—or if there be several such ends, the sum of these will be the Good.[21]

Perhaps then we may arrive at this by ascertaining what is man's function. For the goodness or efficiency of a flute-player or sculptor or craftsman of any sort, and in general of anybody who has some function or business to perform, is thought to reside in that function; and similarly it may be held that the good of man resides in the function of man, if he has a function.[22]

Are we then to suppose that, while the carpenter and the shoe-maker have definite functions or businesses belonging to them, man as such has none, and is not designed by nature to fulfill any function? Must we not rather assume that just as the eye, the hand, the foot, and each of the various members of the body manifestly has a certain function of its own, so a human being also has a certain function over and above all the functions of his particular members? What then precisely can this function be? The mere act of living appears to be shared even by plants, whereas we are looking for the function peculiar to man; we must therefore set aside the vital activity of nutrition and growth. Next in the scale will come some form of sentient life; but this too appears to be shared by horses, oxen, and animals generally. There remains therefore what may be called the practical life of man as possessing reason.[23]

The words from Aristotle quoted above have become so familiar to so many that one might wonder why I have recited them. But is it not possible that Aristotle's words may have become so hackneyed that no one heeds them anymore? That is why I propose to underscore and to comment briefly upon four features of Aristotle's account, which, if one reflects upon them sufficiently, may be seen to provide us with criteria for determining just what the good for man—his natural end or *telos*—must consist of.

21. *Ibid.*, 1097a, 15–24.
22. *Ibid.*, 1097b, 24–28.
23. *Ibid.*, 1097b, 30–1098 a 4. I have slightly altered the translation of the last line of this quotation.

First, there is the criterion of what may best be called "activity," or a certain way of functioning. This criterion means that living well, or being well off, at least for a human being, involves functioning in a certain way, actively living in a way that best befits a human being, actively getting on with one's business of living as a human person. In this respect, one needs to contrast Aristotle's conception of happiness or well-being with the more usual view of man's end or goal. For would not most of us, considering the matter uncritically, be inclined to say that what we want in life, and what all of us strive for unceasingly, is to acquire the so-called goods of life, and as many of these as possible? Thus the customary Utilitarian formula for man's end or goal—and, indeed, the formula of almost any hedonistic theory or interest-theory of ethics—is the maxim: maximize goods and minimize evils; or get all the goods you can and avoid the evils.

And yet the Aristotelian view of man's end or *telos* is notably different. This is not to say, of course, that as human beings we do not have many wants and needs and desires and that the greater part of our waking hours must be directed toward acquiring such goods as will satisfy our needs. Thus no individual could be said to be really well off if he did not possess at least the bare necessities of life such as food, clothing, and shelter, and probably not just the bare necessities; for, in addition, there is a sense in which a human individual might be said also to need—albeit in a more tenuous sense of the word—not simply to be fed, clothed, and housed but to be well-fed and well-clothed and well-housed. Nor is it only material possessions that a human individual may be said to need. For clearly and by implication, he needs life and health as well; he needs society and human companionship; he needs a variety of knowledge, not just a practical knowledge of how to do or make things but also what Aristotle would call a theoretical knowledge, a knowledge of the entire order of nature and reality. And not only does a person need knowledge; he also has a recurrent need for play and recreation, for refreshment and relaxation. Nor is it necessary to stop with these particular enumerated needs, for surely, one can think of any number of others as well.[24] But for the present, we can perhaps let these suffice, at least for purposes of illustration.

Given this variety of needs, the life of any individual in this world—

24. For a particularly satisfactory enumeration and discussion of the goods of life that human beings need if they are to live well, see John Finnis, *Natural Law and Natural Rights* (Oxford, 1980), chaps. III and IV, esp. pp. 85–95.

the work that he does, the various activities that he engages in over the course of his life—is largely directed toward satisfying that person's countless human needs and requirements, physical, psychical, and spiritual. All the same, does it require too much imagination or reflection to see that however successful an individual may be in coming to possess such goods—all wealth and all health, all knowledge and all power, all friendships and all reputation—this mere possession of goods is still not the whole story, so far as an individual's well-being, or his truly living well, is concerned? For in addition to having the necessities of life, to say nothing of comforts and amenities, is it not also important that one be able to use properly what one has? It is in this sense that the end or goal of human life can hardly be said to consist of mere possession of such goods as will satisfy our human needs, but rather in an ongoing business of employing these goods of life wisely and intelligently and as they ought to be used and employed.

After all, have we not all had occasion to observe that the mere possession of wealth and position does not in itself guarantee that a person will not be a fool—as witness Sir Walter Elliott? Yes, even having a brilliant and well-trained mind and possessing no end of scientific knowledge or scholarly learning still does not guarantee that one will not be an unfortunate individual—self-centered, untrustworthy, perhaps even rash and foolhardy. And, of course, although possessing unbounded life, energy, and physical vigor undoubtedly means that one is an excellent physical specimen, it by no means guarantees that one is a good man or excellent as a human person. What is it, then, that is still lacking, if not the simple consideration that human happiness or well-being must involve a further and decisive factor over and above the acquisition or coming into possession of the needed goods of life? And what is this further factor if not simply the business of using and employing these goods in the day-by-day business of living out our lives? Only in this sense may we be said actually to live well, as opposed to merely having what it takes to live well.[25]

25. In this connection, reference might be made to Robert Nozick's illuminating discussion of the "experience machine," an illustration which has become something of a commonplace in the contemporary literature (Robert Nozick, *Anarchy, State, and Utopia* [New York, 1974], 42–45). Translated into Aristotelian terms, it would seem that the life of any beneficiary of the experience machine would be lacking in "activity." To the same effect, see J. L. Mackie's remarks in "Can There Be a Right-Based Moral Theory," *Midwest Studies in Philosophy*, III (1978), 354–55.

And here we can perhaps point to an analogy between the living of our lives and the practice of various of the arts and skills. Let us take, for example, the case of a surgeon who plies his craft in a modern-day hospital. Here there can be no question that he needs many instruments and facilities and much equipment if he is to do his job well—x-ray facilities, the resources of modern anesthesiology, various machines and surgical instruments within the operating room, a trained staff of nurses and assistants, and so on.

Suppose, though, that our hypothetical surgeon does have at his disposal all of these "goods," if we may so call them, which are necessary and requisite for the successful practice of surgery in a modern hospital—still, if he does not know how properly to take advantage of such goods, or how really to use them, then one would not call him a very good surgeon, or one who practices his art well. And why is not this example of someone's being a good, or a not-so-good, surgeon, similar to one's being a good, or a not-so-good, human being? In both cases, it is a question of how well one actually practices one's art—in the one case the art of medicine, in the other the art of living. So also in both cases, the decisive factor is not merely possessing what it takes to do well whatever one desires to do but also actively doing the job, carrying on the business, functioning as one ought to function in the relevant capacity, be it as a surgeon or as a human person. Yes, if the business of living one's life as a person may be compared to plying one's trade or craft as a person with technical skill or know-how, the excellence of one's performance is surely to be found in the actual performance and not in merely having all of the requisite tools, goods, materials, and even capacities needed for such a good performance.

So be it: the natural end or *telos* of a human being is attained only insofar as one actually lives and functions in a certain way. But what is this way? Here Aristotle's answer is that the proper activity for a human being cannot be merely a matter of performing the vital functions of nutrition and growth—after all, plants can do this; nor is it merely a matter of performing the animal functions of sensation and locomotion—after all, even horses and oxen are capable of this. We come, then, to the second criterion: man's characteristic activity must consist of the practical exercise or use of reason. That is, the distinguishing activity of a human being consists not just of living but in living intelligently—in being guided in one's day-by-day conduct by a knowledge of what ought or ought not to be done in the particular case.

Moreover, in thus saying that the end or goal for man must consist of the exercise of reason or intelligence, Aristotle is not talking about reason and intelligence in the sense of their being a mere function of a person's having a high I.Q. or even of such reason and intelligence as eventuate in outstanding scientific or scholarly achievement. Aristotle has in mind what can only be called a practical reason or intelligence—the reason or intelligence that is operative in determining our day-by-day decisions and choices in life, which we hope will not be marked by such follies and mistaken judgments as presumably were reflected in the lives of such men as Sir Walter Elliott or the earl of Shaftesbury or General Grant or Macbeth, or of whomever.

One might object that making wise decisions is scarcely a matter of knowledge, even of practical knowledge, in any meaningful sense. For how can one say that it is a matter of knowledge—certainly not of scientific knowledge—that, for example, I ought not to have still another drink of whiskey, or that I ought to respect another's judgment, even though he is a smug "intellectual," or that it is high time that I take my family on vacation because that is what they need. Surely, these are matters of guesswork, not of knowledge, one will say.

Such a line of criticism, however, unfortunately betrays a decided lack of understanding and appreciation for practical knowledge. And once again, by appealing to the analogy of the arts and technology, it should be possible to make this point clear. For does not the skilled surgeon know—really know—that the incision should be just so deep and no deeper? True, if you were to ask him in advance and in general how deep one should make the incision for an appendectomy, he probably would say that he cannot tell you because it depends upon the particular circumstances. And so likewise, the expert cook may not be able to tell you in principle how much salt should be added to a particular stew, or the skilled game fisherman how much line one should let the smallmouth bass have and then how fast one should reel him in. Still, it certainly is true that the truly skilled surgeon, or cook, or fisherman, is able, in the particular concrete case, to make a right judgment of what ought or ought not to be done, whereas the tyro, or the inexpert person, unfortunately does not know, and that is why he botches the job.

And as with skill in the arts, so also with skill in what might be called the art of living. For the latter is truly a skill—a matter of know-how no less than is the former. Thus the good man—yes, the morally good man—is one who knows what should be done and whose judgment can therefore be relied upon in the day-by-day circumstances of our lives, when we have to decide whether we ought or ought not to do this or that. Accordingly, it is just in this sense that one of the criteria of a human being's living well, of his having attained the proper perfection or end or goal that befits a human being, will be the criterion of practical knowledge or intelligence: the activity of the good man, in other words, will be precisely the activity not of just staying alive but of living wisely and intelligently and rationally.

Being possessed of a practical knowledge and even exercising that knowledge is still not all there is to a human being's succeeding in actively living wisely and intelligently. In addition, there is the third criterion: the matter of choice. For it is obvious that for many of us less fortunate souls, there is many an occasion when we might be said to know perfectly well what we ought to do, and yet we do not do it: we fail to choose to do what our own better judgment tells us we ought to do. "For the good that I would I do not; but the evil which I would not, that I do" (Rom. 7:19).

And what is the source of our thus losing control of ourselves and not being able to abide by our own better judgments, if not the factor of desire and in addition all of the attendant feelings, passions, and emotions—ambition, lust, greed, gluttony, ill-temper, apathy, laziness, self-indulgence, and so on? These are the factors in our human makeup that impel us to do all sorts of things that in our better judgment we know to be unwise or improvident or foolish or whatever. Accordingly, if as human beings we are ever to bring ourselves to the place at which we do not merely possess a practical knowledge and intelligence but actually act upon it, we must somehow learn to bring our desires and impulses into line with what our knowledge and better judgment tell us is the right and better thing for us to do. And what is it that can thus bring us to the place at which we will indeed be disposed to act in accordance with our own knowledge and understanding of what we ought to do, if not what Aristotle calls "moral virtue"? That is, in addition to the so-called intellectual virtues, which are simply virtues of knowledge, and in the light of which we can come to know and to judge what we ought to do, be it in morals or in the arts, we need also to cultivate the moral virtues, which are virtues not of knowledge but of choice, and as a result of which our choices and desires and preferences will, we hope, be made to accord with our better judgment.

And right here, of course, what I have heretofore somewhat sentimentally termed the art of living will part company from all of the other arts and skills. For in ordinary skills, the factor of choice, and therefore of moral virtue, is hardly relevant. Thus the gamefisherman, in playing out the right amount of line to the fish that he has hooked and in reeling in at the right time and with the right amount of pressure, taking full advantage of the pliancy of his rod, the test weight of the line, and so on, performs these actions not in the face of contrary impulses of greed, anger, bad temper, resentment, lust, or whatever. No, all that is necessary for the fisherman, or for skilled person generally, to perform the actions that he should perform, and as he should perform them, is the factor of skill or know-how. But when it comes to being a good man, and not just a good fisherman or a good accountant or a good computer expert, in addition to a knowledge of what to do there must also be an inclination or disposition to choose to do what one knows to be the better and wiser course. And this is why, for a human being ever truly to live as he ought to live, and thus to attain his end as a human person, he must not only have and exercise practical knowledge of what ought to be done but also be disposed to choose in the particular case to do what his better judgment tells him he ought to do.

Perhaps I should mention a fourth feature that pertains to the good life or to what I have been designating as the true end and goal of human life. This fourth feature is not mentioned explicitly by Aristotle; and yet certainly it is implicit in nearly all that he says. This feature is the individual human being's own personal freedom and autonomy in the living of his life. For is it not evident that not only does a human being not attain his natural end by an automatic process of development and maturity after the manner of a plant or an animal? In addition, no human being ever attains his natural end or perfection save by his own personal effort and exertion. No one other than the human individual—no agency of society, of family, of friends, or of whatever can make or determine or program an individual to be a good man, or program him to live the life that a human being ought to live. Instead, attaining one's natural end as a human person is nothing if not a "do-it-yourself" job.

It is true that one can be helped in a variety of ways in attaining one's natural perfection. Friends, family, the various institutions of society—even good fortune—can all contribute mightily to a person's attaining his goal or natural end; but the actual business of attaining the end—living wisely and intelligently—is something that only the individual can do. Moreover, he is able to do it only by coming to understand what his natural end is and then by figuring out what steps need to be taken to achieve such a goal, as well as bringing himself to act on the judgments that he has determined with respect to what he ought to do and be and how he ought to go about doing it and being it. In other words, it is precisely the acquisition and the exercise of the intellectual and moral virtues that is the do-it-yourself job that is incumbent upon every human being, simply as a rational animal. How else can we characterize this fourth feature of the good life for a human being unless by calling it an autonomous life, or a life that is freely determined upon and carried out by the individual himself? Indeed, no human being can ever be said to live well, or to live as a human being ought to live, unless it is on the basis of his own decisions and choices made in the light of his own understanding of what is best for him and what the good life demands.

Natural Laws as Determined by
Man's Natural End

Surely, the foregoing should suffice as an account as well as an argument, demonstrating both that man does have a natural end or purpose or *telos* and what that end is. Given that human beings are by nature ordered to an appropriate end or goal of human perfection or fulfillment, may we not now also see how in the light of such an end, it becomes possible to determine what those moral rules and "oughts" are that human beings must observe if they are to become what they naturally ought to be? As I have said, such moral laws being no more and no less than the naturally determined "how-to-do-it" rules for attaining our natural human end or *telos*, it thus becomes clear that such moral laws are natural laws in a precise and literal sense of that term.

They are not natural laws in the sense that they merely determine and reflect the natural changes in a person's life and development that happen regardless of whether we are aware of them or seek to put them into practice. Instead, these are natural laws of human life and human existence that become operative only insofar as we, as human individuals, come to recognize what they are and then deliberately put them into practice and consciously abide by them in our practice. All of this discussion might be illuminated by returning briefly to the passage that

85

I quoted earlier from Hooker, this time paraphrasing it and commenting on it in the light of those further determinations and specifications regarding both "nature" and "law" that I have been through and tried to detail. Thus we might say:

> Human beings, like all things else in nature, have a characteristic "operation not violent or casual." Nor does a human being, any more than any other natural being, "ever begin to exercise the same without some foreconceived end for which he worketh." Indeed, in the case of human beings, it is important that they become consciously aware of such a foreconceived end as it pertains to them simply as men, and that they deliberately strive for it and seek to attain it. Moreover, "the end which one worketh for is not obtained, unless the work be also fit to obtain it by"— i.e. unless as human beings we allow ourselves to be guided by such how-to-do-it rules as prescribe for us the way our end is to be attained. "For unto every end every operation will not serve." Hence so far as man's natural end as a human being is concerned, that which doth "assign [unto a man] the kind, that which doth appoint the form and measure of [a man's] working, the same we term a law," and more specifically, a natural moral law.

QUESTIONS AND DIFFICULTIES

Why the Way of Aristotle
and Not the Way of Nietzsche?

Let no one be under any illusion: after all of the blood, sweat, and tears of this tortuous and arduous chapter, why should I have any confidence that I have convinced anyone? My thesis is that without natural ends there can be no basis or justification for natural laws in ethics. Yet who in this day and age can ever bring himself to believe that there really are natural human ends—particularly that the natural end for man is simply that of living wisely and intelligently and thus of cultivating and then exercising the intellectual and moral virtues? Undoubtedly, any such contention is bound to be dismissed out of hand by contemporary moral philosophers, notwithstanding any evidence that one might adduce to the contrary. For have not these philosophers all been nurtured on the argument from queerness, as well as the argument from relativity, and nutured on them from the days when they sat at their mothers' knees, or at least were at their day-care centers? Why, then, imagine that any of our latter-day moralists, indoctrinated as they have been, would ever give so much as the time of day to my attempted refutations of their arguments? For in philosophy today it is fashion that would seem to determine all.

Still, before I become wrapped up in this mantle of injured virtue and enlightenment and explain my own ostracism on the sole ground of prejudice, would it not be well first to consider a line of criticism that could be aimed at the argument of this chapter and that I have scarcely attempted even to meet honestly, much less successfully? For may it not be recalled that when I attempted to counter the line of argument from queerness and relativity, I appealed largely to experience—even to common-sense experience? For did I not in effect say—to take but one example—that anyone ought to be able to "see" that a Sir Walter Elliott was pretty much of a fool, whereas an earl of Shaftesbury was brilliant perhaps but was strangely unstable and misguided, being in large measure corrupted by his own vanity, envy, and ambition? In contrast, was it not equally patent and obvious that Socrates was a truly wise man, one who had succeeded in realizing our true human potentialities for living wisely and intelligently, never allowing himself to lapse into the common and easy ways of the "unexamined life"?

To all of this, I can imagine someone making the rejoinder that such an appeal to the testimony of literature or of history is anything but a bona fide appeal to the evidence of experience. And even if one were to insist that there is warrant for relying upon the testimony of poets and historians and novelists as to which ways of life or modes of living might be adjudged successes and which ones failures, one could still respond to such a defender of the testimony of literature that such literary testimony scarcely speaks with one voice. For although writers such as Jane Austen and John Dryden and Plato spoke out of the firm conviction that only the rational life, or the examined life, was worth living and that any departure from such a norm could only lead one in the direction of becoming either a knave or a fool, still it is not hard to find countless examples of contrary testimony from poets and writers and historians, even within our so-called Western tradition.

For example, let us consider the testimony of that singularly gifted poet of the late seventeenth century, the earl of Rochester. So far from testifying to the need for a human being to live rationally and wisely, and so to cultivate the intellectual and moral virtues, Rochester jauntily contends that the lesson to be learned from human experience is the ultimate value of such things as drunkenness and debauchery:

> Were I, who to my cost already am
> One of those strange, prodigious Creatures *Man*,
> A spirit free to choose for my own share
> What case of Flesh and Blood I'd please to wear,
> I'd be a *Dog*, a *Monkey* or a *Bear*,
> Or anything but that vain *Animal*
> Who is so proud of being Rational.[26]

But is such testimony from the earl of Rochester to be reckoned as amounting to anything more than a reinforcement of the argument from relativity? It is that, to be sure. And yet there are many contemporary philosophers who would see it as signifying even more. Thus we hardly need to be reminded that we are continually being flooded with new theories of language and literature—Sausurean linguistics, Heideggerian hermeneutics, the structuralism of Claude Lévi-Strauss, and now the several varieties of post-structuralism, culminating in the new fashion of deconstruction, as perpetrated by the proudly egregious Jacques Derrida and a great miscellany of associated deconstructionists.

Be reassured, though. I have no intention, nor do I have the scholarly competence, to bring all of these newfangled theories of language and literature under a single common denominator. But although they may not all have a common denominator, do they not at least all point to what I earlier designated as being the way of Nietzsche—as if this latter amounted very largely to the view that the character and determinations of all things, be it in ethics or in respect to human nature, or indeed in being and reality generally—are what they are solely in virtue of the exercise by human beings of the will to power?

For is it not the upshot of many of the new theories of language and literature that human language, with all of its manifold structures and devices and strategies, syntactical, rhetorical, and logical, never operates in such a way as to *disclose* the truth about things or about reality but rather in such a way as to "interpret" reality—that is, to *construct* it according to our human interests and projects? And so it is that reality or the nature of things, at least as we know them or talk about them in language, is never reality as it is in itself but only reality as we make

---

26. "A Satyr: Against Reason and Mankind," *Selected Lyrics and Satires of John Wilmot, 2nd Earl of Rochester*, ed. Ronald Duncan (1948, rpr., Devon, 1980).

it to be, or structure it, according to our own logical and linguistic spec-ifications. In other words, there is no way in which we human beings can possibly think about things, or talk about them, save in terms of the language forms, or the language structures, that we happen to be op-erating with. And what are these language forms, and where may we imagine them to have come from, unless they are reflections of the var-ied and various purposes and values that we happen to have as human language-users?

Does not this all begin to approximate something similar to the Kantian view that as human knowers—which is to say as human logic- and language-users—it need not be our concern to try to make our *ideas* conform to facts; rather, the *facts* should be made to conform to our ideas?[27] Curiously, this distinctively Kantian flavor that would seem to have come to attach to modern linguistics and hermeneutics is now coming to be echoed and to receive confirmation in any number of the new and fashionable developments that have been occurring within the field of the philosophy of science. For we hear it proclaimed repeat-edly that rather than the data of observation serving as the test of our scientific theories and hypotheses, it is, rather, that the empirical data, so far from having an independent character in their own right, are themselves determined entirely and take on the characters that they do depending upon the theories and hypotheses in the light of which they come to be interpreted and understood. "No data, but what they are theory-laden"—so the familiar slogan runs. And, indeed, one is accus-tomed to hearing this slogan more and more from our present-day philosophers of science.

Very well, then, whether it be as language-users that we try to talk about the facts of human life and of our human situation, or whether as scientists we seek to reckon with the data of empirical observation, in either case the supposed facts and data are determined entirely by the language forms or by the scientific hypotheses and theories that we use to interpret them, rather than that our changing scientific theories and our manifold devices of speech and of rhetoric are thought of as needing to be brought to book by the facts of observation, be it in the world or in our own human situation. Besides, if one asks the origin of these theories or how we happen to come by such various forms of

27. *Immanuel Kant's Critique of Pure Reason*, trans. Norman Kemp Smith (London, 1929), "Preface to Second Edition," B xvi–xviii.

speech, and indeed "forms of life," that are said to "inform" the entire order of being and reality after their own image, the answer would seem to be that our manifold human values are the sources of the judgments we make about things, whether we make these judgments in our capacity as scientists or as literary men and philosophers and historians.

And what are values, in turn, and where do they come from? To such a question, Terry Eagleton blandly replies: " 'Value' is a transitive term: it means whatever is valued by certain people in specific situations, according to particular criteria and in the light of given purposes." And from this it immediately follows that all of "our factual statements" are but functions of "the largely concealed structure of values which informs and underlies [such] factual statements." Eagleton immediately says that this can only mean that all of our presumed factual statements are but so many reflections of what our ideology happens to be, an ideology being but those "ways in which what we say and believe connects with the power-relations of the society we live in."[28] In other words, it is the will to power that imposes our human values upon the facts and thus gives the facts the character they have for us, as opposed to such character as they may have in themselves.

There we have it, then. It is not the facts of the world that determine our judgments about the world but rather that our particular values determine the facts—at least for us. And what is the agency that imposes our values upon the facts if not man's will to power? Indeed, what else is the will to power if not the determination to bring things, facts, other people, and indeed reality into conformity with what we human beings want them to be? Moreover, following this line, are we not well along toward following what MacIntyre calls the way of Nietzsche and what I might call "the primrose way to the everlasting bonfire." For surely, if this so-called way of Nietzsche is to be countenanced, then the entire case that I have sought to make out in this chapter for an ethics based on the observed facts of nature and reality collapses.

Consider again how I sought to invoke the testimony of such writers as Jane Austen and John Dryden and Plato to show that there is a firm empirical warrant that there is a true end or goal or *telos* of human life and that this end or goal consists of living intelligently and bringing

28. Terry Eagleton, *Literary Theory: An Introduction* (Minneapolis, 1983), 11, 14.

oneself to the place at which the very living of one's life will consist of the exercise of the intellectual and moral virtues. Immediately, though, one can imagine how a devotee of the new fashions in linguistics and rhetoric and the philosophy of language—someone like Terry Eagleton—would knock into a cocked hat my entire case for the way of Aristotle. For how can one possibly appeal to the testimony of Socrates, Thucydides, Shakespeare, John Dryden, or Jane Austen, all of whom appeal to the evidence of our human experience to establish that "the unexamined life is not worth living"? Far from it. For, as Eagleton says, "The so-called 'literary canon,' the unquestioned great tradition of the national literature [and perhaps of Western culture as well] has to be recognized as a *construct* fashioned by particular people for particular reasons at a particular time."[29]

And let it not be thought either that an advocate of the so-called way of Nietzsche would necessarily applaud the earl of Rochester's advocacy of a life of drunkenness and debauchery, as contrasted with an examined life such as was specified by Socrates or Aristotle. No, the way of Nietzsche is not one of always applauding the deviant view as against the received view, or the respectable view, as to the true values in human life and existence. No, for in a sense truth and falsity have nothing to do with the case. Instead, the earl needs to be reckoned as operating with a very different construct from that, say, of his contemporary, John Dryden. After all, the earl's values are different from those of Dryden, and as one's values are different, so also will one's entire world-view be different, and even the facts will be different. For what are the facts but what our will to power makes them to be, construing them and constructing them, now according to one set of values and now according to another?

What, then, can we say to obviate this way of Nietzsche, so-called? For there is no doubt that it would serve to undermine my contention that there is an objective goal or natural end in human life and that the whole of ethics is thus based upon there being such and such an end and such and such an objective good for man. Clearly at this point, neither time, nor space, nor my own competence will permit me to track down the several errors that have developed in modern philosophy particularly since Kant and that in recent years have spawned the many hidden sophistries concealed behind the often rather pretentious fa-

29. *Ibid.*, 11.

cades of latter-day linguistics, hermeneutics, structuralism, poststructuralism, *et al.*

Still, foregoing a fundamental critique, I would like to point out a couple of superficial difficulties, which, though obvious, nonetheless discredit the way of Nietzsche at least to enable us to get on with our business of further developing and defending a natural-law ethic. First, is it not apparent that this so-called way of Nietzsche, at least as I have expounded it, begs the precise question that my own rendering of the way of Aristotle is designed to raise? For to judge from the quotations from Eagleton cited above, the latter-day advocate of the way of Nietzsche assumes that values can never be objective. And yet it is the point of this chapter, and indeed of the book as a whole, that values are objective; and not only values but the entire gamut of moral distinctions as well—good and bad, right and wrong, "ought" and "ought not," and so forth. Besides, was I not at pains to try to answer both the argument from queerness and the argument from relativity by upholding the objectivity of value? How, then, can the latter-day advocates of the way of Nietzsche proclaim the subjectivity of value as if it were patent and obvious and needing neither further evidence nor argument in its support? And yet have I not raised any number of considerations to show that such a thing is by no means patent and obvious and that argument and evidence are what their supposed truism of the subjectivity of value most definitely needs? But if this does not beg the question that any present-day defender of the way of Aristotle is bound to raise, then what is it?

And now finally I will make a few brief suggestions by way of a dialectical refutation of the way of Nietzsche, at least as it is represented by many of its current advocates. Thus Eagleton, for example, is fond of heaping scorn upon that supposed truism of so much modern philosophy that there is an absolute separation between fact and value. "Ridiculous," says Eagleton in effect. "For do they not realize—those who would thus keep facts and values separate—that while there may indeed be values without facts, there could never be facts without values?" And why not? The reason is that there could not be any facts—at least not any statements of fact—but that they must be informed and based upon "the largely concealed structure of values" that constitute our judgments of fact in the first place and that therefore give to the facts such character and structure as they come to have. "Interests are *constitutive* of our knowledge," Eagleton says, "not merely prejudices which imperil it. The claim that knowledge should be 'value-free' is itself a value judgment."[30]

Very well, then, but does Eagleton mean to advance it as a fact that "our interests are constitutive of our knowledge"? Surely, he does. But then must not this supposed factual statement upon which his entire position rests not be regarded simply as Eagleton's own value judgment, as well as the value judgment of other like-minded advocates of the way of Nietzsche? What, then, can these thinkers say to someone who comes along and says that, given his values, he does not see it as being a fact that our interests are constitutive of our knowledge? On what grounds can Eagleton possibly say that his purported factual judgment, being the product of his own particular set of values, must be reckoned as true, whereas its contradictory opposite, reflecting the very different set of values of an opponent, can only be false?

Surely, a philosophical position that finds itself debarred in principle from showing that its own basic principles are any more true than are the very contradictory opposites of those same principles is a poor philosophy indeed. And yet such would seem to be the predicament that any philosopher who would go the way of Nietzsche must necessarily face. Why is not, then, the way of Nietzsche little more than the primrose way to everlasting bonfire?

Can the Way of Aristotle Provide
an Exit from the Dilemma of Teleology versus Deontology?

Recall that in the preceding chapter we found that, in its character as a desire-ethic, any ethical teleology must appear ultimately to run aground on a single question: Why, merely because human beings like to do something, or find it to their advantage to do it, should they suppose that it is therefore morally right for them to do it? This question promptly turns out to be no less unanswerable than it is ineluctable and unavoidable—at least for an ethical teleology. For what must be the bottom line for any desire-ethic if not that the basic reason, and ultimately the only reason, that a human being has for doing anything is that he wants to do it, or that he thinks it to his advantage to do it, whether it is to his individual advantage or to the advantage of mankind generally? Clearly, though, if our merely desiring to do some-

30. *Ibid.*, 14.

thing or liking to do it seems not to offer the slightest moral or ethical warrant for our doing it, the inevitable consequence must be that no desire-ethic, and therefore no ethical teleology, can claim to be an ethics at all.

Nor would the situation appear to be any less desperate were we to renounce ethical teleology as a bad job ethically and were to embrace a duty-ethic or ethical deontology instead. For although it cannot be denied that a so-called deontology, or duty-ethic, has all of the earmarks of being an ethics, it unhappily turns out not to have a leg to stand on, either as an ethics or as anything else. For what is the mark of any duty-ethic or "ought"-ethic if not that "oughts" are absolutely ultimate in such an ethics: the reason that I ought (that is, morally ought) to do thus and so can never be because I like doing it, or because it is to my advantage to do it—for that would return us again to the quicksands of a desire-ethic. No, the only reason that I ought to do thus and so is because I ought; and that ends the matter.

Unhappily, if that ends the matter, our purported "ought"-ethics turns out to be without basis or foundation. For the question "why?" is always proper and legitimate with respect to any assertion of moral obligation. Nor is there any other way that such a "why"-question can ever be answered with respect to an "ought" save by considering what our human desires and wishes and supposed advantages turn out to be. And with that, what was purportedly an "ought"-ethic collapses into the arms of a desire-ethic, and again, the fatal dialectic breaks out anew. The logic of any ethical teleology seems to force us to embrace a deontology, and the logic of any deontology takes us right back to the arms of a teleology. And so our dilemma would seem to be one from which there is no exit.

But what now may be said regarding the fortunes of a so-called natural-law ethic: is there any way that it can escape the dilemma of either teleology or deontology? Apparently not. For certainly, there is no denying that a natural-law ethic—or, as it might better be termed, a natural-end ethic—is a teleological ethic. True, it may not be a teleology in the vein of either a Utilitarianism or a Rational Egoism. But a teleology it surely is. For if the capstone of such an ethics is but the notion of a human being's natural end or *telos*, and if the end or *telos* of a person is that toward which that person is oriented, as being that which he desires and toward which his aims and purposes are ultimately directed, then there is no question but that it is a "teleology" that one must contend with—and not just etymologically but in deed as well.

Nor is that all, for I have been at considerable pains throughout this chapter to show that any and all moral obligations—obligations that can be shown to be either a matter of natural law or derived from natural law—are such that if it is asked why and on what grounds and in what sense they may be held to be duties that are binding upon us, the answer can only be that they are duties for us insofar as they contribute to the attainment of that which is the natural end or goal or *telos* of each and every one of us as human beings. Immediately with this answer, though, that fatal dialectic seems to be triggered all over again.

Appearances to the contrary notwithstanding, I think that a natural-law ethic can successfully obviate the dilemma simply by escaping between the horns. The way it is enabled to do this is by showing itself to be neither a teleology in the usual sense nor a deontology. And yet how is it possible for a natural-law or natural-end ethic to purge itself of the obvious taint, particularly of its being a teleology, when by etymology, as well as in its content, it seems to proclaim itself to be nothing if not teleological?

To the end of such a purgation of a natural-law ethic, I propose to pursue a roundabout and circuitous course by first considering the somewhat eccentric but very illuminating case of two quite eminent contemporary natural-law philosophers, Germain Grisez and John Finnis. For what is interesting about the Grisez-Finnis position—at least so far as I understand it, which I must admit is not very far, the position being most elusive—is that Grisez and Finnis would appear to want to escape from the dilemma of teleology-deontology by seeking to convert natural-law ethics into a seemingly almost unequivocal deontology, and yet at the same time without having to sacrifice the teleological character of their ethics. Morover, so far as I can determine, the resource that they would fall back on to effect this union of seeming incompatibles is to deny that such human ends or *tele* as play a role in a properly teleological ethics are *natural* ends at all. Or at least, they would say that the ethical or moral warrant which we have for pursuing such ends cannot be provided by mere facts of nature. It can never be because as human beings we naturally tend toward, or pursue, such ends that it may be adjudged right for us to pursue them. In other words, it is as though these ends had a deontological character in their own right: they are ends that we ought to pursue, just because we ought. But how can this be?

I cannot but think that this Grisez-Finnis attempt to obviate the dilemma of teleology versus deontology is ultimately unsuccessful. It is almost as though they were trying to salvage a natural-law ethic by denying that moral laws are really natural laws. But successful or not, I think this Grisez-Finnis position is singularly illuminating, and its failure can be most instructive. First, let us see just why and how Grisez-Finnis would appear to go about denying that our supposedly natural human ends and goals are really natural ends.

For example, with respect to an issue that has been of concern in the moral theology of the Roman Catholic church, particularly in recent years—the issue of contraception—Grisez has argued that it does no good for Roman Catholic moralists and theologians to argue that the practice of contraception is contrary to nature and for that reason immoral. Or likewise, as regards the issue of homosexuality, it is of no consequence morally, Grisez insists, to argue that such practices are either natural or unnatural. No, Grisez would reply, there is "no naturally given structure of the sexual act as a human act." "The given structure of sexual action is a matter of fact, and since it is natural, it *can not* be violated. The morality of sexual acts is a matter of *ought*, and the very meaning of 'ought' implies that the subject matter is in our power to such an extent that what will in fact occur is contingent on our freedom." And so, Grisez pointedly concludes, it is therefore at once futile and ridiculous for anyone to "waste time trying to deduce morality from anatomy, physiology, or psychology."[31]

This is not to say, of course, that in presumably giving up the notion that our human ends are in any way natural ends, he therefore would also give up the notion that as human beings we do have ends, and properly human ends as well. In fact, both Grisez and Finnis have repeatedly and on various occasions put forward very helpful lists of what our several human goods may be taken to be. For example, here is one of Grisez's lists: "Human life, including health and safety, all the arts and skills that can be cultivated simply for the sake of their very exercise, beauty and other objects of aesthetic experience; theoretical truth in its several varieties; friendship, both as relationship in immediate liaison and organization in larger communities; the use of intelligence to direct action; the effective freedom to do what one chooses

31. Germain Grisez, "A New Formulation of Natural Law against Contraception," *Thomist*, XXX (1966), 343–44.

with the whole force of an integrated personality; and a proper relationship to the fundamental principles of reality—i.e. to God."[32]

How could one respond to all of the items on this list with anything other than hearty agreement? Indeed, within the framework of my own account of human well-being and of the good life for man—which I have characterized as being simply the wise and intelligent life or a life involving the cultivation and exercise of the intellectual and moral virtues—I can and would be only too ready to acknowledge that such goods as Grisez here enumerates are indeed necessary and indispensable for a full and perfect life for a human being.

Grisez at the same time appears studiously to avoid considering this assemblage of ends or *tele* of human life as constituting man's natural end or *telos*. But why not? In answer, consider the following quotation:

> Throughout the history of ethical theory, the proposal has been made repeatedly that the ultimate standard of morality is simply given by nature. Man has in fact certain obvious needs, or wants, and cannot help but seek to satisfy them. He will proceed in a more or less efficient way, depending upon how well he uses the mind with which nature has provided him as an instrument for obtaining this satisfaction. In naturalistic theories of this sort the ends [and here Grisez would seem to imply not just the ends of individual acts but the ends of the organisms or individual substances taken as wholes] are established by nature, and the imperatives become hypothetical.[33]

Unquestionably, this passage seems to imply that Grisez wants firmly and decisively to repudiate any and all "naturalistic" theories of ethics, as he calls them. Why? The answer is suggested in the quotation. For no sooner does one set up a list of human goods as being both things which as human beings we naturally desire and tend toward, as well as things that serve as the ultimate standards and reference points for what we morally ought to strive for and to be, than at once our moral imperatives would cease to be categorical and become mere counsels of prudence: they are binding upon us only insofar as they specify the means whereby we can attain what we desire or tend toward naturally. And what, pray, is particularly moral about "just doin' what comes naturally"?

But having gotten this far in his moral philosophy, where would

32. *Ibid.*, 348.
33. *Ibid.*, 346.

Grisez go from here? He wants to recognize that there are certain ends or goods that are proper for us as human beings. Yet apparently, he does not want to call them natural ends; or at least he does not want to recognize them as natural ends, in the sense of their being ends that we are naturally ordered to, or disposed toward, simply in virtue of our nature as human beings. And this prompts me to say that though the hands are those of Germain Grisez, the voice is that of Immanuel Kant. Was it not Kant, after all, who decisively turned his back on Aristotle and on the entire tradition of natural-law ethics, in his unequivocal repudiation of nature as being able to provide a foundation for morals or ethics? Accordingly, just as Kant in his ethical deontology sternly refused to make even the slightest concessions to natural teleology, may we say that Grisez would appear to be following Kant's suit?

Surely, though, this conclusion seems scarcely credible. For do not Grisez and Finnis realize that supping with Kant could be like supping with the devil—one needs a very long spoon. And with all due respect to Kant, could not one say that Kant's own spoon would seem never to have been quite long enough? In any case, let us put Grisez-Finnis on hold, for the moment, and see what some of the toils, to say nothing of the trials and tribulations, were that Kant found himself caught up in when he attempted to work out an ethical deontology without appeal or apology to teleology. Wishing most emphatically to distance himself from teleology or desire-ethic, Kant saw himself as being committed to saying that all such things as human ends, purposes, or desires, being but so many facts or phenomena of nature, turn out to be irrelevant in providing human beings with any guidelines or direction in morals or ethics.

But this idea immediately turns out to be exceedingly embarrassing for Kant. For as I have often reiterated, Kant would be the last to want to say that "oughts" and duties are entirely arbitrary and lack either rhyme or reason in their support. And yet how else can any "why"-question with respect to an "ought" be answered, unless one appeals to some purpose or end that one wishes to attain thereby, and in terms of which the "ought" becomes intelligible as being that which one needs to do if one is to attain such and such an end or achieve such and such a purpose?

But surely, Kant would not want to allow himself to be caught in any such trap as that of saying that heeding the injunction of moral "oughts" or duties is utterly without ground or reason. For in many ways, the hallmark of Kant's ethical position—and the hallmark with which Kant himself was determined that it be stamped—is that his position is preeminently rational, even almost rationalistic. Thus is it not precisely "practical reason," as Kant called it, that calls the tune in morals and ethics—which is only to say that never under any circumstances can anything be thought of as being required of us morally if its practical reasonableness is not clearly recognizable? And yet how may a course of action be recognized as being practically reasonable unless it is seen to subserve in some way either an individual's end or interest or advantage or mankind's end or interest or advantage?

No sooner, though, is the practical reasonableness of any action said thus to depend entirely upon its subserving some human end or purpose than immediately the distinctively categorical character of the Kantian moral imperatives would appear to be irreparably undermined: Kant's much vaunted categorical imperatives would then turn out to be no more than hypothetical imperatives. And with that, Kantian ethics would surely be undone. Or put another way, from pretending to be a deontological ethics of the strictest observance, Kantian ethics would collapse into a teleological ethics.

Indeed, it is this point of seeming inconsistency in Kant that Robert Paul Wolff, in his brilliant commentary on the *Groundwork*, points out most tellingly: there would seem to be no way in which moral imperatives could be both categorical and at the same time practically reasonable. Thus consider how Wolff exposes the radical inconsistency of Kantian ethics. For Wolff insists that Kant saw very clearly that the only way practical reason could give us any instruction in the matter of what we ought or ought not to do would be in terms of the ends and objectives that we seek to attain by our actions: "Since according to Kant there is an objective good which all rational agents *qua* rational take as their end (so-called obligatory ends), it follows that the principle of practical reason corresponding to such an imperative is a valid principle for all rational agents whatever."[34]

Then Wolff goes on to aver that Kant seems to take back with his left hand what he has just given with his right: "The principal source of the confusion (in Kant) is his habit of describing imperatives as commanding actions without reference to ends. In paragraph 16 [Kant]

34. Robert Paul Wolff, *The Autonomy of Reason: A Commentary on Kant's Groundwork of the Metaphysic of Morals* (New York, 1973), 130.

writes: 'A categorical imperative would be one which represented an action as objectively necessary in itself apart from its relation to a further end.' . . . Finally, in paragraph 22, Kant repeats, 'there is an imperative which, without being based on, and conditioned by, any further purpose to be attained by a certain line of conduct, enjoins this conduct immediately.'"[35] On this, Wolff's comment is at once sharp and decisive:

> Now this way of talking just doesn't make any sense. Rational action is purposive action. It is behavior which is caused by the agent's conception of the state of affairs to be brought about by that behavior. . . . So a categorical imperative cannot "directly command a certain conduct without making its condition some purpose to be reached by it," for that is the same as saying that it commands an agent to engage in purposive action which has no purpose. Instead, the logic of Kant's theory of imperatives ought to lead him to define a categorical imperative as an imperative which commands us to pursue a purpose which we *must* (insofar as we are rational) adopt.[36]

How else can one respond if not with an enthusiastic "Bravo!" For if Wolff's interpretation of Kant is correct, not only would it appear that Kantian moral philosophy turns out to be completely undone by this sudden turn in the argument, but it also looks as if Kant's own spoon were indeed not long enough for supping with the devil! And if Kant's spoon was not long enough, what about the Grisez-Finnis spoon? First, though, it needs to be admitted that there would seem to be nothing amiss with the Grisez-Finnis spoon, at least not at first blush. For is it not that interesting turn in Wolff's argument—the turn that exhibits for the first time the very fruitful notion of so-called "obligatory ends"— that one could say was the idea the Grisez-Finnis line of argument was all along trying to point up? Indeed, Grisez and Finnis would apparently want to establish that there are "categorical" ends—that is, ends that are binding upon us as human agents, but which for that reason are not to be regarded as being natural ends or ends that we seek because we are naturally inclined to seek them. And what is this if not what Wolff was getting at when he put forward the notion of ends being "obligatory"?

Nor is it only Grisez-Finnis who can rejoice in this tantalizingly

35. *Ibid.*
36. *Ibid.*, 130–31.

fruitful notion of an "obligatory end." For surely, I can find solace and comfort in such an idea. Indeed, is it not precisely this notion of a so-called obligatory end that can provide the means of distinguishing an Aristotelian teleology from such ethical teleologies as are exemplified by the likes of Utilitarianism and Rational Individualism? Moreover, if the teleology that is to be associated with a natural-law ethic is distinctively different from the teleologies that the term normally suggests, why will this not enable us to move between the horns of the dilemma? So far from its having to be either teleology or deontology, it would now appear that there is an entirely different sort of teleology, one that at the same time seems to incorporate features of an ethical deontology as well. In fact, is not this the sense and import of a notion such as that of an "obligatory end"? And why might this not enable us to escape either around or through the dilemma of teleology versus deontology?

To confirm that a natural-law ethics (or a Grisez-Finnis ethic) provides an exit from the dilemma, let us but call up again the distinction that I have already alluded to, which is pointed up by the so-called *Euthyphro* test: are things to be reckoned as good merely because we desire them or tend toward them; or is it rather that we should desire and tend toward such things as we recognize to be really good or objectively good?[37] Suppose, then, that it is the first of these two alternatives, *viz.*, that things are good or of value only because we happen to like them. At once, we can see that with this alternative, the fatal weakness that I have repeatedly suggested seems to attach to most teleological ethics becomes unavoidable: merely because as human beings we want something or desire it or tend toward it may not be taken as being ground or evidence that it is therefore morally right for us to have it or that we ought to have it. And so it is that on this alternative of the *Euthyphro* test, no teleological ethics can claim to be an ethics.

Suppose, though, that we opt for the other alternative under the *Euthyphro* test in interpreting a teleological ethics. Immediately, we see that it no longer follows that what we desire or tend toward is not to be reckoned as being either morally good or right. On the contrary, if our desire or liking for a thing is determined by our recognition of its true excellence or goodness or value, we have to deal with something that is objectively good; and because it is objectively good, it is in the nature of an obligatory end—something that we ought to desire or seek after

37. Plato, *Euthyphro*, 10a.

or value whether or not we actually do. On this basis, however, a teleology can most appropriately be reckoned as an ethics. And the dilemma of teleology or deontology ceases to be a dilemma. So far from its being a case of mutually exclusive alternatives, either of desires or of "oughts," it now turns out to be an obligatory end: it is something that we come to desire because we see that we ought to desire it.

Still, our business is not quite done. For the question still remains: granted that the notion of an obligatory end is viable, how do we know either that there really are such ends or what they are specifically and concretely? And it is precisely with respect to this question that I suspect that Grisez, Finnis, and company would appear to part company with the classical natural-law tradition in ethics—the tradition that I am suggesting is that of Aristotle and Aquinas and Hooker. Indeed, as I see the matter, in the natural-law tradition, the evidence for there being obligatory ends and for their being specific is derived from nature. Thus, for example, Aristotle opens his *Ethics* with the declaration that "the good is that at which all things aim"; and Aquinas suggests that good (*bonum*) may be "defined" as an object of desire—that is, as something desirable or appetible.[38] In the same vein, Aquinas is no less insistent that, good being simply by definition that which is desirable, it is to be regarded as always and inescapably an end or *telos*. Nor is the reason for this other than that the good of anything is simply to be recognized as being that which is perfective of that of which it is the good or end: "It is manifest that each thing is desirable (*appetibile*), just in so far as it is perfect: for all things desire their perfection." Or again, "In so far as one being in its very actuality is perfective of another or conserving [or preserving] of it, it has the notion (*ratio*) of an end in respect to that which thus comes to be perfected by it." Or again: "Two things pertain to the notion (*ratio*) of an end: viz. that it be desired (*appetitum*) or sought after (*desideratum*) by those things which have not yet attained the end."[39]

How, then, do we human beings come to recognize what the true end is at which we all aim, or what the true good is which is perfective of human nature, and which is therefore desirable for every human

38. Aristotle, *Nicomachean Ethics*, 1094 a, 3; St. Thomas Aquinas, *De Veritate*, Qu. XXI, Art. 2 (*cf.* note 10 above).

39. St. Thomas Aquinas, *Summa Theologiae*, I, Qu. 5, Art. 1; St. Thomas Aquinas, *De Veritate*, Qu. XXI, Art. 1 (this is my own free translation); *ibid.*, Qu. XXII, Art. 2.

being—how do we come to know whether and what this is, if not simply by a regard for what we might call the facts of nature and of human nature? Thus, to cite my earlier example: just as from experience with trees and their growth and development we come to recognize full growth or flourishing or perfection in the case of trees, so also from our experience with human beings in our everyday life, as well as from history and art and literature, we come to learn what the perfection or full flowering of a human being is, and is by nature.[40] In other words, from nature and in the light of our understanding of human nature, we come to recognize what our natural end or *telos* is simply by virtue of our nature as human beings. Moreover, our natural end being thus no more and no less than our true human good, which, as Aquinas says, is that which is to be done and to be pursued, just as evil is to be avoided, it follows that the natural end of man that is discoverable by nature is an obligatory end for each and every one of us.

What, then, in the eyes of Grisez-Finnis is amiss about this appeal to nature as the source and evidence of all of our knowledge of ethics? The answer to this question is hard to come by, at least from a reading of the sometimes cryptic discussions of Grisez-Finnis. Nevertheless, I suspect that Grisez-Finnis have perhaps uncritically accepted the standard view of nature that has been regnant ever since the seventeenth century, according to which all distinctions between right and wrong, good and bad, "ought" and "ought not" are totally absent from the natural world. Accordingly, rather than undertake a radical reexamination and reassessment of the current views of nature—to be followed by a possible rehabilitation of a natural teleology that would have unequivocal moral and ethical implications, discoverable directly in nature itself—Grisez-Finnis would apparently prefer to write off a knowledge of nature, even of human nature, as ever being a possible and proper source of ethical knowledge and certainly as being a source of knowledge of anything like "obligatory ends."

But, then, if Grisez-Finnis would repudiate any and all appeals to nature as the means of discovering what our true human ends and goals are, within the context of a presumably natural-law ethics, what evidence do they cite in support of their view that the obligatory ends of

40. Just as this book was going to press, I came across a telling article by Gilbert Harman, in which he seeks to level a critique at the idea of a "natural human flourishing" as providing a basis for ethics. See Gilbert Harman, "Human Flourishing, Ethics, and Liberty," *Philosophy and Public Affairs*, XII (Fall, 1983), 307–22.

human beings are very largely the same as those natural-law thinkers in the past have always taken them to be? In other words, the obligatory ends that Grisez-Finnis would recognize as being incumbent upon us human beings would be pretty much the same as such thinkers as Aristotle and Aquinas have long thought them to be; but in the methods of evidence and demonstration by which Grisez-Finnis would try to show that such ends really are our ends, they would appear to depart radically from the natural-law tradition. For presumably, they would deny that as human moral agents our knowledge of our true ends can ever be based on nature. Rather, such ends need to be held to be self-evident to us or perhaps known to us simply by intuition. But does this not sound like Kant and modern deontologists all over again? Moreover, just as I noted earlier that Kant's appeals to self-evidence in support of his categorical imperatives, or the appeals of latter-day deontologists to moral intuition, will not do, so also I suspect that the Grisez-Finnis tactic in the matter of moral evidence will not do either. After all, a purportedly natural-law ethic, from which all appeals to nature have been excluded, is in danger of coming out looking and smelling like a very curious sort of *Unding*. It is neither fish nor fowl.

Has Creativity a Place in a Natural-Law Ethic?

The Romantic movement of the last century foisted upon us a strange heritage, which, it would seem, we must continue to live with. This heritage is that all of us are somehow fascinated, perhaps mesmerized, by the idea of "creativity." There was a time, no doubt, when it was thought that only God could create. But not so any more. Nowadays, in the schools, from the pulpit, in the streets, and, of course, in advertising, just about everybody is constantly urged to be creative. Is it any wonder that contemporary ethics and moral philosophy also should have become infected with this same passion for creativity? As a consequence, any system of ethics that does not place a high value upon creativity in the life of the human individual is bound to suffer in the opinion of most modern philosophers. Nor is it surprising that a more old-fashioned moralist such as Aristotle should have come in for his share of downgrading on this account.

Prominent among such recent downgraders of Aristotle—albeit this downgrading seems to be somewhat restrained and sober—is the eminent Cambridge philosopher, Bernard Williams. Speaking from his pride of place as master of Trinity and sometime professor of moral philosophy in Cambridge University, Williams has taken it upon himself, in his little book *Morality*, to try to teach old Aristotle a thing or two. Specifically, his tactic has been to confront Aristotle—with an explicit bow in the direction of the Romantics—with what he calls the "Gauguin problem": "A moralist who wants to base a conception of the right sort of life for man on considerations about the high and distinctive power of man can scarcely disregard the claims of creative genius in the arts or sciences to be included preeminently among such powers; yet he will find it hard to elicit from, or even reconcile with, an ideal of the development and expression of such genius, the more everyday and domesticated virtues and commitments of which morality has to give some account."[41]

Faced with such a passage, one can hardly avoid viewing it with irony, considering that the Cambridge don takes it upon himself to be not a little condescending toward a rather benighted Aristotle, who, after all, was only from Stagira and not from Cambridge, and who in addition is no more up-to-date than the fourth century B.C. Overlooking the irony of the situation, and speaking directly to the issue that Williams' criticism raises, one wonders if the criticism may not be, in at least one respect, seriously confused and misdirected. For surely from Aristotle's point of view, two different issues are raised by what Williams calls the "Gauguin problem"—issues that Williams would seem to have carelessly confounded. Thus to judge the excellence—even the "creative genius"—of a person in the arts or sciences is one thing; and to judge the excellence of a person with respect to the living of his life as a human person—that is, his moral excellence—is very different.

True, Aristotle is never averse to stressing the analogy between the practice of the various arts and skills and the practice of what one might call the business of being human. But it is only an analogy. Hence it is one thing to say that someone is a good painter or even a great painter—or for that matter a great general, or a good farmer, or a great speaker, or whatever—and another thing to say that someone is a good man or even a great man. And so it would be entirely consistent with Aristotle's principles to recognize that Gauguin could well be a great painter, even though as a human person he might not stack up too favorably when compared, say, with Socrates. True, we do not know that Aristotle

41. Bernard Williams, *Morality: An Introduction to Ethics* (New York, 1972), 61.

would have reacted to a painter such as Gauguin in quite this way—though personally I have my suspicions. But in any case a response along such lines is very telling against one feature of Williams' critique.

Besides, even granting that Williams' criticism of Aristotle, in this respect at least, is decidedly askew, there is another sense in which Williams does raise a real issue to which many of us can hardly fail to be sensitive, being as we are heirs of Romanticism, like it or not. And, indeed, the issue could be described as being that of the "creative genius." For why not suppose that there is a place for creativity, not only in the arts or sciences but also in the living of our lives—in morals and ethics? And must it not then be conceded that Aristotle, in his insistence that human beings in the living of their lives ought to conform to the dictates of natural law and need ever to respect that single end or goal or *telos*, which I have insisted is an obligatory end for any and all human beings, leaves absolutely no room for creativity in the actual living of our lives and the development of ourselves as human persons?

And indeed, this must in a measure be conceded. For if we contrast the Aristotelian or natural-law position in ethics with the ethics of, say, Kierkegaardian or Sartrian freedom, there is no denying that Aristotle leaves no room for anything like Sartrian "projects." Nor does he leave any room for the position in ethics that has become singularly widespread and popular in the present day and is exemplified by thinkers who otherwise are as different from one another as R. M. Hare or John Rawls or even Bernard Williams himself. Even though none of these latter thinkers comes out smelling exactly like Jean-Paul Sartre (or even Kierkegaard), nevertheless, when it comes to what Hare would call "decisions of principle" in regard to one's overall way of life, they all would insist that a human being is entirely free to decide which way of life is to be the way for him.[42] It is just this freedom which presumably has to be presupposed in any ethics that is open to a genuine Romantic creativity and that thus tends to extol such creativity, not only in artistic production but equally in living our lives and developing our personalities as moral agents. And although a Sartre might be more blatant in his preachments of such a creativity, a Williams or a Hare or a Rawls would be no less determined in his insistence that a creative freedom such as this needs to be reckoned as being basic and central to the moral life of any true individual.

42. R. M. Hare, *The Language of Morals* (Oxford, 1952), pt. I, chap. 4.

But not so Aristotle, I am afraid. And not so Aquinas either, or Hooker, or indeed any other major thinker in the natural-law tradition. As they view our human condition, if there indeed are natural moral laws and if further there is a specifically natural and obligatory end toward which human life is ordered and oriented by nature, then there is no way it could be maintained that human beings are free to choose their own ends in life. At least they are not free to do so, in the sense of its making no moral difference which ends they choose, as if all that was important was that they choose.

Nevertheless, is this failure to make any provision for such a creativity a disability on the part of the natural-law moralists? Remember that the only reason originally for anyone's advocating so radical a freedom in the moral life of a human being was the conviction that there are no natural moral laws or morally obligatory ends in nature; and hence, as Sartre would say, there are no guidelines in fact or in reality that can help us to determine what we ought to do and be as human individuals. And if there are no guidelines anywhere in the world, then why not simply make up our own guidelines? This is what it means to be creative in a moral or ethical sense. And this is also why someone like R. M. Hare can insist that any choice of ultimate ends in human life cannot be anything other than what he calls "a decision of principle." Immediately, though, it has to be added that such a decision of principle can never be a decision *from* principle. That is, there can be no reason, no ground, no justification for embracing any one such end over another. The choice, in other words, can never be other than a purely arbitrary one, and thus it is not a principled choice at all.

Once, though, it is viewed in this light, can we any longer say that the cult of creativity in the matter of our moral ends offers so attractive a prospect for us after all? Do we really want to have to live under conditions of existence such that it would make not the slightest difference morally whether our choice of a moral ideal were the ideal of a Socrates or that of a Stalin, that of a St. Francis or that of an Ivan the Terrible, yes, maybe even that of Paul Gauguin, or perhaps that of a Bernard Williams? Little wonder, then, that no sooner is it shown that Mackie's arguments from queerness and from relativity can be successfully rebutted, and that there really are natural ends discoverable in nature, than many of us would be only too happy in the prospect of a life based on knowledge and understanding rather than one given over to the exercise of an utterly irrational and uncontrolled freedom and creativity.

Nevertheless, it would seem that we still have not fully parried the thrust of Williams' criticism of Aristotle on the score of Aristotle's failure to reckon with the factor of creativity. For however willing you or I or the next person might be to forego the dubious advantages of an absolutely unfettered creativity in the living of our lives, and thus to settle instead for rational guidance and direction in what we make of ourselves, still must it not appear to many to be unduly restricting and constricting that on the Aristotelian view there is but a single end for each and every human individual—the end of simply living wisely and intelligently? For what other effect might this be supposed to have but to usher in a drab and depressing uniformity of human existence, in which all people would need to be tailored according to the same pattern and cast in the same mold?

Once again, it would seem that we are up against a misplaced argument in support of a supposed need for creativity in human existence. For is it true that if all men are under the same obligation to live rationally and intelligently, and that the natural end or goal of human life must therefore be the same for all, even to the point that it might be said that Socrates represents the one ideal which it behooves all of us to try to follow, would it then necessarily follow that insofar as we approximate this ideal, we will all turn out to be but so many replicas of old Socrates? Hardly. And to see how farfetched this supposition is, let us again appeal to the analogy between morals and ethics on the one hand, and the various arts, skills, crafts, and techniques on the other.

Take game fishing, for example; or if you prefer, carpentry or accounting or the practice of medicine. In each and every case the goal of the particular art will surely be roughly the same for all of the practitioners—landing the fish, completing the house, curing the patient, and so on. Likewise, the how-to-do-it rules for the practice of the art will be likely to be generally recognized as being largely the same—for example, in fishing, how to handle the rod, how to thumb the reel, how to make a cast, how to play the fish, and so on. Yet this clearly does not mean that every skilled fisherman's performance and style of fishing must therefore be uniformly the same. Far from it, for has one never had the delight of watching a group of truly skilled fishermen in action? Each will be seen to have developed his own style of doing the very same things that all of the others are doing as well. And each will display no end of variation and resourcefulness in dealing with the particular circumstances he meets on the particular occasion in which he is plying his art.

Besides, when one considers the more complex and sophisticated arts and skills, one can only be impressed with the individuality of the performance of every truly skilled practitioner. One has only to ask oneself: what good is the surgeon who merely operates by the book or the general who would conduct a battle only from his old West Point manual? And indeed, in the moral life no less than in any one of the various arts and skills, it is never merely a matter of following mechanically the how-to-do-it rules of the art, important though those rules are. No, for the know-how, be it of the good surgeon or of the good man, must always be an affair of applying the rules in particular circumstances; and because particular circumstances are potentially of infinite variety, the exercise of any true skill calls for a constant resourcefulness and ingenuity on the part of the practitioner.

There is a definite sense in which in morals and ethics, following the rules and doing as one ought to do will require an even higher degree of individuality on the part of each practitioner than is the case in any other art. And the reason is that as Aristotle insists, morality is unlike all of the other arts in that in all of the other arts all that counts is knowing what needs to be done and being able to do it—in other words, know-how. But whether one loves one's job or delights in one's skill makes not the slightest difference: a surgeon might conceivably hate what he is doing; but as long as he does the job well, his dislike of his work is no reflection on his skill and excellence as a surgeon. In contrast, in the sphere of morals and ethics, it is not enough merely to know what the just or courageous or temperate course of action is and then to do it. No, if one is to be a just or courageous or temperate person, it is not enough merely to do what one ought to do—to perform just and courageous and temperate actions. One must also love justice and courage and temperance as such and for their own sakes. Otherwise, one might perform just or courageous actions out of a desire, say, to be well thought of or because of a fear of consequences if one did not do what was expected of one; and under such circumstances one could hardly be said to be a truly just or courageous person.

Clearly, then, we can see that the good life for a human being, the moral life, if you will, is not merely mechanically doing a particular act. Rather, it is knowing what ought to be done and then doing it. Nor is it a matter of actual know-how, as against a mere knowledge of general principles. One must have one's heart in what one is doing as well. Otherwise, one may do what one ought to do and yet without necessarily being the kind of person one ought to be. Accordingly, is it not apparent that living one's life as one should is not only a do-it-yourself job; it is also a job in which one has to "work out one's own salvation in fear and trembling"? Why, then, worry about creativity, as if it were the only means of cultivating and preserving an individuality of one's own? No, for just living the moral life as one should in accordance with the precepts of natural law is entirely a business and undertaking of oneself and for oneself as an individual person, which no one else can do for you or can ever condition or program you to go through the motions of the doing. You are either into the business yourself, wholeheartedly, and as the individual that you are, or else your business is not the business of the moral life or the examined life.

Suppose that we consider briefly what it might mean if all of us were determined to pursue the Socratic ideal of the examined life. Socrates would be at once our mentor and our ideal, so far as living the good life is concerned. Will the result be but a set of uniform, or uniformed, individuals, all stamped with the Socratic image and thus totally lacking in individuality and creativity?

Of course, we all know that Socrates has often been set up as the ideal to be followed in the moral life, particularly in the Aristotelian and natural-law tradition. Some scholars have even suggested that it was Socrates whom Aristotle had in mind in his account in the *Ethics* of what the good life must consist of and what the great-souled man must be like. Likewise, I have noted that the key factor in such human excellence, as thus exemplified in Socrates, is what I have termed a characteristically practical wisdom. It is a knowledge and a wisdom that are directed precisely toward living in a truly human way and in the way that a human being ought to live, considering that one's human nature demands that one live and act as a rational animal. Accordingly, such a practical knowledge turns out to be for Socrates a self-knowledge— which is to say a self-critical knowledge, in which the individual human being is ever aware of how in his day-by-day choices and behavior his judgment is likely to be colored, and his choices thereby perverted, by feelings and impulses of pride, fear, vanity, greed, selfishness, lust, laziness, ambition, or whatever.

Let us now shift from the example of Socrates to a dramatically different and yet profoundly similar example, that of one of Jane Austen's heroines, say, Anne Elliott in *Persuasion* or perhaps Fanny Price in *Mansfield Park*. As Douglas Bush has aptly noted in his little book on Jane Austen:

> We have seen in the earlier novels—and shall see in *Emma* and *Persuasion*—how much Jane Austen stresses the attainment of rational and emotional self-knowledge and self-control, responsible maturity, and nowhere is that idea or ideal so much emphasized as in *Mansfield Park*. The lack of self-knowledge is explicitly noted, usually by the author, with varying degrees of seriousness, in Mrs. Norris, the Bertram sisters, the Crawfords, Dr. Grant, and Mr. Rushworth. And the lack of self-knowledge, while related to all defects, is most closely linked with selfishness, an insistent theme throughout Jane Austen, not least in this novel. Fanny alone—since Edmund falls well short of her—gains the full self-knowledge and integrity born of almost unfailing self-discipline. And hers, like Anne Elliott's, is acquired through years of trying experience and much lonely reflection.[43]

Superficially, what could appear more diverse than the circumstances and concerns of Socrates' life in fifth-century Athens and those of a character such as Anne Elliott in England at the end of the eighteenth century? Socrates' companions and associates and adversaries were the likes of Glaucon and Adeimantus, Thrasymachus and Protagoras, Alcibiades and Crito, Meletus and Anytus, whereas Anne Elliott's were the members of her own family, together with those of the other country families of her Somersetshire neighborhood and the families and individuals among the various visiting naval personnel—Sir Walter Elliott, the Musgroves, Admiral and Mrs. Croft, Captain Wentworth, Lady Russell, *et al.* Moreover, Socrates' abiding concern, in his own words, was "daily to discourse about virtue, and of those other things about which you hear me examining myself and others. [For this] is the greatest good of man, [it being simply the case] that the unexamined life is not worth living."[44] In contrast, it might be thought—indeed, by those around her it was thought—that the primary concern of Anne Elliott should have been what it nearly always was for other young ladies of her class and station in life, *viz.*, to find a husband.

Nevertheless, despite these manifold and striking and by no means

43. Douglas Bush, *Jane Austen* (New York, 1975), 112.
44. Plato, *Apology*, 38 A.

superficial differences between a Socrates and an Anne Elliott, is it not remarkable how basically and fundamentally an Anne Elliott in her way, no less than a Socrates in his, turned out to be occupied with leading an examined life? True, Anne Elliott would doubtless not have put it that way. But then, was the common human situation in which she found herself so unlike that in which Socrates found himself, or, for that matter, in which any and all human beings find themselves if they reflect upon the matter sufficiently?

Likewise, is it not to be conceded that their (and our) respective ends or goals in life, and their (and our) conceptions of what the good life for a human being consists of, can hardly be reckoned to have been so different either? And yet one could never say that the lifestyle of an Anne Elliott was a mere copy of that of a Socrates. Her situation in life and the particular conditions of her existence, although fundamentally like those of Socrates, were at the same time poles apart from his, at least on the surface. Hence the particular problems and difficulties, as well as the particular triumphs and successes, of Anne bear little resemblance to those of Socrates. Nor does this signify anything other than that each and every one of us as human beings, for all of the basic likeness and similarity of our human situation, has each to do his own thing, live his own life, and work out his own salvation in fear and trembling. And as for creativity, why worry about that fetish of the Romantic movement? For surely, the development and cultivation by each of us of his own individual personality will be found to be but part and parcel of the business of leading an examined life.

CHAPTER III

LAW AS THE IMPLEMENTATION OF ETHICS WITHIN THE POLITICAL SPHERE

Individual Good and Common Good

Just what did we accomplish in the chapter just concluded? Our objective was to try to find an ethics that could serve as a proper and adequate basis for law and for legal systems, such as they either are or ought to be within human communities and societies. Could it be that in what I have called a natural-law ethic, we did indeed find the ethics that was needed? And yet would it not seem that the law, which was to have been grounded and justified in terms of that ethics, somehow got lost in the shuffle?

For just consider: what may be understood by "law," in the sense of the civil law or common law of a political society or community? Earlier on, of course, I put forward my definition of "law" as being any rule of action that is aimed at attaining an end or *telos*. And yet the one end or *telos* that was considered in the preceding chapter was the end or *telos* that an individual human being has simply as an individual. Clearly, though, law in this sense would hardly suffice in the sense of the law of a human society or community. St. Thomas Aquinas gives as his definition: "Law is nothing else than an ordinance of reason for the common good, promulgated by him who has the care of the community."[1] And yet how can law, considered as being aimed at the common good of an entire community, ever be univocally the same as law, considered as being aimed at the individual good of a private person?

A problem seems to have arisen, for moral laws—at least as we considered them to be in the preceding chapter—turned out to be no more than "how-to-do-it" rules directed toward the attainment of the good of the individual. Yet now in the light of St. Thomas Aquinas'

1. St. Thomas Aquinas, *Summa Theologiae*, I–II, Qu. 90, Art. 4.

113

definition, civil laws, in the sense of the laws of a political community or society, turn out to be rules—no doubt, "how-to-do-it" rules—but this time rules aimed at the good not of the individual but of the entire community. Is there any way of reconciling these two apparently disparate conceptions of law, each of them central to the entire so-called natural-law tradition in ethics and politics, a tradition which it is my concern in this book to try to resurrect and defend?

Law as Aimed at the Private Good
of the Individual or at
the Common Good of the Community

With respect to ethics, there would seem to be little doubt that a natural-law ethics, such as I sought to present in the preceding chapter, is a self-determining and even self-regarding enterprise for its practitioners. The natural end or *telos* toward which a human moral agent needs to direct his efforts in life is unmistakably that person's own natural perfection. More specifically, this same end or *telos* of the individual person could consist simply of that individual's living wisely and intelligently—exercising intellectual and moral virtues. But what does this entail if not the sharp recognition that no one else can possibly provide a person with such virtues or exercise these virtues for him? No, this is exclusively a "do-it-yourself" job. Or, as I expressed it earlier, and in a more contemporary idiom, there is no way in which a human person could ever be "programmed," either by his family or friends, by the state, or by any of the agencies of society or of the community, to live well, or to live as he should, or to do what he ought to do, or to be the human person that he ought to be. No, the human individual himself must do this by himself and for himself.

Of course, such a way of characterizing the enterprise of morals or ethics from within the context of so-called natural-law theory is patently different from almost every one of the currently fashionable theories of ethics that are prevalent in the present day. For it is characteristic of neither the Utilitarians nor the Kantians for morals and ethics to "begin at home." Rather, they see morals or ethics as being almost exclusively a question of altruism as against egoism, of being concerned for others as contrasted with being concerned for oneself. "So act," Kant says, "that you can will that the maxim of your action should become a universal law." Or again, "Always act so as to treat human nature, whether in your own person or in the person of others, always as an end and never merely as a means."[2] And similarly, as I noted in the first chapter, what might be called the moral gravamen of Utilitarianism lies not in the moral agent's pursuing merely his own pleasure or advantage, but rather in his being concerned about the greatest good or the greatest happiness of the greatest number—that is, about the good or happiness of others.

Nevertheless, against every such tendency to construe morals and ethics exclusively as being altruistic, a natural-law ethics—or better a natural-end ethics—sets its face firmly and resolutely. For in such an ethics, the end being simply the perfection or flourishing or well-being of the individual person, it follows that the moral life of the human individual seemingly cannot be other than a self-regarding enterprise, first, last, and always. And yet must not this presumed egoism-in-principle that would appear to attach to a natural-law ethic occasion no end of difficulty the minute one turns from the notion of law in the context of ethics to law in the context of politics? Already Aquinas' conception of law as a rule of reason ordered to the common good seems at variance with the notion of law that I have put forward as being a rule of reason ordered to the individual's own good.

Nor is that the only difficulty that we now need to face. For recall that at the beginning of the first chapter, I announced that my ongoing concern in this book is to try to defend and provide an adequate basis for human rights. But must not any consideration of rights, even of our own individual rights, immediately project us into an inescapable regard for others? For one thing, my claim of a right to, say, my life, my liberty, and my property at once entails my insistence that others have a duty to respect these rights. Not only that, but in claiming a right for myself, on whatever grounds—be it in virtue simply of my being human or in virtue of some particular deserving action or achievement on my part—must I not thereby find myself at once implicated in still further acknowledgments that others, no less than I, have claims to rights similar to mine, given that they too are human beings or that they too are deserving? In other words, any concern with human rights, even when I try to make it exclusively a concern with my own rights, must immediately carry me beyond the narrow context of my own ends and

2. Immanuel Kant, *Groundwork of the Metaphysic of Morals*, chap. 6, 421, 429 (pagination of the Royal Prussian Academy in Berlin).

purposes and bring me face to face with that entire web of rights and duties that are involved in any properly ordered human community and that presumably are spelled out in the civil law of that community. And so once again, it would seem that even on our own principles, we are led out and beyond any mere concern with law in the sense of laws ordered to our own individual good and are brought face to face with law as something that is ordered to the good of the community. And yet just how are we to reconcile these two patently disparate conceptions of law with each other? Indeed, how are we to go about trying to find a proper justification for duties to the community, much as we earlier sought to provide a justification for our duties to self? Or likewise, is there any way in which a right concern with our own individual and private good can ever implicate us in a concern with the public or common good?

Toward a Reconciliation of Personal Ends and Political Ends, of Private Goods and the Common Good

Faced with questions and challenges such as these, why should we not again tear a leaf from Aristotle's book—this time from his *Politics*—and invoke the well-known dictum that man is by nature a political animal?[3] For what, after all, may we take to be the import of such a pronouncement if not that man has a dual end or purpose—on the one hand, his end or purpose simply as a human individual, and on the other hand, his end or purpose insofar as he is a citizen and a member of a political community? Nor perhaps is it too much to suppose that in Aristotle's eyes there was not necessarily any radical duality or even conflict between what should thus be reckoned as being man's end or *telos* as an individual and his end or *telos* as a member of a political community. In fact, the more one reflects upon the matter, the more it is borne in upon one that there is no way in which a human individual could ever possibly attain his natural end as an individual without also attaining his natural end as a political animal. Nor would the converse seem any less true. For again, it would seem that there could scarcely be any right or proper attainment of political ends without there being a comparable attainment at the same time by the members of the po-

3. Aristotle, *Politics*, trans. H. Rackham (London, 1932), Bk. I, 1253 a, 2–3.

litical community, each of his own natural end as an individual.

Yet hardly is it to be expected that there can be any convincing reconciliation of public and private ends unless we first take steps to remove a number of roadblocks that are sure to stand in the way—particularly in the present day—of any right understanding of the public and the private spheres. For one thing, there seems to be a false opposition between a supposed state of nature and the state of civil society. Indeed, it would seem that much of present-day thought, just as much of political thought ever since the seventeenth century, has been obsessed with the notion that the natural state of human beings needs to be contrasted sharply with their state in civil society. Surely, though, it is not just incredible but almost perverse that anyone should suppose that human beings might have purely private or personal interests or ends that, at least in principle, might be thought capable of satisfaction and realization entirely outside of the *polis* or civil society.

Moreover, to bring the point home, why not remind ourselves of that initial or starting condition in which we all find ourselves, insofar as we are newborn infants or small children? Already I have quoted the Book of Common Prayer to the effect that "we come into this world bringing nothing with us." Likewise, in thus coming into the world, we surely do not recognize ourselves as having been born into any so-called state of nature, apart from all civil society. Quite the contrary; we are born to parents, and the parents either are, or should be, the nucleus of a family; and, in turn, the family is normally a part of a larger community or society. Moreover, in thus coming into the world bringing nothing with us save our native capacities and potentialities, there is scarcely a one of us who does not soon learn that the business of life is largely an affair of having continually to bestir himself to be the individual that he is, of needing to try to actualize his capacities and potentialities, and of thus having ever to try to put himself into a position in which he can provide himself with those multifarious goods and necessities of life, which in his initial and comparatively deprived condition at birth he does not bring with him but which he increasingly comes to need and want: food, clothing, and shelter; association and companionship with others; knowledge and understanding; and opportunities for rest and relaxation, and for aesthetic enjoyment, for the practice of religion, and, indeed, for all of the so-called finer things of life.

Besides, the signal feature about this initial human condition of ours, which can never be completely disregarded, much less eradicated, even when one is fortunate enough to be born with a silver spoon in one's mouth, is that everyone has to recognize that his condition as a human being demands that he exercise unremitting self-help. For is it not the lesson that we all need to learn, and that some of us fail to learn to our cost and our peril, that always and in principle it is but we ourselves who have ever and ceaselessly to work to provide ourselves with those manifold goods of life that we so need and want. There is no way, in other words, that anyone can simply count on "letting George do it."

At the same time, and of equal evidence with the need for each and every individual to recognize his own responsibility in the matter of providing himself with necessities, there is no possible way in which a human individual, working simply on his own and solely by his own unaided efforts, can ever properly or adequately acquit himself of the responsibility to help himself. Instead, it is only through cooperation and collaboration with others that the human individual can ever hope to satisfy his own diverse and seemingly never-ending needs in life. And what does this come down to if not to a recognition of the absolute necessity for every human being—if he is to flourish or to achieve a modicum of well-being—to be a part of a society or a *polis*, in which there is a proper division of labor, one individual doing one job, and another another, each according to his specialized talents and abilities. In other words, it is only by cooperation and collaboration with others that the individual can ever begin to hope that even his own needs will be satisfied.

Once more, though, for all that this division of labor may be indispensable for the attainment of the common good within any human community or society, and so by derivation for the attainment of the greater number of our own individual goods as members of such a community and society, still a division of labor so understood and conceived never comes about naturally or automatically. For the institution and implementation of any such division of labor requires that individuals first deliberately associate themselves with one another in a *polis* or community; and being thus associated, the division of labor among the individuals within the association can come about by virtue of the devices and doings of the individuals who make up the community. All of which is but to say that divisions of labor between human beings can never be expected to be produced purely instinctively and with no deliberation by the individuals concerned. Nor can any such social division of labor be explained as having been brought about as a result of genetic programming or determining of the individuals involved, as might be the case with bees, ants, termites, or whatever. No, the efficient ordering and coordinating of the individual efforts of the many who make up the political community can only be an order, which, if not always deliberately contrived, must still at least be humanly instituted by the participating and cooperating individuals within the community.

Need we, then, say more to confirm both the sense and the truth of Aristotle's dictum that man is by nature never a mere individual animal but a political animal as well? So far from its being possible for us seriously to think of human beings as being born into a supposedly either real or hypothetical state of nature, the state of civil society being but a subsequent and thus purely artificial development, it is rather the case that, outside of a *polis* or of civil society, a human being could scarcely be conceived as being human at all. Rather, it is as Aristotle remarked: a man who was not a member of a *polis* would not really be a human being but rather either a beast or a god.[4] Or, to use a more contemporary example, one might say that on Aristotle's view to conceive of a human being as naturally independent of human society, and thus as able to opt into a *polis*, or to opt out of it, whether by whim or by preference, such a human being, so far from leading a recognizably human existence, would rather present a spectacle more like that of the reputed "wild boy" of Aveyron. And under such circumstances a human being would be scarcely recognizable as properly human, his life being but "solitary, poor, nasty, brutish, and short," presumably in a far worse sense than even a timid and fearful Hobbes would have dreamed in his philosophy.

And now, given the resources of the immediately foregoing discussion, let us work toward a more adequate understanding of the common good. Are we not provided with a handful of trumps that may be used to take in more exciting tricks than could ever have been done by playing only the poor, old, battered, but now recently again fashionable state-of-nature theory? For one thing, does it not become possible to see how the natural end or goal of any human individual may no longer be conceived as being simply an affair of the individual's at-

4. *Ibid.*, Bk. I, 1253 a, 28–29.

taining only his own private good? And no less may it not now also be said that there can be no attainment of any so-called common good of the community as a whole without this entailing the happiness and the individual good of the individual citizens who make up the community?

Nevertheless, properly to appreciate this latter point, one needs also to consider more carefully just what a so-called common good really is and how it may best be conceived and construed. Thus have we not already intimated that the common good of any society involves a system or order for the provision of the so-called goods of life, which human individuals need and want if they are to attain their full life or their natural perfection? For example, a properly functioning economic system for the procurement, production, and exchange of goods surely needs to be included in one's notion of a common good. No less so, too, would be a legal and political system for the redress of wrongs to individuals and the rewarding of just deserts. And as still further examples of such institutions and social facilities as are necessary for the common good of any community, one might mention educational systems, systems of health care, recreational facilities, and the like.

Moreover, if at this point someone were to protest—say, some hard-headed, two-fisted Libertarian—that educational systems, economic systems, health-care systems, *et al.* should be left to private rather than to public enterprise, my answer would be that the question private versus public is not at issue here. For whether a system of education within a given community, for example, were the creation of the government or of the public authorities, or whether it had been brought about solely at the instigation and on the initiative of private individuals, it would nonetheless be an example of what would need to be reckoned as an obvious common good. That is, education is a good that needs to be made available to all of the citizens of a community, whether they all take advantage of it or not. But whether it is made available by public or private means is, at least on the face of it, largely irrelevant. Rather, what is relevant is that education be recognized as an integral part of the common good of the community, whatever the means for bringing it about.

For that matter, it might be remarked that in saying that insofar as education, for example, is reckoned a common good that should be available to all, it does not follow that it is therefore a good that should be made available to all without cost, as if it were a dole to be handed out indiscriminately. For there is no reason why such goods of life as can be made available to human beings only through their cooperative endeavors or through a division of labor within society must be made available to them free. Quite the contrary. If I am a doctor, who has neither the time nor the talent to grow what I need for the bread that I eat, it does not follow that I therefore need not pay the farmer or the baker for the bread that is made available to me. Nor does it follow that the farmer and the baker are to be excused from reimbursing me for my medical services, which they are not able to provide for themselves but which become available to them through me in virtue of the division of labor that is made possible by human beings being associated with one another in communities and societies. In other words, the common good of any human community is to be understood in general as being a system or order for the provisioning of the individuals within the community with the goods they need, but without necessarily specifying the particular and concrete arrangements for such a provisioning.

Moreover, this argument suggests still another feature of the common good, as I am here trying to characterize it. For does it not now begin to emerge that the so-called common good of a community or society cannot be treated as something final, or as an end in itself? Rather, it needs to be understood as an intermediate end, designed to provide to all the individual citizens, without discrimination, the necessary means for each of them to achieve his own *telos* or perfection.[5] Why not borrow from our earlier discussions in Chapter II to illuminate further what the bearing of the common good is with respect to the natural ends and goals of citizens considered as individual human beings. For when discussing those criteria of human good or human well-being, I emphasized that human happiness or perfection needs to be thought of as consisting of the exercise of rational activity that is the characteristic virtue of human beings; and therefore, not, as many would suppose, consisting of the possession of goods such as wealth, honor, knowledge, pleasure, and the like. True, one's life would be gravely impoverished were one to come up lacking in any of those goods of life. Still, the fact remains that human happiness or excellence or well-being must not be thought to lie in mere possession but in the intelli-

---

5. For this point I am greatly indebted to discussions with my friends, Douglas Den Uyl and Douglas Rasmussen.

gent use and employment of such goods. Therefore, as Aristotle insists, a true human flourishing will consist of a person's living wisely and intelligently—that is, of his using wisely and intelligently the goods that he presumably needs if he is to live well.

Applying this idea, then, to the matter of the distinction and the ordering of the one with respect to the other of the common good of the political community, on the one hand, and the private goods of the individual citizens, on the other, we can now see that in principle there should be, or need be, no conflict between the two. For although the individual citizen will doubtless need frequently to neglect some of his private concerns so as to do what he can to further the common good, it must be borne in mind that any such common good is not and should never be regarded as an end in itself. Quite the contrary; a "common good" should be taken as connoting institutional arrangements within a given *polis* or human community as will make possible the availability to the individual citizens of such goods of life as are necessary conditions of their living well and living as their human nature requires them to live. In other words, there can be no well-being of individual citizens unless a common good of the entire community is achieved; and vice versa, there is no reason or justification for such a common good unless it makes available the necessary means for the individuals who make up the community to realize their own ends and so to become what their nature as human beings morally requires them to be. "Oh," but you will say, "there is bound to be at least a certain tension that will repeatedly manifest itself in the life of any individual citizen of a community between what we may call his public duties as a citizen and his private duties to himself as a human individual." To which challenge the answer is that of course there will be tensions between public and private duties; and yet such tensions will not in principle be very different from the tensions that as individuals we repeatedly feel between the competing claims of our so-called purely private duties. Thus, for example, is not any human being, simply as an individual human being, under obligation to achieve a certain knowledge and understanding, theoretical as well as practical? And yet how often will the demands of research and study or of reading and reflection be at variance with the demands of friendship and family ties or maybe even with the mere need to get on with the business of earning a living or sometimes with the need for refreshment and relaxation? Clearly, it is precisely in making judgments about such competing moral or ethical claims between one's private duties that one needs to exercise what Aristotle called one's practical reason.

Nor are the deliberations of practical reason in such instances very different from the deliberations that skilled practitioners in the various arts are constantly having to engage in: should surgery be used in this case or would treatment by radiation be better; given the geological structure of the river banks, ought the bridge to be built in this way or in that; is it better to dispose of AT&T stock now or should one wait a little longer to see how the company behaves following the divestiture of its subsidiaries? Clearly, when it comes to judgments that need to be made by skilled practitioners in the various arts and skills—in medicine, engineering, business, and so forth—we all will acknowledge that the more skilled the expert or the technician is, the more reliable his judgments will be. Accordingly, given the analogy between skill in the various arts and skill in the art of living, there is no reason why the wise man—that is, the man who understands the business of living—should not make the better judgments about what a person ought to do when confronted with the competing claims among moral duties, just as it is the skilled practitioner in any of the arts who is best able to judge in the concrete case whether it is better to do this rather than that, to proceed in one way rather than in another.

Accordingly, returning to our earlier question about competing claims between so-called public duties and private duties, why should this pose any more of a problem in principle than does the problem of competing claims between conflicting duties within the confines of an individual's purely personal or private life? To take a trivial case, is it not conceivable that I might be confronted with competing claims of certain public duties on the one hand—such as doing jury duty, serving on a government advisory board, or running for public office—and various private duties, such as carrying on with my research, straightening out my private business affairs, or taking my family on vacation? Surely, the resolution of such competing claims between public and private duties calls for the same weighing and judging between the alternatives as does the resolution of competing claims in any set of duties, be they public or private. An individual has to bring his practical knowledge to bear and exercise his practical judgment. Moreover, if his knowledge and judgment are good, then all is well and good; and if not, not. But the point is that questions of whether concern for the common good ought in a given case to take precedence over one's legitimate concerns for one's private good are in principle no different from questions as to which of one's various duties toward oneself ought to take precedence in a given instance.

The Stereotypes of Hyper-organicism and Hyper-individualism

By now my strategy in this chapter should have begun to emerge. In Chapter II it seemed that ethics was a purely personal and individual matter. Beginning with this chapter, however, I made the abrupt declaration that man is by nature not just an individual rational animal but a political rational animal as well. Moreover, considered as a political animal, it would appear that man's natural end—even his end as an individual person—cannot be merely the good of himself as an individual person but the common good of his *polis* or society as well. My strategy, then, has begun to take the seemingly odd turn of seeking to show that, rather than there having to be any conflict between the claims of the individual's own good and the common good, almost the opposite is the case: the common good or well-being of the entire community has to be reckoned as being an integral part of the individual's own private or individual good; and no less would it seem that the common good reduces to, and ultimately needs to be unpacked, and unpacked without remainder, into the individual goods of the persons who make up the community.

Still, you will ask: "But just how can this be?" How can it ever be maintained that in being public-spirited, the individual citizen at the same time, and by that very fact, is being "private-spirited" as well? Or putting it the other way around, how can one's duty to oneself, or one's love of self, be supposed to involve a love of the common good and thus of one's fellows as well?

Presumably, if the seeming paradox, not to say almost seeming contradiction, that is suggested by these formulations is to be alleviated or obviated, we must first digress and have a look at some of the false starts, as well as false solutions, that have sometimes been advocated for resolving the ever-perplexing individual-society problem. For no sooner does one so much as broach this problem than seemingly two opposed and equally untenable stereotypes tend to obtrude themselves upon the scene in such a way as to render a proper resolution of the problem impossible. On the one hand, there is the stereotype of

124

what has been called a "hyper-organicism," in which it is held that the claims of the individual ought always and in principle to be subordinated to the claims of the organic whole of the social organism. On the other hand, there is the stereotype of a "hyper-individualism," in which any claims that might be made on behalf of the society or social whole, with respect to its own proper unity and interests, are held to be nullified by the inevitable atomism that is both rightly and effectively exercised by the individuals who make up any such social or political whole.[6]

First, let us examine hyper-organicism. Not infrequently, this condition is held to be a direct consequence of the Aristotelian contention that man is no mere individual animal but a political animal as well. And this may be taken to mean—at least so it is argued—that the *polis* is to be regarded as standing to the individual citizen much as a biological organism stands to any one of its several organs or functioning parts. I have insisted that a *polis* needs to be understood as a society or community in which a division of labor among the several citizens is implemented to promote the common good of the community as a whole. Why, then, should not any such so-called common good of the *polis* or community be understood as roughly analogous to the well-being or flourishing of a biological organism? Thus just as the hand, the foot, the head, the heart, and so on are to the human body, so in like manner this, that, and the other citizen, each with his own appropriate function to perform within the whole, should be thought of as being ordered to the common good of the community.

No sooner, though, does one thus conceive of the *polis*, or the human community, on the analogy of a biological organism than immediately the idea of the sanctity or inviolability of individual persons or of their rights against those of the community as a whole must be given up entirely. For if the individual is to the social whole much as a particular organ of the body is to the body as a whole, the consequence is inescapable: just as no individual part or organ of the body can be said to have a life of its own, much less individual rights as against the functioning of the entire body, so likewise it would seem that no individual citizen may be thought of as having rights of his own as against the *polis*. Instead, his entire life must be acknowledged to be completely subor-

6. The terms "hyper-organicism" and "hyper-individualism" I owe to William A. Galston, *Justice and the Common Good* (Chicago, 1980).

dinated to the particular role he is supposed to perform within the body politic. One needs in this connection but to call up the celebrated illustration that Plato used, in pressing for his notably organicist or collectivist model of the state. Consider a statue, he said.[7] Since the eye might be held to be the noblest part of the countenance, why would it not be right and proper to paint the eye of the statue crimson, that being the noblest of colors? But no, Plato replies, for only that is proper to each part which contributes to its function in the whole. And so individuals within a political community surely have no rights as individuals; on the contrary, their very being is subordinated entirely to such functions as they perform within the community as a whole. Or to lapse into a more mechanistic idiom, the individual citizen, so far from having rights of his own as an individual human being, turns out to be little more than a cog in the machine of the state. Accordingly, given any such a hyper-organicist model of human societies or communities and of the individual citizens that make up such communities, the ideas of the integrity of individuals in their own right and of their personal ends and goals and purposes, as against the common good of the community, will have to be given up as being ill-founded and out of place.

Happily, though, there is no need for anyone to be taken in by such a hyper-organicist model of the state or of society. And the reason is that the minute one reflects upon the matter, it is apparent that a *polis* or a society of human individuals cannot be what Aristotle would call a substance, or an entity in its own right. And if it is not a substance, then clearly a human society cannot possibly be subject to organic growth or development in the manner of a biological organism. And if it is not subject to a natural development in this literal sense of an organism, then a community or a *polis* cannot be said to have its own natural *telos* or end. True, one can speak of the aims or objectives or ends of a human community; and yet any such end or goal of a social grouping of human individuals can only be one that is recognized and projected for the community by the individuals who make it up. Not that the end that is thus projected for the *polis* by the citizens need therefore be purely arbitrary and without any basis in nature. Rather, the basis or justification of such ends or goals as the *polis* may have will lie in the fact that the individual human beings who make up the *polis* are political animals by nature, and thus it will be the ends or goals which

7. *The Republic of Plato*, trans. F. M. Cornford (Oxford, 1949), Bk. IV, 419.

these same individuals recognize as being their own ends or goals, insofar as they are politically organized and associated, that then by extension may be said to be the end of the *polis* or the community. In other words, the natural end of the *polis*, once it is so conceived, turns out to be an end or a good which each of the individual citizens had made his own in the sense that any so-called common good is literally a good common to each and all of the individuals of the community and thus is to be shared by each and every one of them individually.

In contrast, the good or end or goal or natural perfection of any biological organism in the strict sense could not properly be described as a common good because it is not common to a multitude of individuals but rather is the good simply of the individual organism. Moreover, in the light of this contrast between the natural end or goal or good of a biological organism, as not being a common good at all, and the natural end or goal or good of a *polis* or human community as being a good that is common to each and all of the members of the community, we should now be able to understand more clearly how the common good of the community can be no less than an individual good of each and every one of the members of the community. As I noted earlier, the common good of any social whole is never an ultimate end or end in itself; instead, any such common good needs to be conceived as a social system or social organization or social order designed and disposed so as to make various of the goods of life available to the individuals who make up the community. That is why any individual, in working to promote the common good, is working to promote no more and no less than his own personal good, along with that of each and all of his fellow citizens as well.

If by such means we may have managed to obviate the stereotype of a hyper-organicism, what now of the opposite stereotype of a hyper-individualism? For the latter is no less inimical to a right understanding of the individual-society relationship, or of the relationship of private goods to the public good or the common good, than is the former. No doubt, there is no single or univocal way of characterizing such a hyper-individualism. And yet perhaps we can project a reasonably plausible model that may enable us to see how this stereotype, in turn, may be as successfully obviated as was its opposite number, the hyper-organicism.

To begin with, may we not take it for granted that many contemporary Libertarians subscribe to a form of hyper-individualism? Their basic assumption would seem to be that the human individual, rather than being by nature a political animal, is someone who, in the state of nature, may be reckoned as rightfully and in principle enjoying a freedom or liberty to do with himself and with his own property whatever he pleases. Sooner or later, of course, it comes to be acknowledged, even by the Libertarians, that such a fundamental liberty must be qualified, either by the application of the principle of universalizability or as a result of prudential considerations; and individuals may consequently be expected to enter into a social compact, in which they will concede to each other various rights and liberties comparable to those that each claims for himself. And from this, it is thought that there will arise a social situation or condition in which each individual is held to be by nature entitled to do with his own life and property whatever he pleases, so long as he does not interfere with a like right or entitlement belonging to his fellow citizens. On such a model of hyper-individualism, the metaphor is not strained if one insists that human individuals are no more naturally associated or in community with one another than are atoms in a void.

Nor is it proper either, on such a conception, to speak of any truly common good of the society or of the community as being a good that is common to all of the members of the community as individuals. For rather than pursuing the common good of the community, the individual is to be regarded instead as directing his efforts exclusively toward attaining his own private good, as he conceives it to be. He may well see himself as entering into social arrangements with his fellows, which presumably will provide for systems of law and government, with their attendant machinery of police protection, guaranteeing individual rights, adjudicating personal differences, and so forth. He may even concede to other individuals, through such social and political arrangements, various rights, which he may accept as his duty to honor. Nevertheless, such arrangements, on this Libertarian view, even if they establish a so-called minimal state, are not to be construed to have been entered into for the common good of the entire community. Rather, each individual enters into these arrangements for the sake of his own private good and for his own self-interest.

Supposing, then, that the hyper-individualist repudiated the idea of a common good as a proper goal or objective of individuals organized in a *polis*, then how may an advocate of such a common good, as this is understood within the natural-law tradition, make rejoinder to the hyper-individualist? We have seen that the answer to the hyper-organicist is that an individual citizen cannot possibly be or become fully himself as a human being unless he is concerned about the common good of his *polis* or community. And yet such a common good turns out not to be a proper end in itself, as if it were the good of a social whole or social organism existing in its own right. Rather than an ultimate end, the common good, rightly conceived, can be only an intermediate end, or a means to the perfection or well-being of each and all members of the community. And so it is that an individual, in devoting himself to the pursuit of the common good, is by implication devoting himself to the promotion and furtherance of the individual goods of each person with whom he is associated. Could not one almost say that a true love of self, entailing a love of the common good, will thus entail, at least in principle, a love of each of the others in the community as well?

Curiously, though, would it not now seem that a similar response would answer the hyper-individualist? For much as the hyper-organicist fails to recognize that a good that is common to, and sharable by, all of the members of the community needs to be reckoned as an integral part of the good or end that the individual wishes for himself (instead the hyper-organicist thinks of this good, not as common to all, but as peculiar to the social organism or social whole), so also the hyper-individualist seems to deny that any good that is common to all, in the sense of a common weal or common wealth, is ever to be integrated into the natural end or goal of the individual. And yet surely, the hyper-individualist would seem here to overlook a patent fact about man's natural end, insofar as man is by nature a political animal. For how can a human individual be thought to live a full life without enjoying the love and association of others? Moreover, to love and to be loved by others, when translated into a political context, means to devote oneself to furthering goods that are common to these others. Thus to further the common good, as we have seen, ultimately furthers the individual good or well-being of each and every member of the community. In fact, just as one might say that a human being who is indifferent to knowledge and understanding does not know what is good for him and does not recognize what the perfection of his human nature demands of him, so likewise the individual who is indifferent to the love and well-being of his fellows and who contributes to the common good only by accident and only because he thinks it will advance his own narrow self-interest surely leads a sadly incomplete and impoverished existence.

Even granting the plausibility of these answers to the hyper-organicist and the hyper-individualist, there may still be qualms about accepting my key contention. This is the contention that a pursuit of the common good and a pursuit of one's individual good are not irreconcilable, but rather that one's individual good necessarily entails a concern for the common good, just as concern for the common good necessarily implicates one in concern for the well-being of the individuals for whom the common good is a means to their well-being and perfection. Some of the qualms might be alleviated by resorting to some concrete illustrations and analogies. Various models might be invoked of relationships between individuals and the groups of which they are members, which are analogous to the relationships between individuals and the political societies of which they are members. We are all familiar with the model of individual athletes and the team of which they are members, or the model of individual musicians and the orchestra of which they are a part. Clearly, one can hardly say that these individuals exist only for the sake of the whole. Instead, the group seems to exist for the enjoyment and flourishing of the individuals who constitute it. Thus suppose that one were to imagine basketball players or orchestra members who were in a situation that gave them no possibilities for solo performances just on their own. Instead, the only way they could perfect their skills and gratify their love for the game (or for their music) would be through playing with others in concert or on a team. Here the only reason for being either a member of the team or of the orchestra would be for the individual players to have a chance to play.

At the same time, no individual player ought to think only of himself and of his own playing, be it either in a concert or in a game, as if it were but an occasion for displaying only his own excellence and for his thus outshining all of his fellow players. Such a one would hardly be fit either for a team or for an orchestra. Rather, the individual's efforts would need to be directed toward promoting and achieving the common good of the group, even though this common good can be enjoyed by no one other than the individual players (assuming that there is no audience). Once more, though, this is not to say that an individual player will not do his utmost in the service of the group, even though the group exists for no other purpose than to give the individual members a chance to do their own thing and thereby to gratify themselves by their playing. In terms of such models, then, is it not possible to understand how an individual can work for the common good as being his own good, and how at the same time the common good needs to be understood as being no more and no less than the good of the several individuals concerned?

Still another model is that of the human family as it is normatively understood in the Hebrew-Christian religious tradition. One advantage a model of the family has over that of an athletic team is that the element of competition with other like groups is not essential to it. Also, as compared with the model of the orchestra, the excellence and flourishing that is associated with the life of a family does not need to be thought of with reference to the appreciation and enjoyment of an audience. Of course, this family model is somewhat idealized and hence scarcely the picture of the family that has become largely current today. For with the institution of the family having fallen into disarray in the last several years, and even having come to be in rather bad odor, any talk of the family nowadays is likely to conjure up in the minds of many accounts and pictures such as those given by François Mauriac in *Le noeud de vipères* or by Lillian Hellman in *The Little Foxes* or by countless recent historians, who have delighted in relating the horror stories of dynastically minded families like the Vanderbilts, the Medicis, the Habsburgs, the Bourbons, the Howards, and others. And yet surely, these families illustrate more the corruptions of the institution of the family than the characteristic perfections of which a family in the true sense is capable.

The basic attitude which members of a family should, and ideally do, manifest toward one another is one of mutual regard, or love, or what Aristotle would call friendship. As Aristotle describes it, in true friendship of one person for another, one friend wants for the other the same excellence or virtue that he wants for himself.[8] He truly loves his neighbor as himself.[9] Moreover, this regard or love that characterizes true friendship is reciprocal, so the love that one member of a family bears toward the other members—wishing for them the best that he wishes for himself—ought to be a love or devotion that is reciprocated by the other members of the family toward him and toward each other.

But given this familial setting of mutual regard and friendship and

8. Aristotle, *Nicomachean Ethics*, Bks. VIII and IX, *passim*. Note especially Bk. IX, 1166a,1–1166 b, 29.
9. St. Thomas Aquinas in discussing the Christian virtue of love or charity (*caritas*) describes it as being a form of friendship (*amicitia*). See. *Summa Theologiae*, II–II, Qu. 23, Art. 1.

love of the members of the family toward one another, how is the co-operative enterprise of family life to be regarded by the individual family members? For surely, the institution of the family is a cooperative undertaking, aimed primarily at the nurture and care of the children. More basically, however, it is aimed at the common good or well-being of all of the members of the family. How, then, ought the individual member of the family to regard such a common good or common weal of the group? Certainly, save in cases of the perversions one finds in the ambition associated with the "great families," with the family being regarded by its members as a transcendent unit or as an ongoing organism that perdures and endures and presumably triumphs for generations, the family normally is not something that can be regarded as enjoying a well-being in itself and of its own. For one thing, there is no "it" that is capable of enjoyment in any proper or literal sense. Instead, only the members of the family as individuals are capable of enjoying familial well-being.

But does this mean that the individual members of the family can regard the common good, or the common achievement of the family, simply as a means to their own personal or individual well-being? True, the family is a means of the individual's well-being in the sense that without the family—at least in normal circumstances—the individual would be sorely bereft and miserable. And yet this scarcely implies that the individual may properly regard his family as existing solely to promote his own well-being in indifference to that of the other members. For much as in the case of the orchestra or the athletic team, so also in the case of the family, any such self-centeredness or egoism on the part of an individual member would surely be a perversion of the situation as it ought to be. No, is not the truth that any individual family member needs to recognize that the family exists for the sake of the well-being of each and all alike, and not for the sake either of the family unit alone, considered as an entity in its own right, or for the sake of any one member of the family, considered alone and to the exclusion of the others?

Likewise, just because the end or goal of the individual family member is the flourishing and well-being of each and all of the members of the family, this does not mean that the individual must entirely forget about his own well-being and work only for the well-being of others. Quite the contrary; the well-being of all includes his own well-being. The injunction that appears in the Summary of the Law is that one shall love one's neighbor as oneself. (Luke 10:27). Hence willfully to neglect oneself is, in a Christian context, to contribute to one's neighbor's lack and impoverishment as well. And so it is that only insofar as the individual member of the family achieves his own perfection as a person of reason and responsibility and understanding is the true commonweal of the family achieved, which is, after all, the well-being of each and all alike.

Now there is no denying that when one attempts to carry over this family model, and to make it the model of the political community as well, the fit will be far from perfect, and the operation of *mutatis mutandis* will need to be constantly repeated. Still, one wonders whether for our purposes, the model might not serve well enough. For what needs to be avoided is, on the one hand, a picture of the political community as an organism or entity in its own right, such that the individual members of the community will possess no rights as individuals; rather, their every activity and undertaking as individuals must be made to subserve entirely the supposed good of some fancied social whole or organism. And on the other hand, and equally to be avoided, is a picture or model of the human individual as enjoying by nature a completely egoistic freedom, and for whom therefore life in society or in the community is no better than a necessary evil, and one whose legal and moral structures can claim no basis or lasting justification.

In place of these false models, however, why not consider that human beings are naturally political animals in the sense that they cannot exist or be truly human outside of a *polis*? And yet, what is the natural end of such a *polis* or political community? In one sense, a *polis* as such is not capable of envisaging an end; only the individual members of the political community are able to do this. And what, then, might be the natural and proper end of a human individual, insofar as he is a political animal? It can hardly be his own well-being, to the exclusion of that of his fellow citizens. But then must it not be the common good or the common weal of the whole community; and must not the work and activity of the individual citizens be directed toward helping to bring about such a common good or common weal? Yes, but again, it needs to be asked how such a common good of a whole community is to be construed. Will it not be a general condition—economic, political, legal, and cultural—that can afford the conditions for a true and proper flourishing of the individual members of the community, considered as individuals? And what does this entail, if not that insofar as the individual citizen works to bring about such a common good of the community

133

as a whole, he is in effect working to bring about the well-being and flourishing of all the individual members of the community as individuals—his own included?

But with this we see why an individual's moral activity in the pursuit and enjoyment of his natural end ties in directly with, and is almost indissociable from, his political activity, which is to be understood as something directed toward making provision for a common good. For those same goods of life, which are not themselves the end but which any individual must concern himself with as conditions of his own living well, or well-being as an individual, are goods which no individual, acting alone and relying only on his own resources, can ever adequately provide himself with. On the contrary, such goods require common action by individuals participating in common enterprises, which are directed toward providing the participating individuals with what I have been designating as their common good. Such a common good offers, then, some of the necessary conditions for the living of the good life by an individual, without which the life of a human being would be no less than "solitary, poor, nasty, brutish, and short." It is in this sense, accordingly, that Aristotle says that man is by nature a political animal.

ARE INSTITUTIONS OF LAW AND GOVERNMENT REQUIRED FOR THE COMMON GOOD?

I hope that I have made a case in the foregoing sections of this chapter for there being no necessary irreconcilability between one's pursuit of one's own private or personal good and one's pursuit of the common good of the community. If anything, the situation is one in which no individual can possibly attain his natural end as a human person without at the same time achieving the common good of the community or *polis* of which he is a member; and likewise, no community can be said to have reached its natural end or goal of the common good without rendering possible and facilitating the flourishing or well-being of each and all of its members.

But politics and political philosophy are not the same as ethics; nor are the matter and means for achieving the common good identical with those required for an individual to achieve his own good—that is, his natural perfection as a human person. After all, the common good being a good which is common to many, and its constitution as a common good being little more nor less than a proper division of labor among the several members of the community so that the needed goods of life may be made accessible to all, it would seem that there could not possibly be even so much as an initial institution of such a division of labor among many, much less its efficient operation and continued maintenance, without the exercise of some coordinating authority. And what do we understand to be the notions of government and political authority if not this idea of a coordinating authority for purposes of achieving the common good of the entire community or *polis*?

Likewise, with respect to law, we have already noted that law—even natural law—tends to have one meaning if we are thinking of those moral rules that an individual human being must observe if he is ever to attain his natural end as a human person. On the other hand, there is the notion of law in the sense of civil law. And what is law in this latter sense if not those rules for coordinating the manifold activities of the several members of a community for the achievement, by their combined and cooperative efforts, of the common good of the entire community. Not that these two notions of law are so different as to betoken a thorough ambiguity in the very meaning of "law." Instead, in both cases laws may be conceived as being little more than what I have already termed "how-to-do-it" rules for the attainment of certain ends: in the case of so-called moral laws, the end is simply the flourishing or well-being of the individual; in the case of civil laws, the end is the common good of the entire community. And again, as I have already noted, it is the notion of law, in the sense of civil law, that would appear to be effectively captured in what St. Thomas Aquinas designates as being the "definition" of law: "law is nothing other than a certain rule (or ordinance) of reason that is directed toward achieving the common good, and that has been promulgated by such a one (or such ones) as have the charge of the community"[10]—that is, by the public authorities.

Clearly, it would seem, then, that the task that is cut out for us in the remainder of this chapter is to determine, albeit in a very general way, what the institution of government must be and how it must operate if, through the vehicle of civil law, political government is to institute and then maintain a system of division of labor for the produc-

10. St. Thomas Aquinas, *Summa Theologiae*, I–II, Qu. 90, Art. 4.

tion, supply, and distribution of such goods as are needed by the members of the community.

Libertarian Difficulties and Objections

How can the operation of a free market economy ever be compatible with direction by the government or with the laying down of laws by the political authorities? No sooner have we suggested that any idea of a so-called common good must necessarily entail the further ideas of government and law as being the means for the implementation of such a common good than we can immediately hear protests coming from various quarters among the Libertarians. The protests will no doubt be well taken because many of them will spring to a large extent from sophisticated considerations drawn from economics and economic theory. And that will leave me in something of a quandary, considering that my practice both heretofore and in the future must be studiously to avoid all economic arguments. After all, being no economist, I think that in matters of economics discretion is surely the better part of valor.

Still, might I not at least say—and indeed one can readily imagine sophisticated economists among the Libertarians saying—that by the account I have thus far given of the common good, such a good in my sense of the term might well be equated with something like the operation of a free market economy? For did I not specify the common good as being an order or system for what I called a proper division of labor? And was not the propriety of this division of labor to be determined by whether or not, through its operation, the needed procurement, production, and distribution of goods could be secured, such goods being the answers to the several determinable needs of the individuals who make up the political community? Very well, but what other system or vehicle or agency could ever effect such production and distribution of goods with anything like the efficiency that a free market economy affords? And to this I cannot do other than agree.

But no true-blue Libertarian economic critic would stop there. For such a one would immediately go on to insist, and with plausibility, that no free market economy can be subjected to direction or control by any so-called government or political authority. Indeed, the minute there is subjection of this sort, the economy can no longer be said to be free.

Nor is that all. For just as no free market economy can be subjected to direction or control by government, so also no such economy can have the slightest tolerance for civil laws, promulgated, as St. Thomas might say, by the public authorities and designed to effect either the institution or the continued maintenance of such an economy. If anything, a free market has to be thought of as operating under natural laws in the modern sense of "natural law," in which the laws of supply and demand, for example, would need to be thought of as operating in the economic sphere, much as laws of physics and chemistry operate in physical nature. Accordingly, much as one would never think of supposing that one could lay down man-made laws to govern the changes that take place in physical nature, so also one should not imagine that one can ever establish a system of political economy by civil law and then keep it functioning by still more *ad hoc* laws. For this way of thinking would entail what the great Austrian economist F. A. Hayek would call the "constructivist fallacy."

Nevertheless, to bring home to ourselves the seeming absolute irreconcilability and incompatibility of any free market economy with bureaucratic government control, let me invoke at this point a number of felicitous observations which John Gray made in a review published in the *Times Literary Supplement*. Gray appeals to the authority of the so-called Austrian School of economists—particularly Ludwig von Mises and Hayek—in support of "the thesis that market competition and bureaucratic command structures are together the mutually exhaustive means of resource-allocation in complex industrial societies." Moreover, on the account which I have already put forward as to what I think might best be understood by the notion of a common good, why not adopt Gray's term "resource allocation" and say that this is essentially what the common good might ultimately be construed as being—a system for a proper resource allocation to the members of the political community?[11]

But if as the Austrian economists and Gray would appear to argue, given that there are only two mutually exclusive and exhaustive alternatives for such resource allocation—either "market competition" or "bureaucratic command structures"—and given also the justice of the contention of Gray and others that so-called "command economies have ineradicable tendencies to vast waste and malinvest-

11. John Gray, "The System of Ruins," *Times Literary Supplement*, December 30, 1983, pp. 1459–61.

ment," then must it not be concluded that any common good, properly conceived and understood, requires that "market competition" alone shall be the proper mechanism for resource allocation? Moreover, since what Gray calls the "bureaucratic command structures" of all socialist economics are directly linked with government and political authority, then it would seem that we must reverse the suggestion put forward at the beginning of this section that the common good cannot but depend, for its accomplishment, upon institutions of government and of political authority. Instead, is it not just the opposite that would now appear to be the case?[12]

Nor need we stop there, for Gray again cites "the economists of the Austrian School, above all von Mises and Hayek, as arguing for the impossibility of resource allocation under socialist institutions." He continues:

> If we acknowledge, as did Marx, the essentially unconservative character of capitalist enterprises, we will find it incongruous that he and his followers imagine that the prodigious virtuosity of capitalism can be retained while its control mechanism, market competition, is abolished. There is, in fact, no reason to think that the productive achievement of capitalism will even be maintained, still less surpassed, once market mechanisms for allocating resources are removed. It is the insight which explains the vast chaos and colossal malinvestments which are typical of all existing socialist command economies. In Marx's own writings . . . no proposal is ever advanced for the coordination of economic activity in socialist or communist societies: it is simply assumed, with the utmost naivete, that an acceptable allocation of resources to particular uses will emerge spontaneously, without the need for markets or pricing, from the collaborative discussions of socialist citizens. It was indeed to this gigantic evasion that Lenin referred obliquely, when he confessed that the principal task of the Bolsheviks in the USSR was the construction of state capitalism. Aside from the fact that it entails inexorably a concentration of power in bureaucratic institutions which Marx always sought to avoid, but which was realized fully in the Stalinist period, Lenin's project of a state capitalist regime was bound to founder on the absence within it of the central capitalist institution for resource allocation. . . .
>
> [Against a background of such considerations the possibility needs to be reckoned with] that the economic chaos and political repression characteristic of all socialist command economics are not mere aberrations, but structurally inseparable results of such economics. It [Marxism]

12. *Ibid.*

would, above all, need to confront the repressed possibility that the Gulag represents an unavoidable phase in socialist construction rather than a contingent incident in Soviet (and Chinese) experience.[13]

Achievement of a Common Good
through Institutions of Law and Government

What can a poor noneconomist say in the face of these telling and even devastating comments from the Libertarian economists? For the last thing that I would ever want to concede, given the argument of my entire second chapter, would be that the freedom and autonomy of the human individual should ever, or under any circumstances, be sacrificed to the greater good of the greater number—certainly not to the better functioning of any supposed state organism or collectivity. And must that then not mean that no natural law ethics—or natural-end ethics, as perhaps it might better be called—can be reconciled, once the transition is made to the political sphere, with a "socialist command economy," such as John Gray paints? Surely not.

Still, must we agree with John Gray in his apparently uncompromising assumption that market competition and bureaucratic command structures are the only alternatives that we have to choose between and that these are exhaustive and exclusive as alternatives? For I will readily grant the primacy and even indispensability of a mechanism of market competition if a proper common good is to be achieved within a given community or society. Still, does this necessarily mean that such a mechanism can tolerate not the slightest adjustment or correction or control by agencies of government and their associated bureaucratic command structures?

Putting economics aside for the moment, could we not respond to such questions by introducing considerations that may not reflect much economic sophistication but have a certain warrant simply from the common experience of mankind? For instance, would it not seem undeniable, as a general principle, that in any cooperative enterprise of human beings, even if these be but two or three in number, the activities of the individuals involved need to be coordinated to effect a necessary division of labor and coordination of their several labors? Nor would such a coordination of.the efforts of many toward a common

13. *Ibid.*, 1460, 1461.

end or common good seem possible without at least some coordinating authority.

Indeed, the late Yves Simon has tellingly analyzed what he designated as the need for authority in any and all cooperative human endeavors by the simple device of challenging one to try to imagine how any cooperative human endeavor could ever occur without the exercise of at least some authority.[14] True, we all recognize that no common enterprise is likely to be successful unless each party to the enterprise does his part. And we all know that human nature being what it is, we are all likely at times to "goof off," or do a bit of shirking, or perhaps want to enjoy a "free ride" in various of the common enterprises in which members of a community engage—be it in politics or government, business, the family, or even the private clubs and groups which we join for our own recreation and amusement. Hence we are all likely to recognize that in any group activity there needs to be some one, or ones, in authority, who have the power to make us toe the mark, or pull our weight, in the common enterprises in which we are participating.

Going beyond this, Simon urges us to imagine a contrary-to-fact situation in which everyone in a given group enterprise would be thoroughly well-intentioned and never-failing in his determination to do his part. Would it not still be necessary, Simon asks, that even in such circumstances authority would need to be vested somewhere, somehow, in someone? For how could there possibly be a coordination of efforts on the part of many without someone acting as a coordinator, even if simply to give the requisite signals when all were to start pulling, or pushing, or marching, or going on the double-quick, or whatever? When the respective activities of the members of the group that need to be coordinated with one another are complex and require a variety of different skills—as in, say, a performance by a symphony orchestra or the playing of a game by an athletic team—the need for a director or coordinator becomes even more obvious. The leader or conductor of the orchestra, for example, needs to be given the authority to try to get the individual musicians to play in concert. Not that such a conductor of the orchestra, or coach of the basketball team, need necessarily be a better musician or a better player than the orchestra members or the team members. No, it is just that someone has to be responsible for coordinating the activities of the individuals who are participating in the common enterprise.

14. Yves Simon, *Philosophy of Democratic Government* (Chicago, 1951).

The example of the orchestra or the athletic team might be pushed still further. For it could be that in the case of the orchestra, say, the individual musicians might have their own ideas as to how a particular symphony of Haydn, let us say, might best be rendered. And conceivably, all of their differing ideas might be very good, and each proponent of his own idea might be right in his recommendation. For just as there are all sorts of different ways to skin a cat or to play a basketball game or to perform an appendectomy or to build a house, there are all sorts of different ways in which a Haydn symphony might be rendered; and each different way of playing the game or conducting the battle maneuvre or building the house or rendering the symphony might have much to recommend it. The only trouble is that the symphony—or the surgical operation or the battle maneuvre or the construction of the house—could not possibly be performed in all of the different possible ways at once. Instead, someone has to have the authority, in the sense of the final responsibility, of deciding which way the cat is to be skinned on the particular occasion.

And so from considerations such as these, we may not only see why political authority is a natural necessity in any human community or *polis*, but we also may come better to understand why political or government authority need not, and should not, be understood in the way it so often is today. For the primary note or mark of authority is not its ability to exercise a mere power of coercion; rather, its essential function would seem to be one of coordination. Of course, it is true, recurring again to Simon's counterfactual example, that we human beings tend not to be well-intentioned or morally virtuous even much of the time, much less all of the time. Hence in any common enterprise, there is need for some exercise of authority, if not through brute force and coercion then at least through a rational, even if not always a gentle, suasion. Even a rational suasion will tend to institute discipline and need not be without some threat and use of punishment.

Following out this line of argument and abstracting from such difficulties as Libertarian economists might raise, is there any way that one can avoid the conclusion that the common good being necessarily the result of a common enterprise on the part of the several members of any particular group or political community, there must be an authority vested in what we call government for the express purpose of coordinating such work as is devoted to the common enterprise? Is it not equally evident that, in addition to agencies of government, any political community must also have civil laws, and indeed what H. L. A. Hart would call a fully developed legal system? True, laws in this sense would not be moral laws such as those discussed in Chapter II, but rather what I now choose to call civil law, or, with certain reservations, a common law. For although moral laws are to be conceived as how-to-do-it rules that men have devised, based on experience, indicating how as individuals we need to proceed if we are to attain our natural ends or natural perfections as human persons, so likewise civil laws are to be conceived as rules of reason that human beings have determined upon based upon their experience. But this time the rules of reason give us an instruction as to how we ought or ought not to proceed, not merely if each is to achieve his own private good, but rather if the common good of the entire community is to be achieved.

The Libertarian Concession of a So-Called Minimal State

Returning to the issue raised by Libertarians of whether the operation of a free market economy is compatible with the exercise of political authority on the part of what John Gray would call the command structures of government, is it not possible now to glimpse at least a partial resolution of this issue? True, many Libertarians would remain intransigent in their insistence that there can be no reconciliation of market competition with bureaucratic command structures of government. Others, however, would concede the need for at least the "minimal state" as it is called, or of what in the nineteenth century was sometimes referred to as the "night-watchman" theory of government.

Thus it would seem that some Libertarians would buy at least a part of the argument of the late Yves Simon showing the indispensability of some government or political authority in any common enterprise of human beings. For Simon, it will be recalled, made the obvious point that in any common enterprise, it is unfortunately inevitable that there should be any number who will not do their part—the shirkers, the freeloaders, even the crooks and criminals. Almost everyone—Libertarians included—can be brought to recognize that there never has been a free market system known to man which has not had its share of participants who would not hesitate to resort to fraud, theft, and even violence to gain advantages over their competitors. To Libertarians particularly, such criminal behavior would need to be reckoned as both destructive of the rights of individual citizens—rights which Libertarians are determined and devoted to championing, such as life, liberty, and property—and inimical to the proper functioning of free market competition. And so it is that even some Libertarians are willing to relax that supposed absolute incompatibility and mutual exclusiveness of free market competition and bureaucratic command structures of government—an incompatibility and exclusiveness that in other contexts they are so insistent upon. Indeed, the latter—the bureaucratic command structures of government—are held to be necessary and essential to the former—free market competition—in at least a negative way: it is not that government with its command structures should directly take a hand in the economic operations of the free market but that the function of government is to serve as the night watchman (and perhaps the day watchman, too), who is there to prevent the disruption of free market competition by activities that, supposedly, from the point of view even of a true-blue laissez-faire economics, would be deemed either unfair or criminal.

Beyond the Minimal State to a
State Possessed of a Proper Political Authority

Why stop with this night-watchman theory of the role of government in the business of promoting and protecting the common good? True, the Libertarians are surely right in their insistence that the primary function of political government and of civil law may well be to secure and protect the rights of individual citizens. But is it not possible also, as well as proper, to regard law and government as having a further and more positive function, which is actively to implement and further the achievement of a common good? For again, we would call to mind the more basic reason that Simon gave in justification of political authority: not only is authority needed to protect citizens in their just rights as against their fellow citizens; but also there can be no full achievement of any common good without the cooperation and coordination of the efforts of all of the members of the community. And how can there be coordinated action among free and intelligent human beings without an exercise somewhere, somehow, of at least some coordinating authority?

Of course, the more doctrinaire advocates of a free market economy might retort that although Simon's principle might be true in con-

143

texts other than economics, still, in a market economy, the coordination of the activities of different agents would need to come about automatically and without any deliberate direction or intervention on the part of coordinating authorities.

May not such a stance on the part of economists, however, be somewhat overdrawn? For consider once more how the common good is rightly to be conceived. Thus one ought not to think of a common good of a human community or *polis* as being anything more than a system or order, whereby a proper division of labor in the community can be effected, and as a result of which the members of the community will come to have access to such goods as, working all alone and simply on his own, no one individual could provide himself with a sufficiency of. In other words, the common good is and ought to be the common concern of all of the members of the community. And although it may be acknowledged that a common good so conceived is to be equated with the functioning of what in a very broad sense might be called the political economy of the community, it hardly follows that such an economy must always function wholly automatically and without any authoritative direction.

On the contrary, the citizens of any community cannot but be concerned both with the inception and with the continued functioning of their own economy. And although nobody wants to fall into a "constructivist fallacy" by supposing that a free market economy can be devised and imposed from above by a group of experts and economic planners, it would scarcely seem that such an economy could be other than the creation, or the doing, or the work, of those who participate in it. Indeed, it is they—the participants—who, over successive generations, cannot very well consider themselves otherwise than as having been responsible both for getting their economy under way and for seeing to and overseeing its continued functioning. In this sense, an economy is not like the seas or the land, the sun and the moon, the mountains and the rivers, being but the work of seven days or of geological evolution. No, an economy is man's own work.

Besides, an economy so understood has no other purpose than to provide its members or participants with the goods they need. Moreover, as I have already implied, by "goods" here, one is not to understand the mere necessities of life but the so-called goods of life as well—science, learning, the arts, religion, recreation, friendships, peace, justice, and so forth. All of these, I have suggested, are goods that are made possible through the functioning of what I have been calling an economy and, more specifically perhaps, a free market economy. Suppose, though, that such an economy upon occasion fails to function as it should to render goods sufficiently available. Will this not be a matter of concern to the members of the *polis*? And assuming that an economy is no mere act of God (or of evolution), but rather a creation of men, is it to be expected that men will therefore do nothing when their economy falters, or when it fails to make available the goods that are needed, or when it falls victim to inflation or stagflation or deflation or heaven knows what other diseases political economies tend to fall victim to? Why not rather say that the health of an economy is a matter of human concern, much as is the physical health of the body? Moreover, just as modern medicine is able to effect its cures only by reckoning with so-called laws of nature, which are not man-made and in no sense human creations, so also economics might be thought of as being the art that seeks to effect economic cures by reckoning with such economic laws as are not man-made and which therefore need first to be understood, reckoned with, and respected.

Accordingly, if the extreme advocates of laissez-faire economics would respond to all of this by insisting that any interference with the functioning of an economy is bound only to make things worse and eventually to lead to the still more glaring evils of the welfare state, or even of the totalitarian state, why is not the answer to be made along pragmatic lines? For granting that certain specific economic measures that may have been undertaken by government or by the public authorities are found not to work—say, wage and price controls, tariff regulations, compulsory health insurance, free public education, progressive income taxes, old age benefits, or whatever. If such measures do not work, they should be abandoned and not used in the future; or at least, if they are to be used, they should be used more advisedly.

But this, needless to say, is a far cry from taking the stance that merely because any number of deliberately instituted economic measures—all or some of them undertaken by public authorities to promote the common good—have not worked, therefore the government control or direction of economic forces should never be undertaken by anyone, anyhow, anywhere. This would be like saying that just because certain medical cures have not worked—or have even made patients worse—no medical cures should ever be even attempted because they are a fruitless interference with the iron laws of nature.

Final Libertarian Objections

From all of these considerations, should it not begin to be clear just what that issue really is, respecting the functions of law and government within any given community, that I have been discussing throughout the central part of this chapter? For it is not so much an issue of black versus white—of a rigidly planned economy versus total laissez-faire; of a thoroughgoing direction of an economy by the bureaucratic command structures of government versus a complete and untrammeled laissez-faire; of blind devotion to the constructivist fallacy versus what might be called a thoroughgoing Libertarian "deconstruction." No, the issue is rather one of the degree to which in particular circumstances the role of government in the promotion of the common good should be conceived as being largely passive or whether that role should be conceived more actively.

To point up the issue more clearly, we might borrow the language and the terminology that have been used in an article that I happened upon recently in the *American Journal of Jurisprudence*. The discussion there of the issue before us might appear at first to be anachronistic, the title of the article being "*Politeia* and Adjudication in Fourth Century B.C. Athens." Maybe, though, this should be taken to be evidence not so much of anachronism as that the issue before us is truly perennial:

> A passive state is one in which governmental social control is not a significant factor in the life of the community. In such a state, adjudication is passive, or what we shall call "non-political": the state provides a forum for the resolution of private disputes; and it uses as rules of decision norms that have been nongovernmentally defined (as, for example, in custom). An active state, on the other hand, is one in which governmental social control is a significant factor in the life of the community. In such a state adjudication is active, or what we shall call "political": the state uses its courts for dispute-resolution and other purposes, for the formulation and implementation of public policy; and it uses as rules of decision norms that it has previously defined or that it defines in the process of adjudication itself.[15]

15. Dennis Peter Maio, "*Politeia* and Adjudication in Fourth Century B.C. Athens," *American Journal of Jurisprudence*, XXVIII (1983), 16.

I would now argue for the more active conception of law and government as against the more passive one. In the same article, the author, Dennis Maio, uses a quotation from Book VI of Aristotle's *Politics* in which Aristotle states: "The underlying principle of the democratic *politeia* is freedom. (It is commonly said that only in this kind of *politeia* can human beings enjoy freedom, and that the aim of all conceivable democracies is freedom.) One aspect of freedom is political, ruling and being ruled in turn. . . . The other aspect is personal, living as one pleases." [16]

Availing ourselves of this Aristotelian distinction between the two different contexts in which our human freedom may be exercised, why may we not say that the rights of human beings must surely involve rights to freedom in what Aristotle calls the political domain, no less than rights in the area of an individual's purely personal affairs? Moreover, our rights to freedom as citizens will surely lead us to be properly and actively concerned with whether and how the government should act—that is, with what measures the political authorities should take—to promote the common good.

But will this interpretation create an eventual tyranny by so-called big government—the Libertarians and the defenders of the minimal state will ask—as the political authorities assume more and more responsibility for the operation of economic forces, thereby implicating all of us citizens more and more in the toils of something resembling the welfare state? The answer is that of course there is such a danger, inasmuch as moral life and political life are both fraught with dangers resulting from overconfidence, carelessness, misjudgment, and so forth. But so far as political life is concerned, if the common good is recognized as something that all need to work toward, and for the achievement of which all members of the *polis* must share responsibility, then such institutions as those of law and government must clearly rest upon the consent of the governed. Hence if we do not like the direction in which our political authorities are taking us, or if we feel that they are inefficient or guilty of bad management or faulty direction, then why not exercise our political rights as citizens and turn the government out? In other words, the cure for big government or for an excessive arrogation of political authority by public officials would seem not to be the complete abdication of government from any direction of the econ-

16. This reference is to Aristotle, *Politics*, 1317 a 40-b 3, and 1317 b, 11–12.

omy and a resorting to a policy of total laissez-faire. Rather, the cure would seem to lie in institutions of constitutional government, which makes rulers and public officials accountable to the consent of the governed.

At this point, however, I can imagine a still further objection to the idea that institutions of law and government within a political community should adopt not merely a passive role but rather should assume an active role in promoting the common good. For will not this inevitably mean that the private goods of citizens, taken individually, will necessarily be sacrificed for the common good or public good?

Surely, this need not be the necessary consequence of a government's active pursuit of the common good, however much it may be a consequence that, sometimes and unhappily, does indeed result. For have I not already noted that, even in the case of the minimal state, when the public authorities are restricted to a passive role, still they would be charged with protecting the private rights, or the common law rights, or even in certain senses of the term, the constitutional rights of all of the individual citizens? Why, then, suppose that just because any government in a *polis* always runs the danger of arrogating to itself too active a role in furthering the common good, such a government should then forego the responsibility of trying to protect the individual citizens of the community even from possible depredations by their fellows through fraud or violence?

And now for still a last objection that one often hears voiced in Libertarian circles to the idea of charging governments and the political authorities with assuming an active role in the furtherance of the common good. Sometimes one hears it said that it is mistaken to suppose that one could ever properly think of there being any single end or goal appropriate to political society. True, there are ends and objectives that groups, short of the *polis*, may set for themselves—an orchestra, an athletic team, a business organization, a private club, and the like. But—so the argument runs—the community as a whole, the *polis*, cannot properly be said to have an end or *telos*. Even the expression "common good" might be taken to be an empty word, there being no single, specifiable objective that all of the members of a political community may be said to have as their common end. After all, did not Dr. Johnson say that "patriotism is the last refuge of a scoundrel"? And if by patriotism one means a devotion to the common good on the part of an individual, maybe "common good" in this sense will turn out to be not an empty word but even a cloak for scoundrels.

Nevertheless, I wonder if this Libertarian objection may not be quickly dissipated, given a little further reflection. For in an earlier section I noted that some Libertarians would hold that the common good, so far from being an end in its own right, needs rather to be recognized as a necessary means to an individual's own private end. That is, as an individual, I can never hope to acquire all that I need—food, clothing, shelter, knowledge, recreational facilities, health care, et al.—merely working on my own. Some social organization that affords a division of labor is necessary for me to meet these needs. And of course, an order or economy that makes possible this division of labor is properly to be regarded as a common good, in the sense that it is something that each and all can readily see the need of. Nevertheless, as an individual member of the community, my attitude might be but one of seeking and valuing a so-called common good, not because of the benefits that it brings to all and sundry among my fellow citizens alike but only because of the benefits that I see it bringing to me. After all, I noted that the common good can never be more than an intermediate, and thus not an ultimate, end. And so the issue here seems to be whether, insofar as I come to seek the common good as an intermediate end, do I cherish it only because it is intermediate with respect to my own welfare and well-being or do I cherish and pursue it because it is a source of well-being for all of the members of the community?

Given that our Libertarian critic is an Ethical Egoist, as that term is sometimes used, he will tend to suppose that the so-called common good is not a single or univocal end in any sense. Instead, one man will pursue the common good simply because of the benefits he feels it can bring to him, and another because of the advantages it holds for him. Accordingly, the common good would then come to be regarded not as being anyone's proper end or goal but as something that one man pursues for his own purposes and another for his.

The response, though, to this purely Egoistic way of interpreting a notion like the common good would seem fairly obvious. For did I not make the point earlier in this chapter that a human being is, by nature, more than an individual animal, being a political animal as well? But considered as a political animal, the true end or aim of any individual can be nothing less than the well-being of each and all of one's fellow citizens in the *polis*. Not that such a desire for the common good

149

of all necessarily displaces the obligatory end or *telos* that each man has to perfect himself. It is rather that the well-being of one's fellow citizens is regarded as integral to, and part and parcel of, one's own well-being.

Moreover, if you would make the retort that certainly not every individual—indeed scarcely any individual—is given to recognizing that such a good as is truly common to each and all is at the same time part and parcel of the good that one regards as one's own—this is something that most men are blind to—the answer is that just as with other factors that make up one's own private good, the mere fact that a given individual is indifferent to some of these factors, and does not recognize them, does not mean that such neglected factors are not truly a part of one's natural end and perfection. For instance, how many human beings are clearly aware that knowledge—theoretical knowledge, as Aristotle called it—is an indispensable part and constituent of being fully human, whether one recognizes this or not? And so with the common good considered as an end and not merely as a means to an individual's being better off or as something he thinks contributes only to what he reckons to be his personal interest and advantage, the common good of the entire community is no less a part of the human individual's own *telos* and perfection, whether he recognizes it to be so or not, simply because any human individual is a political animal at the same time that he is an individual animal.

There is one facet of so-called laissez-faire economics that might be taken to contribute to the view of the Ethical Egoist that the common good is something that he pursues merely as a means to his own good and not as a true intermediate end. Thus Adam Smith is sometimes represented as holding that in any properly free market economy, the individual needs to work simply to the end of his own private profit and advantage, whereas the overall benefit and well-being of the community results not from the planning of human agents but simply from the operation of a "divine hand." Suppose, then, that one grants this point of Smith's that in one's own individual work and activity the individual needs to work simply to maximize his own profits and without the slightest regard for what may be to the benefit or profit of his fellow citizens. Still, is it not possible to make the point that while in the pursuit of his own economic activity, an individual should have an eye simply for his own enterprise and its success, still, at the same time, that same individual is no less a political animal than he is an economic animal? And as a political animal, and in his capacity as a citizen, even the economic animal will surely not fail to concern himself with whether the "divine hand" is functioning as it should. As evidence, we may note that capitalist entrepreneurs tend to be not simply entrepreneurs but apologists for capitalism as well. Moreover, as apologists for capitalism, they will tend to argue that if the free market is permitted to operate without interference, in the long run everyone will be better off.

Again, it is not my place to assess the validity of this apologia for capitalism. Rather, the point is that such apologias seem naturally to come to the lips even of those who are most actively and often single-mindedly engaged in the purely self-regarding activities of the marketplace. But their offering apologias for a laissez-faire capitalism—and apologias in terms of the common good—is evidence that they are not just economic animals but political animals as well. And once it is acknowledged that man is a political animal by nature, then all of the arguments that I have adduced in these last several sections take on a renewed relevance—arguments to the effect that human beings do recognize the common good as being an integral part of their own ends or *tele* as individuals and that the agencies of law and government all become relevant to the accomplishment of the common good as being a part of man's natural end.

THE COMMON GOOD AND NATURAL RIGHTS

An Unwarranted Assumption and a Telltale Commitment

How could I have allowed myself, in the course of the preceding sections of this chapter, to speak so casually of rights—that is, the rights that human beings may be considered to possess simply in virtue of their nature? Surely, it cannot be assumed that people do have rights. And yet what is it other than a bold assumption that could be said to underlie my occasional references to rights in this present chapter? After all, in my exposition of a basically Aristotelian ethics in the second chapter (what I have frequently referred to as a natural-law ethics), I insisted that the primary and even the continuing mark of such an ethics is that it is self-regarding—the end or goal or *telos* of an individual's life must be his own perfection or fulfillment as a human person, or what Aristotle called happiness or *eudaemonia*. But surely, the mere fact that as human beings each of us needs to be concerned with making something of ourselves, with achieving our own happiness, in Aristotle's sense, would scarcely seem to imply that the human individual, as thus bent on achieving his own happiness, could claim any right to such happiness or even to the pursuit of happiness. To put it bluntly, who says that I have any right to seek after what I have come to recognize as being what is best for me or in my own best interests?

To put it in an exaggerated and misleading way, insofar as I restrict myself to considerations merely of ethics, as contrasted with what Aristotle would call "politics," the question of rights—or, for that matter, the question of duties toward others—does not enter into the moral or ethical picture at all. For that picture is one of the human individual as simply self-regarding; and one might even say that ethics, construed in this same strict and even narrow way, is nothing if not an Egoism.

Of course, this picture immediately changes as soon as one considers the human individual, not just in himself but as being in the *polis*. I have also stressed that from an Aristotelian or natural-law point of view, man is by nature a political animal—that is, he does not first exist in a state of nature in which all arrangements or even contacts with others are only *per accidens* and thus not natural but merely conventional. That is why so many of those earlier defenders of "natural rights," who are familiar from the writings of the eighteenth century, apparently were nearly always hard-pressed to explain how the rights of individual human beings as against other individuals—or the duties and obligations of individuals toward others—could be justified on the ground of their being "natural." For by the very terms of the state-of-nature theory, would they not have to be admitted to be no more than merely conventional?

Still, putting to one side for the moment the problems that may afflict state-of-nature thinkers when they try to explain how rights can be natural, can we say that natural-law thinkers are in any better case, when it comes to having to show how human rights are both possible and justifiable as being things men have by nature? True, as seen from the perspective of a natural-law theory, human beings are naturally political animals and therefore never mere atomic individuals in a state of nature. Still, would it not seem that even if one holds that man is a political animal by nature, one perhaps cannot get beyond being able to insist only that if there are to be rights (or duties), these will exist only insofar as men are in a *polis*? And yet suppose that human beings

are in a *polis*, and that they are so by nature, does that mean that reciprocal rights and duties of individuals with respect to one another are
therefore necessarily a part of the natural scenery of such a *polis*? Remember that even if the *polis* is man's natural condition, man's primary
and natural concern in that condition is with simply being himself—
that is, with being what a human individual ought to be simply *qua* human.

But I will be quickly reminded that in this chapter I have done little else than develop a long and many-faceted argument, designed to
qualify what I have just said and thus to show that as a political animal
man's natural end will be not simply his own good but the common
good. Additionally, considered as an end, the common good is no more
than an intermediate end, the ultimate end being the good of each and
all alike who are within the *polis*. Will this, then, not mean that insofar
as my pursuit of my own good is integrated into the pursuit of the good
of all, and the good of all into the pursuit of my own individual or private good, that I am therefore by nature obligated to have a regard for
the rights of others, just as they are obligated to have a regard for my
rights because all of us are by nature members of the *polis*?

Surely, though, this conclusion does not follow, or at least it does
not follow immediately. For to simplify the matter somewhat, suppose
that it is true that I have a duty to love my neighbor as myself, and he
me, does it follow that I can claim from him, or he from me, such lov-
ing services or ministrations as a matter of right? Thus given the case
of my friend who helps me and gives of himself unstintingly throughout all of my trials and tribulations, can I say that therefore my friend
is doing for me no more than what I am entitled to by right? Of course
not. In other words, from the mere fact that as an individual my end
or *telos* is the common good, no less than it is my own good, it certainly
does not follow that I therefore have any natural rights as against my
fellow citizens or they as against me. Accordingly, the problem is still
on our hands: even as political animals, do people have any natural
rights as individuals, and if so, on what grounds?

And now I must acknowledge another problem, not one of an unwarranted assumption so much as one of an embarrassing commitment. For in my discussions thus far in this chapter of the common
good, in which I have insisted that it ought to be an integral part of the
end or goal of each and every individual to seek the common good and
that the common good, in turn, needs to be construed as implying the

good of all, what is this if not simply Utilitarianism all over again? And what a comedown this would be for an Aristotelian, natural-law ethics (and politics, too) to be seen to reduce to nothing more than a poor, old, threadbare, and now largely discredited Utilitarianism. In charity one might say that perhaps thinkers of the stripe of Aristotle and St. Thomas Aquinas were, after all, only crypto-Utilitarians. Small consolation that, though, for how is being a crypto-Utilitarian any better than being an apocalyptic one?

But to get down to the serious business of differentiating a natural-law ethics and politics—an ethics and politics of the common good—from mere Utilitarianism, let me begin by noting that the problem that I noted earlier in this section, the problem of how a natural-law ethics is an ethics of natural rights as well, is not altogether dissociated from the problem of clearing a natural-law ethic from the taint of Utilitarianism. For have I not already noted in my earlier chapters that the reason a Utilitarian ethics has come to be largely discredited in recent years is that there would seem to be no way that Utilitarians can consistently defend themselves against the charge that, from the Utilitarian point of view, there are no individual rights that cannot be overridden, once it is shown that in a given instance the general welfare, or the greater good of the greater number, can be furthered by suppressing the rights of any particular individual or of several individuals? Supposing that I can show in the course of this present chapter that an ethics or political philosophy of natural law does indeed entail an obligation on everyone's part, be they political authorities or ordinary citizens, rulers or ruled, to respect those inalienable rights that attach by nature to human individuals, then it will be clear that there is no reason why a moral or political philosophy that aims at promoting the common good will need to be equated with Utilitarianism. For the one will hold that the rights of individuals may never be sacrificed for any fancied common good, whereas the other must hold that of course the rights of individuals are always and in principle to be sacrificed if the greater good of the greater number may thereby be furthered.

But then there is another, and perhaps even more fundamental, reason why what we might call an ethics or politics of the common good is never to be confused with Utilitarianism. In both ethics one might say that what is aimed at—that is, the moral end or goal—is a maximization of human good or human well-being. Nevertheless, as I have not just noted but underscored, there is a dangerous ambiguity in the

154

notion of human good. Thus recalling my earlier invocation of what I called the *Euthyphro* test, it makes no end of difference whether things are held to be good merely because they are desired (or are liked or give pleasure or are found satisfying); or is it rather that things are good in the sense that they are what we ought to like or desire or ought to find pleasing or a true source of satisfaction? Utilitarians seem practically without exception in their conviction that goods or values are entirely relative to human desires or to what men most want or find pleasurable. But if there is in this sense no objective standard of goodness, the Utilitarian moralist must be hard-pressed to find answers to challenges to Utilitarianism such as that expressed in Aldous Huxley's *Brave New World*, or, to use a more currently fashionable example, the challenge of the so-called "experience machine," as this has been described by several recent thinkers.[17] That is, if the greatest happiness of the greatest number may be achieved by social or mechanical arrangements whereby human beings can be made perfectly satisfied by being plied with unending streams of pleasurable sensations from which all painful or disturbing experiences have been eliminated, what possible objection can the Utilitarian moralist find to that? For will not the greatest possible happiness or satisfaction of the greatest possible number of individuals have been thereby achieved?

And if to this the Utilitarian would reply that such a criticism is unfair, since in any "brave new world" the greatest happiness of the greatest number is achieved at the cost of dehumanizing people and making them little better than so many pigs for whom the operation of an experience machine could guarantee a perfect contentment, such a rejoinder would appear hardly consistent. For would not such an attempted rejoinder be comparable to Mill's celebrated effort to defend the pleasure principle against such criticisms by seeking to distinguish the quality of pleasures from their quantity?[18] Not only would this argument seem to involve the inconsistency of seeking to make Utilitarianism operate with a double standard—recall Bentham's famous quip, "quantity of pleasure being equal, pushpin is as good as poetry"; in other words, there is no other standard than mere quantity of pleasure, but also it would appear to be an effort either to confound or to play fast and loose with the distinction that is laid down in the *Euthyphro* test. Ei-

17. See Robert Nozick, *Anarchy, State, and Utopia* (New York, 1974), 42–45.
18. John Stuart Mill, *Utilitarianism, Liberty and Representative Government* (Everyman's Library, No. 482, London, 1910), 7.

ther one recognizes that there is an objective standard of goodness and value—that is, real goods or values in nature—to which our human desires must conform or else there is no such objective standard of goodness, goodness or value being entirely relative to human tastes, likings, and whatever human beings happen to find pleasing or satisfying.

And so a natural-law moralist will make a twofold answer to the Utilitarian by posing a twofold dilemma for him. Either the Utilitarian will recognize that there are inalienable individual rights, which may never be compromised no matter what the consequences, or he will deny that there is any absolute inalienability of rights. That would be the first dilemma; and if the Utilitarian should choose to take the first horn rather than the second, he would cease to be a Utilitarian.

The second dilemma may be understood in terms of the *Euthyphro* test: either there is an objective good—a natural good for man—or there is no such natural good or natural perfection of human beings, everything being relative to human interests or desires. Again, should the Utilitarian choose the first horn of this dilemma, he could no longer claim to be a Utilitarian. Instead, he would be indistinguishable from the thinker whom we would term a natural-law moralist or ethicist. And between the common good of a natural-law ethics and the greatest good of the greatest number of the Utilitarians there can be no compromise.

But what if the Utilitarian still refuses to accept such a consequence, being ever one to be ingratiatingly accommodating, even to the point of wanting to be all things to all people (though doubtless not in any Pauline sense)? And, indeed, it is not hard to imagine Utilitarian thinkers who might try to say that in the case of these two dilemmas they would feel that they could accept the first horn in each case and still remain Utilitarians. I could only reply that if, after making such concessions, our Utilitarians still insisted upon being reckoned Utilitarians, the "Newspeak" of *1984* would indeed seem nearer than we think.

The Sorry Record of Previous False Starts in Justifying Individual Rights

Even if a commitment to the common good need not entangle us in the toils of Utilitarianism, we are still left with that other, and far more serious, problem: how is a devotion to the common good consonant with a recognition of certain inalienable rights of individuals? Still more generally, why and on what grounds should it ever have been imagined by anybody that human individuals have any rights at all? For this is not a problem that attaches only to a natural-law moral philosophy. On the contrary, I have already noted that in recent years it has become fashionable to belabor the Utilitarians with the charge that they fail to do justice to individual rights. True, the ordinary Utilitarian is more than ready to acknowledge that the rights of individuals ought certainly to be recognized; and yet this is always conditional upon the ability to show that only by such a recognition of rights of individuals will it be possible for the greater number to be made happier and better off in the long run. And to most contemporary defenders of rights— to Rawls or Nozick or Dworkin or Ackerman, for example—this is far from enough: individual rights need to be recognized as being inalienable or absolute or they do not exist. My right is my right, even if my enjoying it would appear to jeopardize the greatest happiness of the greatest number.

But if it is demanded that the rights of individuals be acknowledged to be inalienable, on what grounds is such an inalienability of rights to be asserted? The answer that immediately comes to mind is that by an appeal to a state of nature, it should be possible to show that certain rights are inalienable simply because they are our rights by nature. The only trouble with this line of defense is one that I have already remarked upon repeatedly: if nature, as the modern scientist understands it, is devoid of all distinctions between good or bad, better or worse, right or wrong, and so forth, does it make any sense to talk about human beings as having any rights by nature?

Nevertheless, why not have a look at the way the rights of individuals have been defended by various of the classical defenders of so-called natural rights in the seventeenth or eighteenth centuries? John Locke notes that one need only consider "what state all men are naturally in, and that is, a *state of perfect freedom* to order their actions and dispose of their possessions and persons, as they think fit, within the bounds of the law of nature, without asking leave, or depending upon the will of any other man." And immediately Locke goes on to suggest that "this state all men are naturally in" is "a *state* also of *equality*, wherein all the power and jurisdiction is reciprocal, no one having more than another; there being nothing more evident, than that creatures of the same species and rank, promiscuously born to all the same advantages

157

of nature, and the use of the same faculties, should also be equal one amongst another without subordination or subjection."[19] Despite exposing myself to all of the pitfalls connected with any attempted Lockean interpretation here, may I not say that it looks as though Locke were saying that all men *being in fact* free and equal in nature, or by nature, it therefore follows that men *ought to be* free and equal—that they have a right to such freedom and equality? But what does this sound like, at least superficially, if not that Locke were simply committing the patent fallacy of trying to infer an "ought" from an "is"? Doubtless I am being unfair to Locke. At least, Eric Mack, in an exceedingly perceptive paper, has argued that Locke may not be accused of having committed the "is"-"ought" fallacy.[20] And yet, however much Locke's own skirts may have been clean in such a regard, one cannot help wondering if the Lockean appearances here may not be deceptive, whatever the true Lockean reality may have been. Besides, whatever may be true of Locke himself, it would scarcely seem that very many of his followers, among the eighteenth-century champions of natural rights, were equally scrupulous as some would repute Locke himself to be about trying to avoid the "is"-"ought" fallacy. Blackstone, for example, in Section II of the Introduction to his famous *Commentaries*, in which he is talking about the nature of laws in general, declares: "In its broadest sense, law signifies a rule of action." In Book I, which is devoted to the rights of persons, Blackstone begins his first chapter with the confident declaration: "By absolute rights, are meant those which are so in their primary and strictest sense; such as would belong to their persons merely in a state of nature, and which every man is entitled to enjoy whether out of society or in it." From here Blackstone proceeds to his general statement of the primary aim of law: "The principal aim of society is to protect individuals in the enjoyment of those absolute rights, which were vested in them by the immutable laws of nature, but which could not be preserved in peace, without the mutual assistance and intercourse of social communities. The primary end of human laws is to maintain and regulate these absolute rights of individuals."[21]

19. John Locke, *Second Treatise of Government*, ed. C. B. Macpherson (Indianapolis, 1980), chap. II, §§4, 8.
20. Eric Mack, "Locke's Arguments for Natural Rights," *Southwestern Journal of Philosophy*, X (Spring, 1980), 51–60. See also chap I, n. 3, above.
21. William Blackstone, *Commentaries on the Law*, abridged ed., ed. Bernard C. Gavit (Washington, D.C., 1941), 26, 68.

Who would not warm to Blackstone's unequivocal declaration that the rights of individuals are indeed absolute? And yet the question is whether such heartwarming pronouncements can appeal to the head no less than to the heart. For what is Blackstone's ground for asserting so confidently that men's rights are absolute? Is it not because they attach to the persons of human beings "merely in a state of nature"? And yet even granting that there is a sense in which human beings may be said to enjoy their lives, their liberties, and their properties in the so-called state of nature, does that mean that they have therefore rights or entitlements to such things? And what would such an inference be if not the fallacious one of inferring an "ought" from an "is"?

If we call to witness various of our contemporaries, Rawls or Nozick or Dworkin, they all would seem to appeal to a state of nature. And yet just how are they able to do so without falling afoul of the so-called "is"-"ought" fallacy? Moreover, if we move away from contemporary thinkers who would try to base their championship of individual rights on appeals either to an actual or a hypothetical state of nature, what resources do these other thinkers have for their advocacy of individual rights? Presumably, if they cannot appeal to nature and to reality in support of rights, they must have recourse to mere logic and language: if rights are not to be justified on the basis of what men are in fact and by nature, then perhaps it can be shown to be on the basis of the way men talk and think that they may be seen to be committed to a recognition of genuine human rights.

For example, suppose that we single out for purposes of illustration the argument that Alan Gewirth has resolutely exploited in an effort to show that human agents are committed to an acknowledgment of rights, at least by language and logic if not by nature. Paraphrasing this argument, it would seem that Gewirth begins with an analysis of the sense and meaning of the notion of human action. Thus to say that a human being acts, or is an agent of action, is necessarily to imply that such action is purposive and free. Moreover, the agent of action values and esteems these features of freedom and purposiveness that characterize his actions simply because they are actions. But thus to esteem and value these features of one's actions, Gewirth seems to suppose, is to imply that they are things that the individual agent is entitled to insofar as he is a free and purposive agent. Immediately, though, for a person to claim that he has a right to freedom of action—again by Gewirth's reasoning—is to imply, by the principle of universalizability, that

159

any and every other human agent has a right to a similar freedom of action. And duties being correlative to rights, the fact that I have a right to freedom of action means that everyone else has a duty to respect this right of mine, just as I have a corresponding duty to respect the similar rights of everyone else.[22]

Unfortunately, the device that is here resorted to, not just by Gewirth but by any number of other contemporary writers on ethics, of trying to establish individual rights simply by logical implication or by the implications of our language use would appear scarcely to work. For one thing, my inability to do anything but recognize the freedom and the purposiveness of my actions as a human agent, as well as my further inability to do other than like and cherish this freedom and purposiveness of my actions, alas, would appear to provide not the slightest ground for my invoking the principle of universalizability. For after all, mere tastes and likings are not universalizable. That I like X or find it to be what I greatly cherish is no ground for supposing that therefore anyone and everyone else must like or cherish X. True, to say that X is mine by right or is what I ought to have would be a ground for universalizing my judgment: if it is right for me, then it is no less right for every other human being who is like me. And with this, the weakness in Gewirth's argument becomes readily apparent: if what in a given instance I happen to like or cherish—say, the freedom and purposiveness of my actions—can indeed be shown to be no less what it is right for me to have or enjoy, then such a right-claim is universalizable and is therefore a right of mine that everyone else is obligated to recognize and respect. But clearly, this elevation of my likes and dislikes into rights and wrongs first needs to be shown, and only then can there be any universalizability of my rights (or my wrongs). But when Gewirth tries to invoke the argument of universalizability as a means of elevating the things he cherishes into rights that he can claim against others, it would seem that he has put the cart before the horse, and his argument collapses of its own weight.

A New Start in Justifying Individual Rights

Why has there been such a record of failures on the part of modern philosophers in providing a proper justification for individual

22. Alan Gewirth, *Reason and Morality* (Chicago, 1978), esp. Chaps. 2 and 3. For a more elaborate statement of the criticism of Gewirth's argument, see my article-review of Gewirth's book in *Ethics*, LXXXIX (July, 1979), 401–14. For a similar and

rights? Could the answer be that recent philosophers have not reckoned sufficiently with what one might call the essential interdependence of various of the key ethical notions that are involved—the fact of rights, the fact of duties, and the fact of ends or goals? In my first chapter I noted that ever since Kant, moralists who have been of a so-called deontological persuasion have allowed themselves to be maneuvered into a hopeless predicament because of their stubborn insistence that "oughts" or duties must be reckoned as being ultimate and underivable in ethics. And yet is it not evident, on slight reflection, that any supposed "ought" or duty for which one can give no reason or justification can only appear as arbitrary and unwarranted? For surely, there can be no ascription of duties without the question "Why?" immediately becoming relevant: "Why ought I?" Nor can it be a proper answer to such a question merely to reiterate, "Well, you ought, just because you ought."

Any "ought" needs to be justified in terms of ends, purposes, or desires. Nor was this found to be so only in the case of morals and ethics. For even in cases of such so-called practical knowledge as may be found in the various arts and skills and in technology generally, the reason the skilled craftsman or technician knows that he ought to go about a particular job in one way rather than in another is because that would be the best way to achieve the end that he has in view. And so no less in the practical knowledge that is characteristic of morals and ethics: the reason one ought not to conduct oneself in the manner of a Sir Walter Elliot is because one would thereby make a fool of oneself; by such courses of action, one will never be able to attain the end or goal or perfection that is proper to a human person. In other words, "oughts" can be understood and thereby justified only in terms of the relevant ends or goals or purposes that are appropriate to the undertaking one has in hand.[23]

---

more recent criticism to much the same effect, see Alasdair MacIntyre, *After Virtue: A Study in Moral Theory* (Notre Dame, Ind., 1981), 64–65.

23. The term "practical knowledge" has been set in quotes here to indicate and thus enable me to take advantage of an ambiguity that this term has come to have in its usage by Aristotelian philosophers. In its narrower use, it designates moral or ethical knowledge in contrast to "productive knowledge" or technical knowledge. In its broader sense, however, it may designate both "practical knowledge" (in the narrower sense) and "productive knowledge," in contrast to "theoretical knowledge."

But now what about "rights"? For that is the specific moral notion that is immediately at issue and for which some rational justification must be provided. Could one reason so many moral philosophers have failed so signally in showing that there are human rights be that they have neglected to consider carefully enough how a notion such as that of rights both can and should be made derivative from cognate moral facts such as those of ends and duties? Instead, it is all too easy to fall back on the notion that as human beings we have rights simply because our deepest moral intuitions tell us that we do. But this answer will never do. Instead, why not consider the possibility that just as earlier we found duties to be understandable only with reference to ends, maybe our rights are to be understood in terms of our duties?

One needs to tread warily here. On the one hand, nothing is more obvious in the present day than that our moral and political lives are lived in the midst of a veritable web, not to say a maze, of reciprocal rights and duties. What else is a legal system, as it pertains to modern states and societies, if not an intricate network that spells out our reciprocal rights and duties to one another as citizens? What, then, would seem more plausible than to take rights—say, the rights of individuals—as being ultimate? It will then follow that correlative to such rights there will be the corresponding duties to respect those rights. In other words, duties here are to be understood simply in terms of rights. The only trouble is the question of the basis for taking either rights or duties to be ultimate. We have seen that to suppose that such prior rights can be founded either in nature or in intuition or in language use or in contract or convention will not do. The rights always come off as no more than sheer, arbitrary assumptions, however possible it might be to argue that once they are assumed, an entire array of reciprocal rights and duties is thereby immediately determined.

Why not go about the matter of justification the other way around? Instead of trying to suppose that duties must be grounded in rights, with the result that the rights then turn out to be ultimate and yet for that reason arbitrary and without proper foundation, why not try making duties ultimate and seeing if rights cannot be grounded in such prior duties? Unfortunately, one must again proceed cautiously, for surely it would seem that whether one chooses to make rights ultimate and then to ground the corresponding duties in the rights, or to make the duties ultimate and then try to ground the rights in the duties, it all turns out to be little more than a triviality on the order of six of one, half a dozen of the other. Thus, for example, suppose that one takes Kant's so-called second formulation of the Categorical Imperative as an independent principle in its own right and not a reformulation of the first formulation: "So act that you always treat human nature, whether in your own person, or in that of another, always as an end and never merely as a means." But by supposing that the duty that is implied in this formulation of the imperative is ultimate and prior to the corresponding rights that human nature is supposed to have as answering to this imperative, has one gained anything by way of offering a sufficient justification for rights? Of course not. For the imperative would have no force if human nature did not already possess the right to be treated always as an end and never merely as a means.[24] In other words, to suppose that one might be able to justify any right of a human being to be treated as an end and not merely as a means simply by appealing to the corresponding duty that is presumed to be incumbent upon human beings always to treat others as ends and not as mere means—so far from really proving anything, this alternative would seem to do no more than beg the question.

But suppose that one takes a different tack. Suppose that instead of trying to justify an individual's rights in terms of the duties that others are supposed to have toward him, one tries to justify his rights in terms of the duties that he has toward himself. Will that make a difference to the cogency of any attempted justification of that person's rights, and if so, how?[25]

Immediately, the suggestion of possible duties toward oneself, as contrasted with duties toward others, carries us right back into the mainstream of my argument about a natural-law ethic. For given the notion of an end or goal or perfection of human life that is determined by man's nature, it follows that the business of living, for a human being,

24. Kant, *Groundwork*, 429.
25. Students of Dworkin will be familiar with his proposition of a threefold classification of political theories—goal-based theories, right-based theories, and duty-based theories (Ronald Dworkin, *Taking Rights Seriously* [Cambridge, Mass., 1977], 169–77). I have not modeled my discussion of the interrelationships between duties, rights, and ends after Dworkin's because his concern, unlike mine, does not seem to be aimed at any particular ordering of rights, duties, and goals. More fundamentally, Dworkin appears to restrict his goal-based theories exclusively to theories of a Utilitarian inspiration..He seems to have no notion of a *telos*-based theory like that of Aristotle's. I believe that this is the reason Dworkin is unable or comparatively indifferent to ordering of duties, rights, and goals.

must consist of an ongoing enterprise of trying to become and be simply what one ought to be. That is, because man's natural end is determined for him by nature, that end will be obligatory, and in consequence a person's every action and his entire behavior will need to be governed by a regard for his duties toward himself. And how did I earlier seek to flesh out this idea of a person's natural end and of his resultant duties toward himself? Was it not in terms of his trying to become and to be at once a rational and a political animal? Accordingly, those duties and obligations that are incumbent upon us simply in virtue of our being human are no less than the duties of living intelligently and wisely and in a responsibly human way. If one should wish to express this notion in specifically Aristotelian terms, one could say that what is incumbent upon any human being if he would live wisely and well is simply that he cultivate and come to exercise both the intellectual and the moral virtues.

If such are the nature and character of our duties toward ourselves, are there, then, any natural human rights that might be supposed to derive from such duties and that others besides ourselves might be under obligation to respect? Surely, it would seem that there are. I would also venture to suggest that those very rights to life, liberty, and property, which I have been so concerned with trying to justify, may readily be seen to derive from those same natural duties toward ourselves that are incumbent upon all of us to live rationally and intelligently and in a politically responsible way.

Nevertheless, before I undertake to sketch out, one by one, the derivation of each of these three natural human rights from our basic duties toward ourselves, I will first indicate, very generally and in the abstract, the overall logic of such a derivation. For suppose it is assumed that a given individual is under obligation to perform a certain action—to hand in a report, to pay his taxes, to contribute to the support of his family, to return something that he has borrowed from a friend, or whatever. Moreover, suppose it is agreed both that the obligation truly is an obligation and that it is recognized as such by everyone concerned, including the person who is under obligation. That is, he not only acknowledges the obligation but is also morally concerned to acquit himself of it. Would it not follow that the person who would thus discharge himself of his obligation could properly claim that he had a right not to be interfered with or to be forcibly prevented or deliberately deprived of the necessary means of doing what he and everyone else recognizes that he ought to do?[26]

Let us take a simple example. Suppose that in my job my boss requires that I prepare a certain report for him, and suppose that I recognize that the report needs doing and that I am indeed the one who ought to do it. But suppose, then, that the boss suddenly gives me several other assignments and loads me down with busy work so that I cannot complete the report, which he and I are both agreed should be given top priority. Under the circumstances, might I not complain that it was not right for the boss to have laid the obligation upon me of preparing the report and then to have deprived me of the time or the chance to prepare it? Moreover, if it is acknowledged that it was not right for the boss to have done this, is there not a further sense in which it could be said that I had a certain right in this matter and that my right was violated by my boss's seemingly inordinate demands?

From this example, can it not be seen that duties do generate rights and yet not merely in the generally accepted sense of the rights of others to whom the duties are due or owed? For in this case there is also the right of the person who is under the obligation; and this latter right, if we may so term it, of being able to discharge oneself of the duty that is incumbent upon one would seem to be no less a right that is derivative from the duty than is the right of him to whom the duty is due or owing.

Moreover, what is significant about this derivation of rights from duties is that it does not simply beg the question. For to say that the

26. At the time my own book was being readied for the press, I chanced upon a very significant article by Gilbert Harman, entitled "Human Flourishing, Ethics, and Liberty," *Philosophy and Public Affairs*, XII (Fall, 1983), 307–312. There to my astonishment I read the following affirmation: "[There is] an argument which I have sometimes heard which goes roughly like this. 'I ought to develop my own potential for flourishing. So, others ought not to prevent me from developing my potential. So, I have a right not to be prevented from developing my potential. So, by the principle of universalizability everyone has such a right.' " What is this, if not a statement in summary form of the very argument that I sought to develop in the text of how individual human rights are to be justified in terms of what I called, perhaps rather infelicitously, our duties to self—*i.e.*, the duties all of us have to perfect ourselves as human persons. Not only do I find it reassuring that such an argument should receive confirmation from such a one as Gilbert Harman, but I was particularly interested that he should refer to it as being an argument "which he has sometimes heard," for I cannot recall having come across this argument anywhere else, either in the literature or out of it.

existence of a duty implies the existence of a right in him to whom the duty is due surely is a truism. On the other hand, to say that my being under obligation to do thus and so implies that I have a right not to be interfered with or prevented from discharging my duty—that surely would be a proper case of providing a ground for a right in what was clearly a prior duty. Indeed, I wonder if the principle that is involved here might not be a variant on the familiar ethical principle that "ought" implies "can." That is, just as it is acknowledged that one can hardly be said to have an obligation to perform any action that one is totally incapable of performing, might it not be a logical inverse of this that, granting that I do indeed have a duty or obligation to perform a certain action, then to render me incapable or unable to perform the action would surely be a violation of my right?

Justifications of the Rights to Life, Liberty and Property

What now of those specific rights to life, liberty, and property that I have been citing as being the primary and basic rights of human beings? Can these rights be justified in terms of what I have been calling our human duties to self and more specifically in terms of that overriding duty to self that is incumbent upon everyone to be and become truly human, or the person that a human being ought to be? First, let us consider the right to liberty. At the outset, would it not seem plausible to recognize that without a certain liberty or freedom of action on our part, we human beings could not possibly acquit ourselves of our obligation to make something of ourselves and to bring ourselves to the point that each of us as an individual might be said to live rationally and wisely and responsibly? But if one's duties imply that one has rights that should not be interfered with or that one should not be deprived of conditions necessary for the performance of one's duties, are we not already in a fair way toward establishing that human beings really do have a right—and a natural right—to liberty?

Nevertheless, to make this human right to liberty somewhat more concrete, let us recall once again my oft-repeated description of the basic moral situation of any human being engaged simply in the business of living his life. Although born a human being, an individual's human nature consists at birth of little more than potentialities, so that any human infant needs to be viewed in terms of what he might be, could be, and ought to be if he is to become what his nature as a human person demands. Moreover, any such natural development of a human being should not be conceived merely biologically but morally as well. For considered morally, every human individual is under obligation to make something of himself, to be and become truly human. And being and becoming truly human means getting to the point at which as a human being one can live rationally, that is, can be guided in his manifold choices and decisions in life by his own understanding and better judgment. Nor is there any other way in which this natural and obligatory end of ours as human beings can be attained save by our own efforts and exertion and enterprise. In other words, it is not enough for us simply to sit back and let nature take its course. For never is a human being able "naturally" to develop into a full-fledged rational and political animal, as an acorn naturally develops into an oak or a human infant into a biologically mature and full-grown person. For as I have often remarked, the business of becoming human, in the true sense, is first, last, and always a do-it-yourself job.

Moreover, that our attaining to our natural and obligatory ends as human beings should be a do-it-yourself job further implies that no one else, no thing, no force, no power under heaven, or even in heaven, can ever make us into true human beings. Parents, friends, society, the state, or forces of nature can never do the job for us. They can help, to be sure; more than that, each of them, and often all of them, are to an extent necessary means to a human individual's attaining his true and natural end as a human person. But however necessary they may be as means, they are never, either any or all of them, sufficient as means. For this, the one and only and absolutely indispensable and decisive means is a self-help or a self-development or an individual enterprise.

But what is this if not to say that ours is a job that we can only do ourselves, that it is only we ourselves who can live our own lives and acquit ourselves of our natural human responsibilities? And if the job is one that we can only do ourselves, if there is no way we can be forced or compelled to be or become what we ought to be as men and women— no way we can have a proper human excellence or virtue provided for us or given to us or bestowed upon us, either as a gift of nature or a gift of our fellowmen—then there is no possible way we can do the job that we are naturally cut out to do and obligated to do, as human beings, unless we are free to do it ourselves.

But does this not provide a demonstration of our natural human right to freedom and liberty? For recall what the logic of such a demonstration of human rights must be: we have a right to liberty to the extent that without liberty we cannot possibly live the life that it is morally incumbent upon us as human beings to live. And is it not now abundantly clear that without personal freedom and liberty, we cannot possibly do the things we are by nature obligated to do? Accordingly, to assert that we have a natural right to be free is to imply that it is only right that as human beings we not be subjected to any compulsion or coercion designed to force us to become good people; that we not be made to undergo any programming or conditioning aimed at making us act in ways that we are supposed to act or ought to act; and that we therefore not be foreclosed from exercising that liberty of action without which we could never acquit ourselves of the overriding obligation that is incumbent upon us to live our lives as human beings and not as mere dogs who can only bay the moon.

In other words, is it not in this sense that our natural human right to freedom or liberty is strictly derivable from our natural human duty to become and be truly human? Our individual rights, in other words, can be derived from the duties that are incumbent upon us as individuals. And of course, once my right or your right or the other person's right to liberty of action is established, then the principle of universalizability immediately takes over: given that I have a right to freedom, based on the duty and obligation that I have to myself, then so also does every other person have a similar right based on the like duties that he has to himself; and likewise, given that I really do have a right to freedom and liberty, or whatever else, then necessarily everyone else has an answering duty or obligation to respect those rights of mine as thus demonstrated and established. Can we not, then, be said to have worked out a logic of demonstration whereby our human rights are derived from the duties that we have to ourselves; and then, once such personal rights are established, the principle of universalizability can be used to show that all other human beings are under obligation to respect these prior rights of ours?

Making the transition from the right to liberty to the right to life—which really means a right to life and limb—and thus a right not to be deprived of life or limb or of any significantly functioning bodily organ—it requires no great wit or argument to see that to the extent to which any human individual may be subjected to being maimed or injured or killed or in any way forcibly deprived of the use of his functioning organs, he would thereby be impeded in being or becoming—even perhaps kept from being or becoming—what he otherwise might be or could be or should be in the way of attaining his natural and full flowering as a human being. Moreover, if it is the responsibility, and hence the duty and obligation, of any human being thus to make something of himself and to be and become what he ought to be as a human being; and if, as we have seen, such duties and responsibilities as an individual may thus have toward himself tend to generate for him various rights such that he ought not be deprived of the capacities and capabilities that enable him to acquit himself of his obligations, then a human being's right to life and limb becomes no less intelligible than his right to freedom and liberty.

It is true that through ill health, accident, or disease, a person could be deprived of life or limb and thus of what might be said to be his by right. And yet although unhappy eventualities such as these could cause problems for theologians—particularly as regards questions of theodicy or of divine justice, when it comes to human justice or what we might call a natural justice—still in human societies or communities, there can be no doubt or question or problem but that human individuals have a natural right to life and limb; and if that right is violated by other human beings, such a violation is clearly wrong, whether the wrong is in the nature of a crime, a tort, an unlawful exercise of power by the state, or whatever.

What, then, is to be said about property and the supposed right of an individual to his own private property? Can this be shown to be a natural right of individuals, no less than their rights to life and to liberty? Certainly initially, any demonstration of a right to private property might seem to bid fair to being far more fractious and difficult than any demonstration of an individual's right to life and liberty. Still, why not try to follow the same general line of demonstration that I used in the other two cases? For if wealth and property can be shown to be, in their own way, conditions that are peculiarly necessary to a human being's achieving that natural human perfection which it is morally incumbent upon him as a human being to try to achieve, then surely it should be possible for people to claim their property as a right.

But can it be shown that private property is a necessary means or condition of a person's achieving his natural end? First, before beginning to address this question, I should give some indication of what is to be understood as constituting wealth and property. I must frankly admit to having neither the learning nor the experience requisite for advancing any very subtle or sophisticated definition of property. Still, without a proper definition, may it perhaps suffice to point to familiar examples of some of the major sources or kinds of property—for example, real as compared with personal property, or perhaps, as the economists might say, capital goods as compared with consumer goods—would not such examples indicate what one is to have in mind in this discussion of wealth and property?

No sooner, though, is property understood in this sense than immediately one can see that any right to private property—supposing that there is one—must be somewhat different in character from our rights to liberty and to life and limb. For after all, we do not create or procure our life and our limbs for ourselves. And though in a sense there could not be such a thing as individual liberty apart from the legal protections of a community or political society, still liberty or personal freedom is not anything that a human being has to procure for himself or provide himself with in the way his wealth and property need to be earned or otherwise acquired.

Supposing, then, that all property has in this sense to be acquired and secured and, indeed, appropriated by human individuals, what is the original source of such an acquired wealth or property? Presumably, it must be gotten from somewhere. But where? To this question, the answer would seem to be that originally and ultimately human wealth or property must be derived from what might be called the primordial goods of the earth, or, perhaps in more theological language, from the goods of creation. Nor would it appear that we would be committing ourselves unduly to any theological presuppositions if we frankly recognized the apparently obvious notion that such goods of the earth have been primevally set before us and made available to us for our use and consumption and exploitation.

At once, though, if the source of all wealth and property is held to be the goods of the earth, and if the primeval setting for such goods can hardly be conceived otherwise than as if these goods were but so many gifts offered to mankind—in other words, gifts not to any one individual to the exclusion of others, but rather to all people equally and alike—then this would indeed appear to create problems with regard to the notion of the rightfulness of purely private property. For surely, it is ridiculous to imagine that the goods of the earth ever originally came to human beings with their titles of ownership written on their face by the hand of God. But then, if people do not have titles to their private property by nature, how do such entitlements arise and by what right and with what justice?

Of course, I must emphasize that here I am raising the question of *quid juris* with respect to private property and not *quid facti*. For whether it be in prehistory or throughout history down to the present day, there is no doubting or denying that human individuals always have and still do take possession of the goods of the earth, simply by exercising their own effort and enterprise and labor. That is, the human individual, at one time or other, appropriates such primordial goods to his own private use, be it the land, the flora and fauna of the land, the minerals in the earth, the water under the earth, the fish of the sea, the fowls of the air, or even the air itself. And certainly all such acts of appropriation involve an unmistakable element of effort and work. Using Lockean language, one might say that property comes to be originally acquired by human beings "mixing their labor" with the various goods of the earth that they find before them.

Still, granting that in fact and in history and even still today, private possessions have come about in this way, that scarcely means that the ownership of private property is for that reason necessarily justifiable. True, most of us have a deep-seated sense and feeling that the fruits of our own labor should be ours. But why? Why, merely because we have managed to take possession of something—granted that it be through our own effort and enterprise, still it was of something that was not originally ours—should such a taking now be considered to be ours by right? After all, Pierre-Joseph Proudhon pronounced all property to be theft. And such pronouncements serve to bring home to us that the question of the right to private property, as opposed to its question of fact, is still very much with us.

Besides, there is more to the story of the generation of wealth and property than any mere business of certain goods of the earth being originally appropriated and so converted into the private possessions of the appropriating individuals. For having been appropriated, such original goods of the earth can then be further exploited by their owners in the sense that they can be made to fructify and be used as materials for the production of still further goods: the soil is made to yield crops, the wood of the forests and the metals of the earth become raw materials for manufactures, and so on. And as a further complication, in these productive activities of human beings, working on the raw materials of creation, the work and the labor of the individuals involved tends to become organized and coordinated to the end of an ever greater and more efficient productivity. And with that, our fundamental question comes round again, directly and with renewed force: can it be said to be by any natural right that human individuals thus come to own and to possess what they have exerted themselves to acquire and to appropriate and to manufacture by their own effort and labor?

Why should not property be common rather than private? For one thing, if all wealth is generated from an original store of goods of the earth, and if such goods are not the property of anyone in particular, but rather are like gifts of God made available for use by the whole of mankind, then how can the wealth that comes to be acquired be regarded as private, when its sources are common and public? Likewise, if such wealth as is not merely taken possession of but is produced by human work and labor is nevertheless the product of a cooperative and coordinated division of labor among many, how can the product that emerges then be regarded as the private property of one, or of a few, rather than the common property of all those engaged in its production?

Still, I have already noted that if private property, like our rights to life and to liberty, can be shown to be an indispensable condition to our carrying out the job of living our lives in a way that it is morally incumbent upon us to do, then it can indeed be claimed that people's private ownership of property can be justified by right, as opposed to being merely established in fact. And given a little reflection, it does seem that a case can be made for private property along these lines. And why might we not begin by asking what is the basic reason why nearly all human beings, everywhere, and for much of the time, seem to be ever striving to acquire goods and possessions for themselves? And why, likewise, are they forever sweating and straining and occupying themselves in all manner of productive activities as well? Must it not be because only by so doing they can get themselves into a condition to live at all, much less to live well? And so it is that there is scarcely any human being who must not concern himself with procuring for himself, and usually for others around him as well, the basic necessities of food, clothing, and shelter. Accordingly, must not such a concern and obligation be a part of our human condition? "If any would not work, neither should he eat" (2 Thess. 3:10).

Nor must it be thought that wealth and property only make it possible for human beings to be provided with basic necessities like food, clothing, and shelter. For wealth is also a prerequisite for the so-called higher things of life—knowledge, learning, friendship, the arts, and the like. It is true, of course, that we do not ordinarily think of a man's knowledge as a scientist or his skill as a musician or his trust and loyalty as a friend or his appreciation and enjoyment of art, television, or ordinary recreation as being a possession of his in the sense of ordinary material or physical possessions. And yet a scientist's knowledge, an artist's skill, or a person's everyday pleasures and recreations would not be possible without wealth and possessions. The scientist must have his laboratory and equipment, the artist his paints, brushes, and perhaps a studio, the television enthusiast his television set, and so on. And so it is that although wealth and material possessions are not the only goods of life, they would seem to be inseparable from them and hence essential to provide what might loosely be called the material conditions of just about anything and everything in human existence.

No doubt, at this point many will interject, "But all of this in no sense demonstrates the need, not to mention the legitimacy, of private wealth and property. True, wealth in the sense of capital, means of production, and material goods generally is undoubtedly indispensable if human beings are to live, much less to live the good life. But that surely does not prove that such wealth has to be in private hands or that the individual human being must have wealth and property of his own if he is to live as a human being ought to live."

Let me give a brief answer in defense of private property. For we are directly and unavoidably faced with the specific issue of private property—that is, the issue not simply of whether one can justify the ownership of property as an indispensable condition of the good life for human beings, but rather of whether one can justify the ownership of property by a private individual as being a necessary means or condition of that individual's making something of himself and living as he ought to live. To meet this issue, I suggest that two lines of answer be followed. First, there is the answer that Aquinas, for example, used and that avails itself largely of what might be called practical or pragmatic considerations.[27] Thus, as should be obvious from the preceding account, that wealth and property should be indispensable means of

27. St. Thomas Aquinas, *Summa Theologiae*, II–II, Qu. 66, Art. 2.

173

human beings living as they ought to live, it is not enough that goods should merely be held or owned or possessed, either as common or as private property. It is also necessary that the goods be exploited—that even the one talent not be simply buried in the ground but that it be invested, put to work, and made to yield further increase. Only in this way can the goods of the earth be made to serve the needs of all mankind. And it is here that pragmatic considerations can and need to be invoked, and with a telling effect. For does it not stand to reason that even if not all human beings, certainly most human beings will be much more likely to conserve, exploit, and render productive property that is their own, rather than property that is held in common, and that is therefore no one's particular concern because it is everyone's. As we have often been reminded, what is everyone's business tends to be no one's business.

"Oh," but you will say, "this is no more than a pragmatic argument, and hence an argument that fails to justify private property on principle, having regard only for human beings as they unfortunately are and not for human beings as they ideally might be or should be." And yet might not this retort be predicated on a mistaken view of human nature, considered even ideally? In any event, we need to see if we can supplement this first and largely pragmatic argument with a second and more principled argument. To this end, may I once more invoke that account of human beings and of their natural human condition that I have repeatedly used throughout this entire discussion? A human being is a being who must make something of himself, who must make a life for himself; and there is no possible way anybody else— and particularly not the society or the community—can do this for him. Not only that, but supposing that the natural end of a man is that he become a truly rational animal in the sense that he learn to act on his own better judgment and to conduct himself in a reasonable and responsible way, must it now follow that, this being a do-it-yourself job, what one might call a continuing self-help and self-reliance must come to pervade and characterize the entire gamut of an individual human being's existence? And so, granting that what I have been designating as being a certain wealth and property, or a certain material base of existence, is absolutely indispensable to any true human flourishing, then surely any and every human being ought to have a concern for, and to engage in, what might loosely be called some wealth-producing activity. Nor would it seem that the individual either ever could or should completely dissociate his wealth-producing activities from his own personal material needs. And what does this mean if not that every person must concern himself with what, in the old-fashioned sense, is earning a living and acquiring at least a modicum of wealth and property and possessions that would be one's own and that one would thus have the disposition of in the planning and ordering of his life and in the use of his resources in the wisest possible way?

It is true that given the division of labor that prevails in modern society, one must not suppose that each and every human individual, in his concern with thus providing himself with the material necessities of his existence, must necessarily assume responsibility for growing his own food, building his own house, making his own clothes, and so on. And yet making allowances for the implications of a proper division of labor in society need not mean that the individual human being should become indifferent to working productively and to receiving a compensation that is his due and that will thus be his own to use as he sees fit and judges best.

Nor does this general line of argument for the legitimacy and propriety of what might be called a right concern for property of one's own necessarily mean that no human being, under any circumstances, can or ought to abstract from all concern with private wealth. On the contrary, there is no reason why some might not have vocations to a religious life of poverty or others be so absorbed in scientific or scholarly or artistic work as to have grown indifferent to having wealth or possessions for themselves. That some individuals may be so circumstanced that they either need not or do not worry about material wealth and possessions for themselves still does not mean that such concerns are not proper for most human beings or would not be proper even for those without such concerns, supposing that their own circumstances were not so special.

Likewise, just because I would insist that private wealth and private property are thus in principle right and legitimate, it must not be thought to follow that private property is therefore never something that can be abused, pursued to excess, or frequently so loved as to blight and ruin an individual's existence. Of course not. And yet just because a private right may be abused does not necessarily mean that it ought not to be a right in the first place or that, being a right, it perhaps should be forbidden to a particular individual because he abuses it. Indeed, an individual's right to liberty, no less than his right to property, may be and often is abused, as when an individual uncritically indulges his chance whims and fancies. Even a person's right to life and limb can be abused, as when a hypochondriac or valetudinarian becomes so preoccupied with his own health as to make himself ridiculous in the eyes of those about him. And so likewise with wealth. For we all know how legendary are the follies of the spendthrift, the repulsiveness of the miser, the displays of those given to conspicuous consumption, and so on. But notice that such abuses of life or liberty or property all reflect upon the personal character of the individuals concerned and thus constitute violations of what I have called the natural moral laws that operate in the ethical domain and with respect to the individual's own personal development and character, as contrasted with such natural laws as are and should be operative in the *polis* and in society. Moreover, just as it would seem that law, in the sense of public law or civil law, ought never to be used as a device for trying to enforce a personal morality, so also it would seem that one ought never to deny someone his natural right to private property merely because as an individual he might so abuse it as to reflect unfavorably upon his entire character as a person.

Having taken account of these exceptions and qualifications, may we not now say that our case for the right of private property can stand the test? It is no less a right than the rights to life and to personal liberty. In addition, it can be demonstrated to be a right much as they can, for all three of them are requisite if we are to acquit ourselves of our basic obligation to live our lives as human beings in the true sense of the word.

But now it is necessary to consider political rights as additional to private rights. With justice it may be said that thus far in this discussion of the natural rights that human beings have, I have confined myself to a consideration only of those old standbys, life, liberty, and property. Beyond these, I have mentioned no others; nor have I attempted even a rough classification of the various rights that people may be reckoned as having or possessing simply by nature. Nor do I propose to remedy this omission except to say a word about what we might roughly call political rights, as compared with private rights.

Earlier I mentioned Aristotle's suggestion in the *Politics* that "one aspect of freedom is political, ruling and being ruled, whereas the other aspect is personal," according to which one orders one's life according to one's judgments and decisions. Accordingly, may it not be said that under what I have dubbed the political aspect of freedom, there may be classified a host of political rights—the right to vote, the right to freedom of speech and assembly, the right to bear arms, the so-called common law rights—habeas corpus, trial by jury, protection against unwarranted searches and seizures, and the like?

Must not all such so-called political rights be reckoned as being ours by nature on the ground that, unless we enjoyed such rights, we could not properly acquit ourselves of those natural duties and responsibilities which we have by virtue of our nature as political animals? After all, being by nature political animals, and political life in the true sense being practically impossible for us, unless we ourselves institute it and constitute it, must we not conclude that any government or political constitution must rest upon the consent of the governed? In consequence, may not the various and sundry political rights that we should be said to have by nature be justified as necessary means to our properly acquitting ourselves of our responsibilities in the way of governing ourselves politically and thus pursuing the common good of the *polis* as it ought to be pursued?

The Issue of Positive Rights Versus Negative Rights

And now a new problem confronts us. Having insisted that human rights can be understood and justified only in terms of those prior duties to self that each of us has by nature, will it not follow that human rights are thus to be understood in terms of our human needs—that is, what is necessary to us if we are to acquit ourselves of our responsibilities as rational and political animals? For was this not precisely the justification that I put forward for our being able to lay claim to having a natural right to life, liberty, and property? Deprived of these rights, we could not hope to acquit ourselves of our reponsibilities to live as human beings ought to live: we need them if we are properly to do our job in life.

This issue, though, appears to open the floodgates to a veritable torrent of rights—rights to food, clothing, and shelter, rights to education and health care, perhaps rights to needed opportunities for rest and relaxation, to a living wage, to old-age benefits, to equality of opportunity, and so on. Such rights appear to be of a different character from the rights to life, liberty, and property. And yet would it not seem that these new-vintage rights would have to be reckoned as rights no less than what we might call the traditional, old-vintage rights—and that, for the reason that no human being could properly acquit himself of his obligation to be truly human if he lacked sufficient food, clothing, or shelter, or if he were without adequate education, or if he were denied proper opportunities for rest and relaxation, and so forth? In other words, adequate food, clothing, and shelter, to say nothing of education and knowledge, as well as opportunities for rest and relaxation and for association with our fellows surely are needs of human beings, no less than are our needs for life, liberty, and property. Accordingly, what would seem to have been a proper justification for rights of this latter and more traditional sort would now apparently prove to be no less a justification for rights of the former sort as well.

But are we not suddenly brought face to face with the question of what Iredell Jenkins has termed "positive rights" as contrasted with "negative rights"? As he poses the contrast:

> It has often been pointed out that the natural and legal rights of classical doctrines were conceived primarily—though not exclusively—in negative terms. Their chief function was to assure freedom *from* various intrusions and oppressions. Men sought the rights of liberty, property, equality, security, assembly, due process, and so forth, in order to be protected against arbitrary power, whether this was political, religious, military, or economic. . . . The case is different with human rights. These are far more positive in their content and intention. Human rights tend to take the form of claims *to* or *for* something. Their function is to assure to people certain goods, benefits, and supports for which they experience an urgent need, to which they feel entitled, and which they are unable to procure by their individual efforts—[e.g. such things as] low-cost housing, a food allowance, minimum income, education, medical assistance, useful employment and so forth, [all of these] on the ground that these are due them as human beings and so are owed them by society.[28]

One might wonder whether Jenkins' formulation of this difference between "negative" and "positive" rights or of the difference between rights that guarantee against interference from the outside, as contrasted with rights that are rights to and for something, can be made entirely precise and definitive. But no matter. For however one chooses to formulate it, the nature and character of the contrast that Jenkins makes is clear, and the import and implications of the contrast are no

---

28. Iredell Jenkins, *Social Order and the Limits of Law: A Theoretical Essay* (Princeton, 1980), 252–53.

less clear than they are disturbing. One might well turn to Jenkins to have it spelled out how troublesome the import of this notion of positive rights can prove to be. For what is troublesome about the so-called positive rights is, as Jenkins remarks, that "they require that government plan and administer society in a manner that assures men a standard of living and a way of life that will afford them a satisfactory existence."[29]

"But what is wrong with this?" you might ask. And in answer does one need do more than point out that no sooner is it maintained that government, or society as a whole, has an obligation to afford individuals "a satisfactory existence," than it quickly begins to appear that there is no way a government can acquit itself of this supposed obligation to guarantee men their positive rights without the government's at the same time, and almost inevitably, having to violate some of men's negative rights in order to do so. And surely, governments are no less obligated to respect and guarantee the negative rights of individuals than they are to promote these presumed positive rights of their citizens. And so what to do?

Let us examine the issue with an illustration: how is it possible for a government even to begin to satisfy the presumed rights of every citizen to "low-cost housing, a food allowance, minimum income, education, medical assistance, useful employment, and so forth" without infringing upon the rights of at least some individuals to their wealth and property and doubtless to their lives and liberties as well? For how can such a social objective be achieved without enlisting the talents, the strength, the energies, and the wealth of individuals in the community who are fortunate to possess such resources? And if an individual's right to what is his own is absolute, then any contributions that he may make to the general welfare, other than purely voluntary ones, must necessarily entail a violation of that individual's rights. It cannot be expected that purely voluntary contributions by the individuals within a society will normally suffice to assure that all the members of a community will be able to enjoy a "standard of living and a way of life that will afford them a satisfactory existence."

Besides, even if on natural law principles one were to hold that an individual's rights to his life, liberty, and property are limited, albeit inalienable, it would still seem not just likely, but practically unavoid-

29. *Ibid*, 253.

able, that any and all social programs directed toward the full-scale satisfaction of individuals' positive rights must sooner or later involve a serious trenching upon any number of the so-called negative rights of individuals. For must not the very logic of any doctrine of positive rights lead to an acceptance of the principle "to each according to his needs, and from each according to his abilities"? Nevertheless, on the basis of that principle, as we have already seen, there is no way negative rights, even limited ones, can withstand erosion even to the point of extinction. For who will deny that in societies that have been erected on the principle of rights as determined by needs, the rate of survival of negative rights has not been high?

And so again the question presses, what to do? My answer must take the form of a simple denial that individuals have any positive rights. There are no such things. Nor do I believe that of all the varied claims that individuals make to their having a right to food, clothing, and shelter, education, old-age benefits, and so on, there are any such claims that may be said to be proper right-claims.

Still, is it not paradoxical, not to say inconsistent, that I should take such a line in regard to positive rights, considering that I have been so insistent that the only way individual rights can be grounded and justified is in terms of prior human duties and obligations, and more specifically in terms of our duties and obligations to our own selves, that is, to make something of ourselves and to be and become truly human? Yet surely to acquit ourselves of our natural obligations as human beings, it has to be recognized that we can never afford to allow ourselves to be deprived of life and limb, and certainly not of our basic freedom and liberty or of our property, considering that wealth and property provide us with the means and resources that are requisite for us if we are to live our lives at all, much less if we are to live them well. Besides, did I not also earlier argue that any such justification of rights in terms of the duties and obligations that we have toward ourselves is a variant on the principle of "ought" implies "can"? The "can" here requires that we not be deprived of such things as are necessary to us if we are to do the very things that it is incumbent upon us to do by virtue of our being human. Yet would not such an exploiting of the principle of "ought" implies "can" serve to justify positive rights no less than negative rights? Indeed, have I not recognized that there can be no denying that food, clothing, and shelter, education and possibly health care, a living wage, meaningful employment, *et al.* are all among the necessary means to our being properly human and to our living our lives fully and rightly as human beings? How, then, can I possibly maintain that right-claims to positive rights are never justified, when exactly the same line of argument that I have used to justify negative rights would appear to justify positive rights as well?

And yet is this really the case? Is it true that the appeal to the principle of "ought" implies "can" would justify positive rights no less than negative rights? Hardly. And the reason it would not is that we might be said already to possess such things as are said to be ours by negative right and that for this reason we are not to be deprived of them, at least not rightfully. Thus, it is surely true that we have or possess simply by nature life and limb, and even in a sense our basic human freedom and liberty. In Jefferson's phrase, they are endowments bestowed upon us seemingly by our Creator. And they are bestowed upon us as being a radically indispensable means and equipment and wherewithal that as human beings we must have if we are to do our job of being truly human. Likewise, although our wealth and property are not given by our Creator—at least not individually—they are nevertheless a means and a resource that as human beings we have come to possess by virtue of our human labor. Moreover, it is as something already possessed and owned that we are said to have a right to our property in the sense that we may not rightfully be deprived of it because it is already ours. In contrast, all of the so-called positive rights are those that human beings who are said to have a right to them do not possess, and therefore it is claimed that they have a right to become possessed of them.

But there is a marked difference here. It is the difference between claiming a right to what is already ours, either by nature or by dint of our own labor, and claiming a right to what is not yet ours but what we want to be ours. To appreciate the significance of the difference, suppose that we once again call to mind what I have described as being our fundamental human situation in which in principle each human being finds himself by nature. For is this not a situation in which we must recognize ourselves as being endowed or equipped with little more than those powers and capacities that as human beings we are going to need if we are to cope with our condition and environment in the ongoing business of living our lives? Furthermore, is not this same human situation one in which we recognize ourselves as being under an unmistakable obligation and as having an ineradicable responsibility to cope with that basic condition of potentiality in which we find ourselves and then to get on with the serious business of actually living our lives in a way that befits us as human beings? Again, this job that we all have of living our lives is emphatically a do-it-yourself job.

True, it is not a do-it-yourself job that each of us can hope to accomplish all by himself and working entirely alone. Rather, it is a do-it-yourself job that people can accomplish only by working cooperatively and in virtue of their being the naturally political animals that human beings are. Still, from within this context, and viewed from this perspective, it should now be apparent that so far from possessing positive rights to food, clothing, shelter, education, health care, a minimum wage, and so on—as if these things were owing to us as individuals and we had a right to have them handed to us on a silver salver—we are not. No, we are not initially entitled to these things because we are obligated to work for and to provide ourselves with them. And indeed, if we fail to provide ourselves with such things, working both individually and collectively, then clearly we will have failed to make of ourselves as human beings what we need to make and ought to make of ourselves, and as a result, our lives may well turn out to be little more than "poor, nasty, brutish, and short."

But this is not anything we can blame others for, as if God, our fellow human beings, or fate deprived us of our rights. We can blame only ourselves. And if in the enterprise of living our lives we end up lacking the food, clothing, and shelter, the education, knowledge, refinement, or whatever that we need, then we can no more say that this lack occurred because we were deprived of what was ours by right than if, in the living of our lives, we should turn out to be foolish, vain, and stupid or lacking in wisdom, practical judgment, and understanding, we could then very well say that this was because we were not given, or provided with, such wisdom and judgment as was ours by right.

The conclusion of the last paragraph may be a little overdrawn, in that all too often in life people find themselves deprived of their means of subsistence and the physical and even moral necessities of life, simply as a result of ill fortune or of forces beyond their control. And hence it must be said that they are often not to blame for such shortcomings in the way they are to blame for their failings in matters of wisdom, good judgment, and self-control.

I will discuss this problem soon. For the present is it not apparent that even if sometimes individuals may not themselves be entirely to blame, as isolated individuals, for their lack of the basic necessities of their existence, it is nonetheless certainly the case that for people to provide themselves with such necessities is one of their inescapable responsibilities as human beings and is a responsibility that they have to take seriously and cannot simply write off, as if their being provided with such necessities were not an obligation of theirs, but rather something that they could blithely claim should be theirs by right? Indeed, do not these considerations return us once again to our earlier considerations in regard to private property? For as I noted earlier, wealth and property are certainly means to the living of human life and even to the living of life well. But people have to work and labor for wealth and property, and they have an obligation to occupy themselves with providing themselves with them—if not each and every one of them working individually, then certainly working in concert and cooperation with fellow human beings. Does this not also account for the fact that once property has been acquired by human beings, it is theirs by right; and, with the qualifications that I have already introduced, it is theirs by right of the labor that has had to be expended for its acquisition and appropriation? But in no sense are wealth and property theirs by right, simply by virtue of their being able to claim a need for such things, however desperate that need may be.

With this, then, may we not be said to have succeeded in dismissing any supposed right-claims to so-called positive rights? All the same, we cannot simply terminate this discussion with the conclusion that was just reached. Rather, it is now necessary to show how many of the substantive elements in so-called positive rights can perhaps be vouchsafed to individuals living in a political community, even though this must be done as a matter of what might best be called public policy, rather than by honoring individuals' natural rights. Indeed, have we not already observed that the policies of political associations are, and need to be, directed toward ends that go far beyond merely securing the rights of individuals? Indeed, the natural and proper end of any political community must rightly be the attainment of a common good. And although, of course, the value of any so-called common good has to be understood in terms of the flourishing and well-being which it affords the individual members of the community, there still is presumably much more to any notion of a common good than the mere guarantee to individuals that their lives, liberties, and property will be respected.

Again, consider how a notion like that of the common good needs to be understood and why it has inescapably to be reckoned as part and parcel of the obligatory end of any and every human individual. For is it not practically, if not absolutely, inconceivable that an individual human being not have at least some concern for the common good of the community of which that individual happens to be a member? For one thing, every individual must recognize that, as Aristotle remarked, although it might be barely possible for a person to live outside of the *polis* or the community, he certainly cannot live well. For only through cooperative and coordinated community action is it possible for individual human beings to enjoy an adequately high standard of living, to pursue the arts and sciences, to have proper facilities for their health, their recreation, and their general pursuit of happiness. And so it follows that outside of a *polis* or a community, it is out of the question for an individual to acquit himself of his natural obligations as a human being to be and become a truly human person. It is in this sense that the attainment of at least some common good of the community as a whole is inseparable from the natural end and goal of every human individual—an end or goal which a person has simply in virtue of being human. There may be no end of differences, disagreements, and disputes between individuals as to what a common good consists of or as to how that common good may best be attained. But that at least some sort of common good must be part and parcel of the natural and obligatory end of each human individual there surely can be no difference, disagreement, or dispute.

Why, then, is it not conceivable that within a given political community there should come to be a general agreement that what the community needed were better educational facilities, better health care, better systems of public transportation, and so on? The particular community in question might not have sufficient resources, either of wealth or of expertise, to accomplish such objectives, or at least to accomplish them all at once. And then, of course, it would be unwise and even wrong to embark on overly ambitious projects. Or again, there might be serious misjudgments on the part of both the public authorities and the community as a whole as to how best these objectives might be attained, even supposing the community's resources to be sufficient for the purpose. An excessive and uncritical reliance, for example, might be placed upon so-called public, as opposed to private, enterprise to accomplish such goals. And so something like the constructivist fallacy might well come to be committed. Or even more serious, per-

184

haps, is the danger that in carrying out such public policies as are aimed at achieving various features and aspects of a common good, the so-called negative rights of individual citizens could be seriously infringed upon and thus irreparably compromised.

Still, for all of this, and for all of the dangers and disabilities connected with fixing upon the wrong objectives to achieve the common good, or perhaps choosing the wrong means to accomplish such purposes, there can surely be no denying that any political community needs to be, and even has the obligation to be, ordered toward the attainment of a common good. Additionally, such a common good as might thus be aimed at could comprise many of those very citizen benefits that on the theory of positive rights were claimed for the individual citizens as being theirs by right. But what we are now envisaging is a situation in which these same benefits for individual citizens would be aimed at simply as a matter of public policy and not as a matter of the citizens' individual rights.

To illustrate how any political community, and certainly any government of such a community, cannot but aim at the achievement of a common good, let me quote from the inaugural address of President Benjamin Harrison. The occasion was March 4, 1889. Not only was President Harrison a Republican, but in addition it is hard to imagine any president of the United States who might be said to have been less given to the idea of anything like the modern welfare state. He could scarcely be said to have entertained such an idea even in his wildest dreams or nightmares. Notwithstanding, upon the occasion of his inauguration, Harrison "drew a contrast between the now 'thirty-eight populous and prosperous States' and the thirteen States of Washington's first inauguration, 'weak in everything except courage and love of liberty.' He recognized, however, that we had 'not attained an ideal condition' for 'not all of our people are happy and prosperous. But on the whole the opportunities offered to the individual to secure comforts of life are better than are found elsewhere and largely better than they were here 100 years ago.'"[30]

With these words, Harrison would seem to be implying that even though not all of the people of the then United States had attained the "ideal condition" of happiness and prosperity, it was nevertheless an

30. James Ford Rhodes, *History of the United States*, 8 vols. (2nd ed., New York, 1920), VIII, 328.

ideal that was devoutly to be wished for; and not merely to be wished for but to be striven for; and to be striven for not merely by individuals but to be sought after by the entire body of the citizens working together. Moreover, recognizing that such an ideal of happiness and prosperity for all was the consensus of all, it was apparently further presumed by Harrison that it was his duty, and the duty of all public officials within his administration, to do what they could to implement this ideal and bring about its realization.

Of course, this did not mean that President Harrison, or even necessarily any of his compatriots in those days, had great visions of trying to effect this national ideal of happiness and prosperity for all by elaborate schemes of state planning. They doubtless were scarcely tempted by the constructivist fallacy in Hayek's sense. Instead, Harrison and the other officeholders of his Republican regime were no doubt convinced that the only way to bring about such a general happiness and prosperity within the nation had to be through the encouragement of what today would be called free enterprise.

Yet for present purposes, what needs to be noted is that whatever their views may have been in 1889 as to the best means for attaining such an end, whether through public or private enterprise, they took their end to be nothing less than the attainment of a common good. Nor did there seem to be much disagreement as to the basic elements of that common good. And no less did they recognize that it was not merely their desire but the duty of both public officials and the nation as a whole to work to improve the lot of all of the individual citizens.

Was this, though, because it was supposed that every citizen had a right to happiness and prosperity, a right for which the individual might sue in the courts to compel the government and the public authorities to provide him with as his by right? Of course not. For that matter, even so indisputable a democrat as Thomas Jefferson never claimed that human beings had an inalienable right to happiness but only to the pursuit of happiness. And so likewise, it would appear that even in Harrison's rock-ribbed Republican regime, it was clearly recognized that the public authorities and the nation as a whole had a clear duty and obligation and responsibility to try to provide for the general happiness and prosperity of all. At the same time, never once was it supposed that answering to such duties and obligations on the part of the authorities and the nation as a whole, there were in any sense corresponding rights—positive rights—that individual citizens could claim as rightfully theirs.

However plausible may have been the argument just concluded, its actual conclusion might strike one as being somewhat anomolous. For how can it possibly be maintained that political communities and the political authorities in those communities have a responsibility and even a duty to try to secure certain benefits for the citizens within the community without its being said that such individuals have a right to such benefits or are entitled to them, at least in natural law? Nevertheless, to show that a situation in which there are duties without corresponding rights is not anomolous, we need to make a quick detour from the domain of public morality to that of private morality.

And here just consider the case of the Good Samaritan. After all, this has been a common illustration in recent moral philosophy. Accordingly, could it not be said that the priest and the Levite who "passed by on the other side" had a duty to do something to relieve the poor man who had "fallen among thieves," been "stripped of his raiment," "wounded," and "left half dead"? They may not have been under any legal obligation to do anything—certainly not according to such public law as may have existed at that time and place. Nevertheless, that the priest and Levite had an obligation under the moral law that they both presumably recognized could scarcely be denied. Likewise, even the Good Samaritan, however much he may have done what he did out of the goodness of his heart, must surely have recognized that he had a moral duty and obligation to do as much, whatever his actual feelings and inclinations may chance to have been.

In contrast, consider the case of the poor man who had gone down from Jerusalem to Jericho and had fallen among the thieves (Luke 10:25–37). Could he be said, either in natural law or in civil law, to have had any right to the ministrations of such strangers as might have come along the same road and could either have turned aside to help him or else passed on the other side? Surely, the answer must be, "No." For however much he may have needed help, he could hardly have claimed that he had any right or title to such aid and comfort. In fact, that such help or assistance should have been his by right would have seriously compromised the very gratitude that we hope he displayed on receiving it. But more than that, and generally, if what a person receives is his by right, then this would indeed appear to compromise, if not actually preclude, any exercise of virtues like those of charity, generosity,

187

beneficence, or whatever. For how could one be said to be generous if what one gives to a person is his by right?

On the other hand, because what a donor or benefactor gives to another is a free gift, and not something that the recipient can be said to have any right to, certainly does not mean that the donor may not be under a duty and obligation to be generous or beneficent or charitable. On the contrary, in the dramatic Chapter 25 of St. Matthew's Gospel we are told that "inasmuch as ye have [not] done it unto one of the least of these my brethren, ye have [not] done it unto me." And what is it that one is supposed to have done to one of the least of these? It is no less than to have fed the hungry, clothed the naked, visited the sick, received the homeless, visited the prisoners, and so on. And what was, and presumably is, the penalty for one's not having exercised this virtue of charity to which one was obligated in such circumstances? The answer that is given is, in no uncertain terms: "Depart from me, ye cursed, into everlasting fire." Needless to say, I do not cite this example on any assumption that because it is scriptural, the lesson it contains must therefore be true. Rather, the point is that in the ordinary use of moral notions and concepts, one can find may examples from a great variety of sources (the New Testament included), all indicating that people are continually being held to have certain duties toward others, even though those others have no right-claims to the ministrations that others are obligated to give them.

"Very well," you will say, "but this all has to do with personal morality, whereas our present concern is with the political community and with what might be called the public morality of public officials in the exercise of their public duties. Is there a like case here, in which it can be said that certain public policies are no less than obligatory and in this sense morally incumbent upon human communities and the public authorities within those communities, even though such morally obligatory policies are not called forth by any so-called positive rights on the part of individual citizens?"

Responding to this challenge, why may it not be said that in the public domain, as contrasted with that of private morality, there are both duties and virtues corresponding to those one finds in the private sphere? Thus I have already noted that the public authorities ought to reflect what is surely no more than the right and proper concern of the community as a whole for the common good. But the common good is indissociable from the good of the individual members of the community. Accordingly, what exactly is the characteristic attitude, or rather virtue, which members of the community should manifest toward their fellow citizens who are engaged with them in their common enterprise?

In an earlier section I made a tentative approach to answering such a question by suggesting that what I then put forward as the model of the human family was a far better model for understanding what the rightful attitude of members of a community should be toward one another than was any model of the state, or of society, as an organism. Still, I insisted that such a family model was far from entirely appropriate for a right understanding of the human community. And one reason is that the model was not entirely apposite presumably because the virtue that individual members of a family ought to exercise mutually toward one another is that of love or of what Aristotle called friendship. Moreover, the example of the Good Samaritan should further remind us that when it comes to a question of membership in Christ's Kingdom, or in the Kingdom of Heaven, it is our Christian duty to love our neighbors as ourselves. The relevant virtue in this connection is the so-called theological virtue of Christian charity, which in many ways is but a theologized version of Aristotle's virtue of friendship.

Clearly, though, one would need to say that it is perhaps far too much to expect that in the ordinary secular human community, the virtue that should be demanded of all citizens in their attitudes toward each other should necessarily be either the virtue of love or friendship in Aristotle's sense or the virtue of charity in the Christian sense. But then, what is the virtue or proper moral disposition that is called for, so far as the *polis* or the secular human community is concerned?

Of course, the virtue of justice is always called for, all men being called upon all of the time to exercise justice toward one another. Still, the virtue of justice is hardly sufficient as the sole political virtue, for reasons that I have already touched upon at least tangentially. For the virtue of justice—at least, so-called commutative justice—would seem to be correlated with human or individual rights; justice being by definition the rendering to each his due, that which is a person's due must presumably be that which is his right—for example, his life, liberty, and property. My point here is that, when it comes to political action aimed at the common good, much of that action is aimed at far more than merely securing and guaranteeing the rights of individuals.

How, then, are we to characterize the virtue or attitude that is reflected, for example, in President Harrison's inaugural—an attitude or disposition which I expounded as being simply one of concern for the securing and preserving of the common good, this being construed, in turn, as comprising the peace, prosperity, and happiness of all of the citizens? What, then, should we call this public concern, which is proper to all public officials and which also should be shared by all citizens in their public capacity as citizens? We cannot call it love or friendship or charity. Nor is it exhausted by the notion of justice either. Should we call it "fraternity"? Perish the thought. For that conjures up, on the one hand, the debasement of the notion of brotherly love that was both sentimentalized and brutalized in the French Revolution and, on the other hand, the literal brotherly love that I have suggested is proper more especially in the family or in the Christian community. As an alternative, what about the idea of a virtue that might be called "public-spiritedness" or perhaps "beneficence"? Perhaps that definition might do as well as any. For why could it not be taken to mean a disposition to contribute to and to bring about as far as possible the well-being of one's fellows?

And now you may well ask, "But what does all of this have to do with law and justice as these are manifested in the legal system of a particular community and particularly in the courts?" May I answer, "Nothing!" For is it not proper to note that the courts have nothing to say about whether the policies of government display a wise beneficence any more than presumably the courts have anything to say about the personal morality of individuals—their courage, temperance, charity, good judgment, even temper, and so on? It is true, of course, that political policies of government often tend to infringe upon the negative rights of individuals; and then a resort to the courts is relevant and proper. For as I have already observed, the business of the courts is, or should be, primarily with questions of individual rights—which is to say, negative rights; for of so-called positive rights, I do not think they exist.

And now for a somewhat different issue. Is it not of significance perhaps that thus far in this discussion of natural rights I have said nothing about equality? And yet does not equality have no less an ancient and honorable title to being one of our basic human rights than do life, liberty, and property? As well as the French revolutionary slogan of "Liberty, Equality, and Fraternity," we certainly all as Americans either are or should be ever mindful of the words of the Gettysburg Address: "Four score and seven years ago, our forefathers brought forth upon this Continent a new nation, conceived in liberty, and dedicated to the proposition that all men are created equal."

No doubt, in Lincoln's mind, and particularly on the occasion of the Gettysburg Address, the notion of equality connoted the notion of the right of all men equally to be to be free and thus not be enslaved. That is, all men should be reckoned as equally human in that the same basic rights and responsibilities are to be recognized as attaching to all men alike, simply in virtue of their humanity. And so it is that no man may be reckoned as any less a man, and therefore any less a responsible moral agent, and thus a political animal, than any other man.

Yet surely, this does not mean that all men have equal talents, abilities, training, or accomplishments. On the contrary, although they are all equally human, this scarcely implies that no distinctions may ever be drawn between individual human beings, either as to what they can do or possibly already have done. Yet does not the fact of this latter inequality generate a positive right on the part of less favored individuals that such inequalities be rectified and that perhaps society or the community should do what it can to bring all persons up to the same level of achievement so far as possible?

And now we can begin to see wherein lies the real challenge of the notion of the equality of men. For that challenge arises, not so much from the notion of all men's being equally human, that is, being equally rational and responsible moral agents, but rather because, being unequal in their resources and abilities, it might seem only right that such inequalities should be remedied so that all men might thereby become the equals of one another in the second, no less than in the first, of the two senses of equality. Moreover, supposing that men do have a right to equality in this second sense—that is, to an equality in their resources and abilities—then that would be what I have been calling a positive right. If anything, equality in this second sense could be considered as the source or matrix out of which all other positive rights arise.

What would seem to give this challenge its peculiar bite is that if men do have a right to equality in the second sense, there would seem to be no way such a positive right could be realized or brought about except at the expense of what I have been designating as those basic negative rights of human individuals, *viz.*, their rights to life, liberty, and property. For how can the level of those who are less fortunate in the community be raised so as to make them equal to their fellows in their resources and their abilities unless it be through the concerted action of the *polis* or the community? And how can this concerted action be brought about except through commandeering the resources of the more fortunate and requiring them to give of their lives, their liberties, and their properties, even against their wills, supposing that the general level and well-being of the members of the entire community might thereby be raised and thus equalized? In short, must not any *polis* or community in which equality is recognized as being a positive right make its own the familiar maxim, "To each according to his needs, and from each according to his abilities"?

Having thus set the stage and drawn the issue with respect to the question of there being a positive right to equality on the part of all, which all may claim as a natural right, is there any way that we can rebut this idea of a positive right to equality? To this end, I propose to avail myself of a trenchant line of criticism that Fred D. Miller has directed at the general Rawlsian position in regard to equality. Miller begins by introducing a most useful terminology. The inequalities among human beings, he says, are attributable either to an inequality of *natural assets* (that is, the varying natural endowments which individual human beings may be recognized as having) or to inequalities in *nonhuman resources* (that is, inequalities in respect to "geographical regions, transportable physical objects and intangible products of human labor"). Moreover, as Miller interprets Rawls, it would seem that Rawls would "argue that the benefits of distribution of natural assets and nonhuman assets are subject to a conception of justice that is essentially egalitarian."[31] In other words, Rawls's famed two principles of justice are thought to operate in such a way as to attempt to compensate the less fortunate individuals in the community for the disadvantages from which they suffer as a result of their inequalities in natural assets and/or nonhuman resources.

But on what basis is Rawls able to argue that justice requires such an equalization among human beings with respect to both their natural and their nonhuman assets? Apparently the Rawlsian argument is based on the notion of "desert." And indeed, it is not to be denied that often-

31. Fred D. Miller, Jr., "The Natural Right to Private Property," in *The Libertarian Reader*, ed. Tibor R. Machan (Totowa, N.J., 1982), 275–85, quotes p. 276.

times, if not most of the time, the more favorable circumstances that one individual finds himself to be in, as compared with many of his fellow citizens—circumstances involving either greater natural assets or more plentiful nonhuman resources—are frequently owing not so much to the individual's own greater desert but simply to his greater good fortune.

And what conclusion does Rawls draw from the fact that inequalities among men are often more the result of fortune than of desert? The conclusion is—and here Miller quotes from Rawls: justice requires "in effect, an agreement [among the members of a community] to regard the distribution of natural talents as a common asset and to share in the benefits of this distribution whatever it turns out to be." Spelling out still further the implications of his conception of justice, Rawls suggests that "no one deserves his place in the distribution of natural endowments, any more than one deserves one's initial starting place in society." And then Rawls proceeds—again as quoted by Miller: "The notion of desert seems not to apply to these cases. Thus the more advantaged representative man cannot say that he deserves and therefore has a right to a scheme of cooperation in which he is permitted to acquire benefits in ways that do not contribute to the welfare of others." And so it is that Rawls feels warranted in enunciating his second principle of justice as a "difference principle": "Social and economic inequalities, for example inequalities of wealth and authority, are just only if they result in compensating benefits for everyone, and in particular for the least advantaged in society."[32]

To all of this Miller replies that a serious non sequitur is involved in this reasoning of Rawls. Miller suggests that there are three main stages in Rawls's argument: (1) An individual does not deserve his or her natural assets. (2) There is no reason to assign an individual exclusive title to his or her natural assets. (3) Everyone has title to the individual's natural assets.[33] Following Nozick, however, Miller insists that there is no warrant for the inference from (1) to (2), for why should it be assumed that "people are entitled only to what they deserve"? And as for the entire inference from (1) to (2) and from (2) to (3), Miller makes the following devastating rejoinder: "It is not at all necessary, 'from the standpoint of common sense,' to prove that I deserve my left

32. *Ibid.*, 278, 276.
33. *Ibid.*, 278. For a similar argument, see Bruce A. Ackerman, *Social Justice in the Liberal State* (New Haven, 1980).

kidney, in order to have a basis for claiming that it shouldn't be real-located to contribute to the welfare of others. From this standpoint to the fact that it is part of my body and is therefore *mine* provides a sufficient basis for a title to its continued possession."[34]

What more need be said to rebut the usual egalitarian argument in favor of making equality a positive right? For does it not emerge clearly from Miller's critique of Rawls that no sooner does one assume that nothing can be claimed to be ours by right than it must first be shown to be ours by virtue of desert? Yet such an argument would clearly undercut any claim we human beings might have even to our so-called negative rights, such as I have laboriously argued for heretofore. For in the light of my earlier analysis of our so-called negative rights to life, liberty, and property, there are things that may be said to be ours simply by nature and thus not things that we must first show ourselves to deserve in order that we may have title to them.

To shift for a moment to a Judeo-Christian theological perspective for purposes of illustration, what human beings receive simply as a result of God's gift in creation, *viz.*, their very being, their lives, their liberty, are not to be regarded as things that God gives to people only on the basis of their past deserts. Indeed, the very idea is ruled out by the notion of a creation *de novo*. At the same time, though, what a man is endowed with by birth and by nature, he is then obligated to use and to exploit so that thereby he may become what as a human being he ought to be. That is the basis of the individual human being's right not to be deprived of what is his, be it by nature or by chance—*viz.*, that such gifts are needed by him if he is to attain his natural end and natural perfection as a human person. Moreover, should one be inclined to say that it is not fair that the Creator should have endowed some with greater gifts than others, thereby giving them a greater advantage in the business of living, the answer must surely be that the fault must lie with God the giver and not with the human beings who have been the more fortunate beneficiaries of such gifts. In other words, it would seem that Rawls should have taken God to task, rather than those who are the recipients of gifts far greater than they deserved.

Of course, this is not to say that those in any given community who have been more fortunately endowed than many of their fellows might not feel called upon—even obligated—either through their own ef-

34. Miller, "The Natural Right to Private Property," 278.

194

forts or working through the agencies of government to try to make up for some of the inequalities in human society that they see round about them. But as I have already noted, this would be to act out of motives of beneficence or charity and not out of regard for what might properly be called the rights of others. For there do not seem to be any positive rights in this sense.

Having completed these arguments, all designed to show that there are no grounds for supposing that there are any positive rights, this discussion must come to a close with a belated and yet unqualified recognition that there is at least one exception to the rule that there are no positive rights. It is a signally striking exception, for it concerns the institution of the human family, and more specifically the children within such families. For may not infants and small children, and minors generally, be able to claim rights to care, nurture, and education from their parents? And presumably, if in given instances parents are unable to provide such care and oversight, then will not the responsibility for such services devolve upon the *polis* or the community as a whole?

I do not propose to discuss in detail this one major exception to the rule of no positive rights. Instead, I merely put it forward as something that should be evident. And why do I abdicate responsibility to treat this case with the care that it deserves? The basic answer is like the one Dr. Johnson once gave to the woman who asked him why he had defined "pastern" as the knee of a horse: "Sheer ignorance, Madam, sheer ignorance!" And so likewise, I do not have the sufficient sociological knowledge or the requisite sophistication to discuss with much intelligence the role of the family in present-day society.

But ignorance may not be the only reason for my sin of omission in this case. It may be uneasiness as well. For when I consider very superficially what some of the implications would seem to be of the notion of the rights of children within the context of a natural-law philosophy as a whole, I find these implications to be puzzling and disturbing. For consider what my overall justification has been regarding human rights generally, be they either negative rights or positive rights.

Basically, that justification has been that human beings have natural rights only to the extent that the needs are ones that individuals could not satisfy simply on their own and without the help and cooperation of others. And of course, there is the further qualification that these right-claims which human beings have with respect to the satisfaction of such needs are valid only to the extent that the needs are ones that people cannot satisfy by themselves. In other words, human beings have rights only to the extent that they have prior duties and responsibilities toward themselves, which they could never acquit themselves of unless the necessary means thereof were vouchsafed to them, and needs which they could never put themselves in a position to satisfy.

Minor children are certainly among those who could qualify for right-claims by this standard. For they can hardly be expected to be able to provide themselves with the proper care, nurture, and education that they need if they are to become the human persons that they ought to become. Yet remember that these right-claims are entirely conditional upon children having the regular natural duties and responsibilities to become the rational and responsible individuals that they ought to become. Consider, though, what must happen to such obligations and responsibilities of a human individual in this regard if he should be found to be a hopeless defective. That is, suppose that on the basis of the best medical knowledge it could be established that such and such an individual was precluded, absolutely and irrevocably, from ever being able to live rationally and intelligently—that is, from ever being able to live such a life as a human being ought to live, in contrast, say, to that of a mere vegetable?

Supposing that such an incurable condition could be determined with reasonable certainty, would a human individual, suffering from such a condition, be said to have the duty to make something of himself or to try to become the person that a human being ought to be and become? And if the duty or obligation of the individual should have thus ceased to exist, what of the right-claims of that individual to care, nurture, and education by his parents, or, if not by his parents, by the community and by the society? Would not such right-claims then lose their validity as well, if the obligation and the duty upon which they were conditioned could no longer be considered as binding? And yet what other implications must all of this have if not to throw open the floodgates to abortion, euthanasia, infanticide, and the like?

Frankly, I am repelled by such implications. And yet I am unfortunately not too clear in my own mind as to just how such implications are to be obviated or rebutted. In the present day the arguments pro and con for abortion, for example, would seem regrettably oversimplified. On the one hand, the Utilitarians think that practices such as abortion, euthanasia, and infanticide may be justified in light of their consequences—that is, if they make for the greatest happiness of the greatest number. The opponents of such practices, however, do little more than contend that these practices are wrong simply because they violate certain absolute principles, be these divine commands or categorical imperatives or whatever.

My earlier arguments all tended to show that neither considerations of a Utilitarian nor those of a Kantian character can serve to find genuinely and rationally determinable moral rules and principles. Nevertheless, in this particular case my justification for proper moral rules would seem hardly to work either. For if duties are conditioned entirely upon our natural ends, and if our rights in turn are entirely conditional upon our duties and responsibilities toward ourselves to try to achieve our natural ends, then what if in certain circumstances these so-called duties to self would appear to be no longer binding? Would not, then, our rights as human individuals cease as well, our negative rights no less than our positive rights? And can one accept any such consequence in the hypothetical cases I have just cited?

The Common Good and
the Safeguarding of the Rights of Individuals

Throughout this discussion of rights, have I not been attempting the impossible—or at least the improbable—of trying to carry water on both shoulders? For continually I have been insisting that what I have called the government or the political authorities of any *polis* or community has a twofold function or responsibility: (1) to promote the common good; and (2) to protect individual citizens in their rights. Yet are these two functions reconcilable with one another?

No doubt it is an integral part of any notion of the common good that the rights of the individual citizens should be respected. Yet surely this is hardly enough to show that the two functions are not bound to come into conflict with one another. For instance, earlier on I made a point that I favored not any mere "passive state . . . in which governmental social control is not a significant factor in the life of the community"; rather, my option was for "an active state . . . in which governmental social control is a significant factor in the life of the community." And yet what must such an active state be concerned with doing if not coordinating the activities and labors of the members of the body politic so that as many of the goods of life as possible—food, clothing, and shelter; knowledge and learning; recreation and relaxation; associations and friendships; opportunities for religious worship; and so on—may be made available to each and all alike? To this end, however, the public authorities would certainly need both to commandeer and to organize the manifold talents and resources of the individuals in the community so as to further any such common good for each and all. And yet how can the state thus avail itself of the lives and liberties and properties of citizens without finding itself compelled to encroach seriously upon the rights of the individuals involved?

Once again, it is of course true that if the citizens should all be disposed voluntarily to give of their talents and resources in order that the common good should be more completely achieved, there would be no problem. But alas, in the world as we know it, it is hardly to be expected that there will be very many communities in which the common good will ever be attained through purely voluntary contributions by the citizens involved. And so the unhappy conclusion would seem inescapable: there is no way in which the business of any political community can ever be properly or adequately transacted save at the expense of the individual citizens and thus in violation of many of their admittedly personal and private rights.

Thus already in this discussion of so-called "positive rights," we have seen that there is no way such rights could be vouchsafed to individuals—for example, the right to health care, a living wage, old-age benefits, adequate education, and the like—unless through expropriation by the government, and against the wills of the individuals involved, of what Fred Miller has called both the natural assets and the nonhuman resources of individual members of the community. Save for the one possible exception of the rights of children to proper care, nurture, and education, I insisted that there might well be no positive rights. And this in turn might help matters somewhat, so far as our being able to reconcile claims made on behalf of the common good with the rights of individual citizens. For if there are no so-called positive rights that the public authorities would have to be charged with trying to satisfy, then governments would surely not have that excuse for raiding private citizens and taking from them what presumably would be theirs by natural right. Yet any such bracketing of these so-called positive rights would seem scarcely to help with the resolution of our immediate problem. For is it possible to get on even with a minimal prosecution of the common good without its quickly being found necessary to trench very seriously upon what I have insisted are absolutely fundamental negative rights of individual citizens? Supposing the functions of government are cut back to the most minimal of states, one wonders whether even then it would not be found necessary to deprive private citizens upon occasion of some of their negative rights if the functions of the *polis* are to be adequately carried on. Accordingly, one is thus led to suspect that doubtless the only consistent position for the maintenance of individual rights would be one in which an unequivocal option came to be made in favor of anarchism, as opposed to archism. That is, it would have to be a case of not the merely passive state, as contrasted with the active state, that would need to be opted for, but rather no government at all.

At first glance this solution might seem a little extreme, this contention that in any consistent defense of individual rights there can be no compromise with government or with archism. Yet recall that in my earlier quotation from Blackstone, he spoke of the rights to life, liberty, and property as being "absolute rights." And must not an absolute right of an individual be one that is not subject to any qualification or restriction? And if our natural rights as human beings are subject to no restrictions or qualifications, they certainly cannot be subject to restrictions or qualifications by government or by political authorities. Moreover, it would seem that Blackstone gives as his reason why our natural rights are thus not subject to restriction, even in the political sphere, the fact that absolute rights are such rights as "would belong to their persons merely in a state of nature, and which every man is entitled to enjoy whether out of society or in it." In other words, it is what we might call the state-of-nature thinking that Blackstone was partial to that led him to think that, people being entitled to rights by nature, no state or condition of civil society could ever justify a purely arbitrary and artificial deprivation of a person of what was his by nature.

Coming down to the present day, one wonders if it is not a comparable state-of-nature thinking that has led a thinker like Nozick to subscribe to a doctrine of rights that would appear to make such rights absolute, almost in the manner of Blackstone. Thus he says that human individuals are "different individuals with separate lives." And a little further on he suggests that as human beings we are all "distinct individuals each with his *own* life to lead." Nozick would seem to conclude that such separateness and distinctness being what characterizes human beings by nature, or in the state of nature, it must follow that "no one may be sacrificed for others"; "there is no moral outweighing of one of our lives by others so as to lead to a greatest overall *social* good."[35] And might this perhaps be interpreted to mean that there is no way any mere socially devised requirements or conventions or arrangements could ever take precedence over what nature has entitled us to?

I find it difficult to see what cogency Nozick's apparent argument for his conclusion here has. Thus the mere fact that human beings are separate existences would hardly in itself seem to warrant the conclusion that therefore human beings have a right to be respected in their separate existences. After all, one oak tree is no less a separate life, or a separate existence, from another oak tree, and yet that scarcely means that oaks are under a moral obligation to respect the rule of "No one of us oaks may be sacrificed for others." Less trivially and more specifically with respect to members of the human species alone, might it not seem that to argue that, because human beings have separate lives or separate existences, be it in nature or by nature, they therefore have a right to their separateness—is not this ostensibly like an inference from "is" to "ought" or from facts of nature to norms of nature?

Waiving these points of criticism, however, and coming to what most would say is the truly substantive import of what Nozick is claiming, is the point not that individuals' rights and entitlements—say, to life, liberty, and property—are evident simply from nature and therefore ultimate and absolute? Accordingly, there would appear to be no way such rights could ever morally, rightfully, or justifiably be sacrificed in favor of a so-called common good. In other words, whatever the needs of the community or of society might be, they could never, either in right or in justice, take precedence over the rights of individuals.

But, then, our question is, How is any political organization possible under these circumstances? For must it not be acknowledged that as soon as human individuals band together into any organization, be it that of a *polis* or even that of a private club, situations are bound to arise in which the common interests of the group will tend to conflict with, and even be inimical to, various of the private interests of various of the individuals who make up the group—in other words, and more

35. Nozick, *Anarchy, State, and Utopia*, 33–34.

specifically, to their lives and liberties and properties and in many different ways.

Thus, for instance, let us take the most farfetched example that one could think of. Suppose that some friends of mine and I decide that we want to organize a club for the obviously innocent and yet nowadays highly gratuitous purpose of meeting periodically to read together certain classics of Greek literature and philosophy. It should be apparent from the context of the present discussion that even so apparently irrelevant and idle an undertaking as that of a small Greek reading club would still by its very nature have to be reckoned as a common enterprise; and as a common enterprise, it would seem necessary that someone be at least tacitly recognized as the leader of the group (call him the "authority") and that the group have some rules, even if only tacit ones, as to times and places of meetings, texts to be read, the order and conduct of the meetings, and so on. Suppose, though, that some one or ones in the group do not like the arrangements: they do not want to expend their time, energies, and resources in the ways called for by the rules and organization of the group. "All right," you will say, "they don't have to join the group in the first place. Or if they did join and did once agree that things would be done in certain ways, but then came later to feel that the common enterprise ought to be carried on on somewhat different lines, there is nothing to prevent them from withdrawing or resigning. And where would there be any injustice or violation of rights in all of that? Is any more involved than either to play the game or get out?"

But is this so easy a resolution in principle of the problem of the individual's rights as it is in practice? For suppose that the dissident members of the group do not want to leave the club; they like reading Greek texts, and in all likelihood there is no place else where they could go to gratify such a desire. After all, Greek reading clubs are not as readily available in most communities, as are, say, drugstores or even pawnshops. So where else are the dissident club members to go if the affairs of the club are not being run as they want them to be, and in consequence their resources are being used in ways they do not want them to be used, and even their liberty of action is being forced in directions they do not want to follow? Hence in these circumstances why could not such dissident club members claim that their absolute rights to their liberty, their time, and in small measure perhaps even to their property, were being infringed upon?

201

To be sure, if the club were to be run in the way the dissidents might want it to be, that would preclude others in the group from having things go their way, and they could then claim that their rights were being violated. But must not the lesson that is to be learned from this petty and insignificant example of the Greek club be anything but petty and insignificant? Whatever the human group may be, whether it be an insignificant group of superannuated professors who think they would like to read some ancient Greek, or whether it be a top-flight symphony orchestra, an efficient business partnership, the New York Yankees baseball team, or the Constitution of the United States— in any and all such cases of common enterprise, the very cooperative, and hence coordinated, nature of the enterprise must in all likelihood involve at least some interference with, or unwanted restriction upon, the private rights of individuals. Hence must not the inescapable consequence be that if rights are to be taken seriously, anarchism is the only proper option—and not just an option on the level of the state so-called but right down the line, including even the most insignificant groups of human individuals. In other words, any taking of rights seriously would thus appear inevitably to involve an across-the-board anarchism.

Perhaps, though, we can find a justification for an archism rather than anarchism. And why might it not consist of a scaling down of the notion of absolute rights to one merely of inalienable rights? For the conclusion reached above would seem to be intolerable. Must we not acknowledge that one both has to take rights seriously and yet also recognize that one has certain duties and responsibilities for furthering the common good? Nor is that all, for surely there must be a way whereby one might be able to accede to both of these demands without having to find oneself caught up in a perennial inconsistency. Unhappily, though, it would seem that contemporary rights-theorists have not found the way to avoid this perennial inconsistency. Instead, it is as if with these theorists their left hand never knows what their right hand is doing.

For instance, have we not often had the experience of one of our latter-day rights-theorists first coming on strong, proclaiming that he is one who always takes rights seriously; and then in the next moment he clears his throat and whispers something to the effect that well, of course, there are times when the absolute rights of individuals will have to be qualified and toned down for the sake of the common good. Or on the other hand, our rights-theorist may first come out loud and strong in support of the notion that in political society there can be no avoiding some such principle as that of "to each according to his needs, and from each according to his abilities"; and then in the next moment, and more quietly, he will say that it is nonetheless important that one never deprive a human being of what is properly his own—his life, his liberty, or his property.

Surely, though, this will never do. Instead, there must be some way to reconcile the claims of the individual that his private rights be respected with the claims of the community that the common weal must be fostered and furthered. And to this end, might we not begin by raising the question of whether, after all, individual rights are absolute, as Blackstone said they were or as Nozick seems to imply that they are? Thus recall the ground on which Blackstone seemed to think that individual rights were absolute. Presumably, it was simply because they were rights which people could be said to have enjoyed within the state of nature. For if people have entitlements to their freedom and their property by nature, and thus independent of any institutions of civil society, then such entitlements may in no way be qualified or restricted by any mere social conventions. On the other hand, suppose that a so-called state of nature is dismissed as no more than a fiction, or even a delusion, and suppose, instead, that man is regarded as being a political animal by nature, will that not tend to put an entirely different construction upon things?

Specifically, why might we not say that human rights are not so much absolute as they are inalienable? For the distinction here hardly amounts to a mere word quibble. In the first place, in the natural-law theory of rights that I have been trying to expound and defend, individual rights have never been presented as being absolute so much as they are derivative and dependent. Fundamentally, that is, they depend on certain prior duties that are not to be reckoned as duties toward others, such as are merely correlative to the rights those others are said to possess in turn. Instead, the entire line of contention in natural-law theory is that the rights of an individual are entirely dependent upon, and understandable in terms of, those specific duties which an individual may be said to have toward himself—and these precisely as contrasted with the duties an individual has toward others. More specifically, therefore, our rights to life, liberty, and property are justified only to the extent that they serve as necessary conditions to our living our own lives, making something of ourselves, and in general acquitting ourselves of our basic responsibility to be and become truly human beings.

And now note the further implications of this distinction between rights thought of as being absolute in a state of nature and rights thought of as being conditioned upon their affording us the necessary conditions for the living of our lives in such a way as is prescribed for us by nature. Thus on the state-of-nature view, it is often averred that there can be no limitations placed upon how we choose to employ our lives, our liberties, and our property so long as we do not interfere with the freedom of others to exercise their rights in any way they see fit. In contrast, in natural-law theory, a man's freedom of action with respect to the use of his life, liberty, and property may cease to be justified if his unimpeded employment of these things outruns his needs and requirements for the attainment of his natural end. Thus suppose, for example, that an individual were to use his liberty not toward the attainment of his natural end but simply to do as he pleased and whenever he pleased—even to wreck his own life, supposing that such a course were the one that he was pleased to follow.

Why not remind ourselves of the earlier-cited example of the earl of Rochester, who devoted his singular talents, both as a man and as a poet, to celebrating the pleasures of drunkenness, licentiousness, and debauchery? Indeed, so far from pursuing man's natural end as a rational animal, which, as we have seen, would consist simply in the exercise of what Aristotle called the intellectual and moral virtues, Rochester made sport of the whole thing, saying that he would rather

> ... be a dog, a monkey, or a bear,
> Or anything but that vain animal,
> Who is so proud of being rational.

Or again, what about someone who, as St. Paul says, comes "to think more of himself than he ought to think"? Did I not earlier cite the example of Jane Austen's Sir Walter Elliott, whose vanity ran alike to his own beauty and his own baronetcy, with the result that those became the most "constant objects of his warmest affection and devotion"? "Oh, the more fool he," you might say—which is certainly correct. And yet is not the real issue for our present purposes the question of whether Sir Walter Elliott might be said to have had the "right" to make a fool of himself?

And so likewise with the earl of Rochester. Was it right that he should have devoted the better part of his life to drunkenness and loose living? Could he be said to have had the right to do this? It is true that the earl might be said to have had the right, in the sense that there was no law against drunkenness or even against debauchery—at least not for an English nobleman at the court of Charles II. But more fundamentally, from the point of view of a state-of-nature theory of ethics, what an individual thus does with his life, liberty, and property could be said to be all right or naturally all right. He even has an absolute right to do with himself whatever he pleases, so long as by his actions he does not interfere with others or impede their freedom of action.

But on a natural-law theory of ethics, in contrast to a state-of-nature theory, the story is very different as regards an individual's natural rights. For here a person's rights are strictly conditioned upon that individual's life, liberty, and property being the necessary means of his living wisely and responsibly and of his becoming and being the person that a human being ought to be. Accordingly, to the extent to which an individual does little more than devote his life to indulging his every personal whim or inclination or to the extent to which he gives himself over to little more than an inordinate love of gain—or even suppose that he so pampers life and limb that he becomes little more than an accomplished hypochondriac, a veritable *malade imaginaire*—then there is no longer a sense in which what he does, in the exercise of his freedom, is any longer necessary to his becoming the person his natural end requires that he be. The actions that he takes and the conduct that he pursues are then no longer right at all; nor can his natural right to life, liberty, and property be said to entitle him so to live in the way he has foolishly and unwisely chosen to do. In other words, that one should abuse one's right must not itself be taken to be right, or even one's right in any strict sense.

Just the same, suppose that one does abuse one's rights in this manner and yet in such a way as always carefully to avoid harming one's fellows by one's conduct. Can that be said to be all right, or one's natural right? Again, the answer must surely be "no"—at least from the standpoint of natural law. Yet note that it does not follow that, merely because one is engaged in conduct that is not right for one to engage in, the state or the community or the public authorities may therefore interfere to set the individual right. For however morally wrong and injurious one's conduct may be toward oneself, this hardly bestows any warrant upon one's neighbors or one's friends or relatives or the public authorities or whomever to intervene and try to correct one's behavior. For this would be to commit oneself to a blatant theory of paternalism on the part of the state and the public authorities. And yet my entire argument thus far has been based on the principle that never under any circumstances is the state or are the public authorities justified in arrogating to themselves the role of Big Brother, or perhaps Big Father, according to any of the familiar patterns of paternalism.

The reason is that there is no individual human being who must not live his life himself. No one else can live it for him; and by the same token, neither family, friends, nor the state can properly intervene in the life of any responsible moral agent in such a way as to threaten or force or compel him to be a good man. Accordingly, it is in this sense, and for a like reason, that it may truly be said that a man's rights to life, liberty, and property are nothing if not radically inalienable: they are no less the necessary means to his reforming himself than they are the necessary means to his making something of himself in the first place.

All the same, suppose that the concern of the community and of the public authorities is with the prosecution of some common enterprise aimed at furthering the common good, and suppose that in the given instance a particular individual's labor or his wealth or his energies are needed in the common cause and that an adequate compensation and recognition are to be extended to him if he will cooperate and make his needed contribution. Under these circumstances can the individual be expected and required to cooperate and contribute, even if he does not want to? This time, the question is not one of whether the community may restrict the use of an individual's life, liberty, and property simply for the purpose of reforming that individual. That is the individual's own affair, and not the community's—no matter how much the individual be hell-bent on "following the primrose way to everlasting bonfire." In contrast, in the case that is now before us, the question is whether the community may make demands upon an individual's life, liberty, and property for the purpose, not of furthering the individual's own good but of furthering the common good, that is, the good of each and all.

And might not the answer to the question this time be affirmative? For just as a human being, as an individual, is under obligation to pursue his natural moral end as a rational animal, whether he wants to or not, so also must not that same individual, as being no less naturally a

political animal than he is a rational animal, likewise be under obligation to work for the common good? True, in his pursuit of his own end
simply as a moral individual, there is a sense in which the individual
has to see this as a do-it-yourself job and hence cannot put himself entirely under the authoritative guidance and direction of someone else.
On the other hand, in the sphere of those common enterprises which
are the normal feature of our political and social life, there, as we have
seen, must necessarily and properly be coordinating authorities. Hence
within properly determined limits, an individual, in his political and
community life, may surely be expected to put himself under the direction of, and to obey, those who are in authority. Nor can he simply
stand on his "rights" and refuse to lend either life or limb or to contribute of his wealth and property or to accept any restriction upon his
liberty when the question is one of the common good—provided always that what is being demanded of him is not sacrifice of such life,
liberty, or property as are essential and necessary to his being truly human. In this regard, and with respect to these truly inalienable rights
of an individual, as Nozick rightly remarks, there can be "no justified
sacrifice of some of us for others."

To anything beyond this, however, that is, to anything beyond that
which the individual has a right to as the necessary means to his acquitting himself of his obligations to himself as a human being, it would
seem that the individual no longer has a right that is either absolute or
that may not in any way be restricted. Rather, if anything, he has an
obligation to contribute his fair share to the common enterprise of the
polis and of the community, the achievement of the common good by
the *polis* being no less an integral part of any human being's natural end
than is his achieving his own perfection as an individual rational animal. Moreover, just as in his own personal life he is under obligation
to heed the dictates and recommendations of his own better judgment,
whether he actually does so or not, so also in his life as a citizen and
member of the *polis*, he would seem to be under obligation to heed the
just dictates and recommendations of the political authorities to whom
the direction and coordination of the common enterprise have been
entrusted. Besides, now that I have shown how the rights of individuals are to be regarded as limited and not absolute, it becomes possible
to understand how and to what extent the various rules, laws, demands, and so on that are directed to individuals by the public authorities are at least in principle just. In other words, it is not necessary

for us to have to make a decision between either not taking rights seriously or else finding ourselves constrained to admit the claims of an across-the-board anarchism. We can perfectly well both take rights seriously and recognize the need and the justice of an archism.

Suppose that by distinguishing inalienable rights from absolute rights, we have provided the means for seeing how there need be no inevitable conflict—at least not in principle—between what we might call public policies and private rights. Still, who may determine when and where and how public policies might be adjudged to be in violation of individual rights and when and where and how not? Must not the answer be that such determinations should be the business of the law and the courts?

Considering the matter more specifically, why not put forward the question: if, as I have insisted, the rights of individuals are inalienable, though not absolute but limited, and if their exact limitation is to be determined in the light of how much liberty or how much property and wealth or how much of a free use of life and limb is needed if an individual is to live his life as a responsible rational and political individual, then how are such questions to be decided and by whom? Surely, in the very nature of the case, it being either the public authorities who would be in violation of the rights of private individuals in such matters, or private individuals who would be reneging on their civic and public obligations, it would scarcely seem that decisions in such matters, to say nothing of the necessary rectificatory judgments, could be left in the hands either of the public authorities or of the private individual, without either the one or the other being thereby made a judge in his own cause.

Of course, it must be frankly admitted that this present book can make no attempt at being a treatise on political theory. Still, there would seem to be no reason not to observe that the conflict situation I have just described would seem to require for its proper resolution some constitutional arrangement of a so-called separation of powers. And more specifically, of course, the necessary separation of powers in this context would call for an independent judiciary. Why not say that it should be the business of the courts to decide when government policies conflict with private rights and when they do not? After all, it is generally recognized that in those reaches of the law such as crimes, torts, contracts, *et al.*, the business of the courts and of the judiciary is to sort out the various claims and counterclaims as to rights and obligations as between individuals. And so likewise, why not consider it to be a further and eminently proper function of the courts to try to resolve those conflicts between the policies of the public officials and such principles of law as guarantee the rights of individuals?

This is not to claim that by thus referring possible conflicts between public policies and private rights to adjudication by the courts, we have thereby provided an automatic means for the resolution of such conflicts. Far from it. For justice as dispensed by the courts can never be automated or computerized; nor can the dream ever be realized that there might be devices for obviating "hard cases." Indeed, such a conception would go directly contrary to the entire theory of natural law as providing the only proper basis for any positive legal and constitutional system.

Thus recall how in my second chapter I drew an analogy between morals and ethics, on the one hand, and the various arts, skills, and technologies, on the other. In the one case, no less than in the other, I insisted, the business always turns out to be one of determining what the relevant how-to-do-it rules must be if the relevant end is to be attained. Thus in ethics the end is simply that of living well, or living as a human being ought to live; whereas in the various arts and crafts the end is the product or the work that is to be accomplished, the bridge to be built, the patient to be cured, or the fish to be landed. One needs to go still further and recognize that in morals and ethics, no less than in the arts, the business never stops with merely determining and learning relevant how-to-do-it rules. Rather, the payoff always comes in actually using and applying the rules in particular concrete cases. And so it is that in ethics, no less than in the arts and skills, deciding what needs to be done in the particular concrete case can never properly be done automatically and mechanically. Just as the good physician is never one who practices his art merely out of a book, so also the good man is never one who simply memorizes the Ten Commandments or some other and more complicated code of conduct, and then assumes that living as one ought to live involves simply automatically applying his learned rules to particular cases. Besides, just because the skilled physician or skilled engineer cannot always come up with some particular rule of the trade that explains why he did what he did in the particular case, that certainly does not mean that the physician or engineer does not know what he is doing or could not justify his practice if called upon to do so. This is what real skill or know-how in an art involves. And what goes for the arts and skills that constitute what Aristotle called the productive sciences also applies in the so-called practical sciences, namely, morals, ethics, and politics.

And so, shifting our attention now directly to politics, which, as we have seen, is aimed at the attainment of the common good, why may we not say that what generally tends to be called "the law"—that is, civil law, common law, statute law, et al.—is nothing but the assemblage of those how-to-do-it rules that a given society or community has worked out over time with a view to achieving its natural end as a human community, that is, the common good? Moreover, should you wish to object that what is generally called "the law" in this sense—the entire corpus of so-called case law and statute law—so far from being an affair of "natural law" is nothing but mere "positive law," I would respond by citing Aquinas and saying that positive law is nothing but the "determination" of natural law or the working out of the principles of natural law as these come to be applied in particular situations and circumstances.[36]

In other words, much as the rules or laws of medicine or of any other technology are but the specification or determination of laws of physics, chemistry, biology, and so on, insofar as these latter come to be applied in particular cases and circumstances, so also the case law of any particular legal system may be regarded as no more than the sustained and ongoing attempt on the part of a community to apply those fundamental principles of a natural justice, and hence of those natural rights and obligations of human beings, insofar as they are political animals, to the particular individuals who make up a given human community or society in a particular age or at a particular time.

Note, too, that just as we have seen with moral laws, as well as with such laws as have come to be observed in the practice of the various arts and skills, so also when it comes to the so-called common law or civil law of a political community as a whole, it must not be thought that skill in the administration of justice involves merely knowing the law in the sense of having memorized a vast array of relevant how-to-do-it rules; it also involves applying these rules in the immediate and concrete cases of the litigants who are before the bar. Here it is, indeed, that litigation before the courts and adjudication by the courts becomes of such importance for the maintenance of justice within the community.

36. St. Thomas Aquinas, *Summa Theologiae*, I–II, Qu. 95, Art. 2.

After all, remember that although in this present chapter—especially in the latter part—our concern has been primarily with the question of how the claims of public policy can be reconciled with the claims of private rights, we must never forget that the ultimate justification even of what is put forward as being simply a matter of public policy can be only in terms of the well-being of the individual citizens and of a respect for their individual rights. Hence any administration of justice, so-called, must always refer ultimately to a justice that is toward individuals and with respect to individuals. And so it is that any body of law within a state or a community can never be, or ought never be, exclusively or even primarily an affair of merely preserving a just balance between the claims of the *polis* and the claims of the individual. Rather, it is in the main an affair of trying to determine and then to secure and to see to it that justice is done in such myriads of claims and counterclaims as the individuals within any given community come to have with respect to one another, and with a view to meeting their demand that their individual rights and duties be properly observed by their fellows. In other words, the law—the civil law or common law of a community—may never be regarded as confined only to public law or constitutional law. Rather, it extends to all of those familiar divisions of common or civil law that we currently designate by such divisions or categories as criminal law, torts, property, contracts, *et al.*

Moreover, in the light of this background, we should now be able to see how the litigation and adjudication of claims before and by the courts needs to be understood not as automatic applications to particular cases of an elaborate set of how-to-do-it rules aimed at the attainment of the common good and of justice for all individuals. For just as the skilled surgeon or civil engineer has to bring the rules of his art to bear upon the particular concrete case, thus determining why he considers that the job needs to be done in this way rather than in that, so also the adversarial proceedings in the courts, in which the lawyers for plaintiffs and defendants seek to cite and to argue the relevance of the leading cases on the subject, are done with a view to trying to determine what it is that justice demands be done, not in general or in the main, but right here and now.

Is it any one wonder, then, that "hard cases" could be the rule rather than the exception in the administration of the law, much as difficult and controversial diagnoses could be the rule rather than the exception in a physician's practice of medicine? But so also, just as one does not say that because a correct diagnosis in medicine may be difficult, and even precarious at times, it must therefore follow that diagnostic medicine can never be an affair of any proper knowledge or skill but only of arbitrary guesswork, so likewise, merely because cases in law are often "hard," it does not follow that lawyers and judges can never hope to know what they are about when rendering justice in particular cases. Similarly, just as the skilled judgment of the physician has behind it a sure grasp of the principles of physics, chemistry, biology, *et al.*, as well as an entire fund of experience that goes with the medical art, so also the skilled lawyer and judge will not fail to have a basic understanding of the natural-law principles of right and justice that must underlie any proper legal system, to say nothing of a fund of experience of cases and court decisions that he has built up in the practice of his profession.

This does not mean that the right decision will necessarily and unfailingly be reached in every case, any more than it does in the practice of medicine. And yet just as the practice of medicine can be pursued in such a way as to be self-corrective of its own errors, so also would it seem to be the case with the practice of law. Moreover, when one hears complaints, as one often does nowadays, of the arbitrariness of judicial activism; or again, when one hears criticisms of attempts to introduce ethical considerations into the law, as if this would make for a certain arbitrariness in the way in which cases come to be decided—the basis of the decision being the judge's own personal moral convictions and not any firm background of legal precedents—all such criticisms and complaints may indeed be well taken in many individual instances. And yet surely they need pose no difficulty in principle for a natural-law legal tradition, rightly conceived and rightly understood. On the contrary, the analogy that I have been here belaboring between the practice of law and the practice of any of the several arts should enable us to defend the lawyers' and the judges' pursuit of right and justice as a pursuit that can be and should be guided by a truly reliable practical knowledge of what right and justice are in general, as well as of what they therefore turn out to be in particular cases. In other words, it is knowledge that offers the true protection against arbitrariness or a mere cynical charlatanry in the law, just as it is true knowledge and skill that offer the only real protection against quackery in the art of medicine.

CHAPTER IV

LAW AND ETHICS IN SEARCH OF A PHYSICS OR METAPHYSICS

Has Our Day of Reckoning Come?

Need any of my readers be reminded that my entire argument thus far has rested on little more than borrowed capital, for which I have never given, and presumably could not have given, adequate security? And is this anything other than to have lived in a fool's paradise? But now the loan is about to be called. How can I possibly come up with the necessary funds?

First, though, let us clarify the deficiency that needs to be covered. From the very start of this book I have insisted that law must be based on ethics, and ethics, in turn, must be grounded in fact and have a basis in nature. And yet how is it possible to show that moral laws are true laws of nature? For certainly in this day and age no one doubts that the only access that anyone can have to nature or to reality or to the physical world generally must be through science—that is, through modern natural science. And yet who is there among us who does not know that science, so far from ever disclosing to us a moral universe, discloses only a world totally devoid of values, devoid of distinctions between right and wrong, of either moral "oughts" or "ought nots," and indeed of anything and everything that could be of any moral relevance?

Is it any wonder, then, that modern moral philosophers have, seemingly almost to a man (or woman), eschewed any effort to find a basis for ethics in fact or in nature? How, then, can I hope to do what others have largely given up trying to do? Is this perhaps not so much a fool's paradise as a case of "fools rushing in where angels fear to tread"?

Is It Also a Day of Reckoning for Our Rivals?

Despite the seeming hopelessness of this situation, have I not la-

213

bored abundantly to show that my recent predecessors and contemporaries in matters of ethical theory are in many ways worse off than I am? But whereas my failure must presumably lie in my inability to come up with a physics or metaphysics that could provide a foundation for ethics, their failure has turned on their having tried to get along without anything like a physics or metaphysics of any kind.[1] In consequence, their various attempts to develop a sound ethical theory have resulted in one sorry failure after another. And indeed, I have even tried to turn my rivals' failure into an argument for my own natural-law position, as if a demonstration that ethics cannot get along without natural law could somehow be turned into an argument that there therefore must be a natural law that ethics can get along with. Alas, such a conclusion does not follow. Still, it might not be out of place to review, at least cursorily, how and why it is that ethics presumably cannot get along without natural law, even if I am eventually forced to admit that there is no natural law that it can very well get along with either. Basically, my underlying argument has been that if morals and ethics are not based on nature or on reality, then what else are or can they be based on?

Of course, this is not to say that modern moral philosophers have not shown themselves to be exceedingly adept at thinking up numerous surrogate facts upon which an ethics might be based, in the absence of any genuine facts, or facts of nature, upon which it might seem to need to be based. In my first chapter I examined several of these apparently bogus claims that modern moral philosophers have put for-

1. In the context of Aristotelian philosophy—and therefore of any natural-law philosophy—"physics" is said to be concerned with the world of nature, that is, with the world of entities or beings that are subject to change and motion. In contrast, "metaphysics" is concerned with beings as such—with "being *qua* being," as Aristotle would say. With the advent of modern science, however, the terms "physics" and "metaphysics" have come to be understood differently. Instead of designating a distinction between changing being and being as such, the words more often than not tend to be used to designate the difference between the domain of science (*i.e.*, modern natural science) and the domain of philosophy, as if "physics" had to do only with entities that are empirically observable, and thus accessible to scientific investigation, whereas metaphysics is held to be perhaps a purely speculative endeavor, or at least one whose findings do not involve a reliance upon empirical scientific procedures. In this book, however, I propose that the term "physics" be understood in the older Aristotelian sense and therefore without the question's necessarily being begged as to whether physics must be ruled to be the preserve exclusively of science in the modern sense, and thus not of philosophy.

ward to try to show that although theirs is not a moral philosophy based on fact in any strict sense, still it is a philosophy that can claim to be a legitimate body of knowledge. Thus oversimplifying the situation a bit, one might say that there are only two main varieties of contemporary ethical theories—that of the so-called teleologists, or partisans of a "desire-ethic," on the one hand, and that of the so-called deontologists, or partisans of an "ought-ethic," or "duty-ethic," on the other.

Consider, then, how the teleologists find surrogate facts as a basis for their ethics. For it must be admitted that they tend to resort to a most curious device. "Let it be granted," they say in effect, "that the world of nature, or the world of fact, is radically and completely amoral. Nowhere can one find in the facts any distinction between good and bad, or right and wrong, or anything else of the kind. But then," they hasten to add, "so far from its being any source of despair or weakness, so far as morals and ethics are concerned, this totally amoral character of the real world turns out instead to be a great boon. For if it is no longer necessary for us to have to worry about whether moral distinctions are written into the very nature of things, we can accordingly turn our attention to the more immediate business of simply living our lives as best we may—that is, pursuing our own interests, doing what we want to do, figuring out what is to our greatest advantage, and so on. And we do not have to worry in the least about whether what we are doing is sanctioned by God, or by nature, or by the facts, or whatever." In other words, a teleological ethic of this sort is actually a "desire-ethic"—that is, an ethics that is devoted entirely to the business of trying only to satisfy our desires and get what we can out of life without ever having to concern ourselves with whether our actions are in some deeper, or perhaps higher, sense right or wrong or good or bad.

All the same, no sooner does one begin seriously to reflect upon the underlying principle upon which such a desire-ethic—be it in the specific form of a Utilitarianism or in that of what is sometimes called an Ethical Egoism—than the radical weakness of such an ethics must quickly disclose itself. For let one ask, "Just how can one justify devoting one's entire life to doing no more than trying to satisfy one's desires, be they those of an individual person or those of mankind as a whole?" and immediately it becomes apparent that such a question is not answered by saying, "Oh, but we do not need to justify such a way of life, considering that neither reality, nor nature, nor the world of fact, nor any truth can ever provide us with such a justification." For what is this answer but the implication that since our way of life is indefensible, we therefore do not have to defend it? And what defense is that? Is it not more an effrontery than a defense?

Suppose, then, that a teleological type of ethics—what I have called a mere desire-ethic—does not fare too well at trying to find a justification for itself that does not require an appeal to the facts of nature or to reality. What, then, of that alternative type of ethics that is so prevalent among modern philosophers and that goes by the name of deontology? For this type of ethics, which traces its origin back to Immanuel Kant, tries, no less than does a so-called teleological type of ethics, to construct an ethics but without basing it on fact. And yet can such a thing be done?

Interestingly enough, any and every such deontological ethics usually starts out by focusing directly upon the weakness that we have already found attaches itself inevitably to any teleological ethics or desire-ethic. Thus say the deontologists: "The trouble with any ethical teleology, or desire-ethic, is that the proponents of such an ethics try to argue that all we human beings need to do in matters of morals and ethics is to find out what it is that we want to do, and that will then be what we ought to do, or the morally right thing for us to do. But this," the deontologists say, "is simply ridiculous: the mere fact that I want something, or desire it, or like it, is no reason to suppose that I therefore ought to have it, or that it is morally right that I have it. This is a *non sequitur.*"

And so it is that all deontologists begin their ethics by insisting that morals and ethics—that is, theories of what we ought to do or ought not to do, of what it is right that we should do or wrong that we should not do—may never be erected on the basis of mere appeals to human desires, ends, purposes, inclinations, or anything of the sort. Instead, moral obligations and duties are, in the final analysis, ultimate and underivable: we ought to do thus and so, not because we want to or because doing so will further our ends and interests; it is rather always a case of "we ought" just because "we ought."

No sooner, though, do the deontologists seek to develop their position along these lines than the entire edifice of such an ethic threatens to collapse from the weight of its own arbitrariness. For surely, for any assertion of an "ought"—of what one ought to do: "I ought to pay my debts," "I ought to speak the truth," "I ought to do no murder," "I ought not to bear false witness"—the question "Why?" is always relevant and legitimate. "But *why* ought I, or *why* ought I not?" To such "why-questions," the ethical deontologist cannot give an answer. He cannot say, "I ought to because it is to my advantage to do so, or because I want to, or because doing so will somehow further my ends and purposes," because such an answer would drive the deontologist right back into the arms of the teleologist. On the other hand, he cannot argue that he ought to because God commands him to because the question "Why?" breaks out all over again with respect to God's command: "Why does God command me as he does—say, that I not bear false witness? For what is wrong with bearing false witness against one's neighbor? Surely, God would not issue His command against such an act unless it were really wrong. And yet that is just the question at issue: why should anyone—God included—think it wrong to bear false witness? And this question one scarcely answers by merely saying, 'it is wrong because it is wrong.'"

Nor, of course, can the deontologist justify his "oughts" or his moral prescriptions on the ground that nature, or reality, prescribes such "oughts" for us. For that would be like saying that water seeks its own level because that is the course of action that nature makes morally obligatory for water, as though a moral obligation were inscribed in the very nature of water—which, of course, is patently ridiculous. Accordingly, being thus precluded, seemingly in principle, from ever being able to give any well-grounded reason for the duties and obligations they want to claim are incumbent upon us, many deontologists of recent years have taken to claiming that, not being able to give any reason for moral "oughts," it is simply by intuition that they come to recognize what human beings either ought or ought not to do. But now I ask you: how is this appeal of the deontologist merely to his own intuitions of the rightness or wrongness of certain actions any different from an appeal to his own entrenched prejudices? And to this question it would seem that the contemporary deontologist has no answer.

Ambiguities in the Notions of
"Nature" and "Natural Law"

Still, is it unreasonable—given that the principal contemporary alternatives to a natural-law ethics all seem to end in failure—that we should thus be led to a further consideration of natural law and of whether nature might not be shown to provide a basis or foundation for such an ethics after all?

To begin with, why not say that the most signal feature of a natural-law ethic is that it cannot be other than a teleological ethic? And a teleological ethic, at least in this present sense, bespeaks no less than a natural teleology as its very foundation. That is, the teleology is a teleology within nature itself. What, though, does this do, if not bring us face to face with a serious, not to say glaring, ambiguity in the notions of "nature" and "natural law"? Indeed, in the very opening chapter, did I not note the fact, and then try to slither around the difficulty connected with the fact, that the notion of a natural law must presumably be a radically different one in the context of ethics and politics from what everybody nowadays understands laws of nature to be within the domain of modern natural science? And surely, if the word "natural" is ambiguous as between "natural law" and "natural science," then the root notion of "nature" must itself be hopelessly skewed in the two contexts.

Did not the late great Leo Strauss, in the introduction to his seminal book *Natural Right and History*, state "Natural right in its classic form is connected with a teleological view of the universe. All natural beings have a natural end, a natural destiny, which determines what kind of operation is good for them. In the case of man, reason is required for discerning these operations: reason determines what is by nature right with ultimate regard to man's natural end."[2]

Moreover, save for certain differences in terminology, is not what Strauss is here saying the substance of the argument of this book thus far? For what has that argument been if not that when determining whether laws are just or unjust or whether our supposed moral obligations are binding upon us, we have to look to man's natural *telos* or goal and thus try to determine whether such courses of action are prescribed for us by positive law or in traditional morality are either warranted or unwarranted, depending on whether or not they are conducive to the achievement of our natural ends as human beings.

Strauss amplifies this notion of "human nature" and man's "natural end" by setting it in the context of ancient Greek philosophy. For the ancient philosophers, the so-called pre-Socratics, were forever occupied with trying to determine the nature of things; and for them this

2. Leo Strauss, *Natural Right and History* (Chicago, 1953), 7.

meant the nature of the whole of being or reality. Strauss continues, however: "Socrates deviated from his predecessors by identifying the science of the whole, or of everything that is, with the understanding of 'what each of the beings is.' For 'to be' means 'to be something' and hence to be different from things which are 'something else.' . . . If 'to be' is 'to be something,' the being of a thing, or the nature of a thing, is primarily its What, its 'shape' or 'form' or 'character.'"[3]

The significance of this argument, at least for my present purposes, is, as Strauss notes, the way Socrates regarded his "deviation" from his predecessors:

> Socrates seems to have regarded the change which he brought about as a return to "sobriety" and "moderation" from the "madness" of his predecessors. . . . In present-day parlance one can describe the change in question as a return to "common sense" or to "the world of common sense." That to which the question "What is?" points is the *eidos* of a thing, the shape or form or character or "idea" of a thing. It is no accident that the term *eidos* signifies primarily that which is visible to all without any particular effort on what one might call the "surface" of things. Socrates started not from what is first in itself or first by nature but from what is first for us, from what comes to sight first, from the phenomena. But the being of things, their What, comes first to sight, not in what we see of them, but in what is said about them or in opinions about them. . . . Socrates implied that disregarding the opinions about the nature of things would amount to abandoning the most important access to reality which we have, or the most important vestiges of truth which are within our reach.[4]

Consider the irony of this theory with respect to our present situation in this book. For notice how in many ways our situation today is almost the reverse of what Socrates considered his situation to have been. For Socrates' predecessors, their concern with nature meant a concern with the nature of things, in the sense of the nature of the whole. For Socrates, in contrast, the concern with nature meant a concern not with the great panorama of nature as a whole, and thus not with the nature of things, but with the natures of things—and particularly with the nature of man—as contrasted with the natures of dogs, catfish, stones, or whatever. Moreover, for Socrates this concern with the natures and characters of things, and particularly with the nature

3. *Ibid.*, 122–123.
4. *Ibid.*, 123–124.

of man or of human beings, represented a return to common sense and to the objects of our everyday world as we know them in everyday life.

When, though, we consider our own situation in today's world, do not the natural scientists fall into a role like that of Socrates' predecessors? Their interests and concerns seem to be far more with the nature of things than with the natures of things; or with the nature of the whole, as Strauss would prefer to say, rather than with the natures of the parts. True, one might say that the research of a modern chemist, for example, is into the nature of silver, hydrogen, coal, or whatever. But do not such expressions have an odd sound about them? Moreover, it sounds not so much odd as forced to say that disciplines such as psychology, anthropology, or physiology are concerned with an investigation of human nature or the nature of man.

If we wished to test still further the analogy that might be supposed to hold between Socrates and his predecessors, on the one hand, and between natural law philosophers and modern scientists, on the other, would it be plausible to say that no sooner does one turn from investigations of nature and of the world of nature, as today's scientists understand them, to the considerations and reflections upon human nature that a natural-law philosopher must engage in with respect to law, morals, and politics than we seem to be returning from "madness" to "sobriety," or from a world that was bizarre and remote to a world that is familiar, and that we immediately recognize as being the world of common sense, the very world that we live in? It is not inconceivable that we might speak in such a vein upon occasion, as if scientists did indeed seem concerned with a nature that is scarcely recognizable in everyday life, whereas all of us in our everyday affairs are familiar with what we might call the natures of ordinary things, and not least with the nature of man. But conceivable though it is that we might sometimes speak in this way, still, given the context of today's world, the import of any such return to common sense would be almost the opposite of what Socrates took it to be—or at least as Strauss represents him as taking it to be. For today, common sense no longer has any authority or enjoys any prestige over science, with the result that any implied return from science to common sense could scarcely be construed in any other way than as a retreat from genuine knowledge to little more than old wives' tales.

Therefore, must not the embarrassment of any present-day natural-law philosopher be rendered alike palpable and unanswerable? For if any defense of natural law as the foundation for law, morals, or politics must inevitably involve an appeal to "nature," as Socrates and the classical philosophers generally understood it to be, and hence a repudiation of "nature," as it has come to be understood by modern natural scientists ever since the seventeenth century, then it would seem to discredit what Socrates took to be the common sense of natural law. For how could there be any sense, common or otherwise, to natural law, if the nature that underlies such a law is irreconcilable with the nature of modern science?

Again, we might turn to Strauss to point the moral of this apparent collapse of our entire natural-law argument thus far. Referring to what he calls the "teleological view of nature," which is associated with the enterprise of trying to determine all such things as human natural rights and natural laws in terms of a regard for "man's natural end," Strauss remarks:

> [But] the teleological view of the universe, of which the teleological view of man forms a part, would seem to have been destroyed by modern natural science. . . . [Indeed,] the issue between the mechanical and the teleological conception of the universe . . . seems to have been decided in terms of the nonteleological conception of the universe. Two opposite conclusions could be drawn from this momentous decision. According to one, the nonteleological conception of the universe must be followed up by a nonteleological conception of human life. But this "naturalistic" solution is exposed to grave difficulties: it seems to be impossible to give an adequate account of human ends by conceiving of them merely as posited by desires and impulses. Therefore, the alternative solution has prevailed. This means that people were forced to accept a fundamental, typically modern, dualism of a nonteleological natural science and a teleological science of man. This is the position which the modern followers of Thomas Aquinas, among others, are forced to take, a position which presupposes a break with the comprehensive view of Aristotle as well as that of Thomas Aquinas himself. The fundamental dilemma, in whose grip we are, is caused by the victory of modern natural science. An adequate solution to the problem of natural right cannot be found before this basic problem has been solved.[5]

So be it. And yet since fools rush in where angels fear to tread, I now propose to rush in and show how this apparently hopeless dilemma that Strauss suggests confronts all moral and legal and political

5. *Ibid.*, 7–8.

philosophers in the modern world can be obviated: neither is it necessary to surrender a teleological view of nature nor to try to carry water on both shoulders and say that nature, as the scientist deals with it, must be nonteleological, whereas the nature of what we might designate as being the object of the human sciences is teleological. Yet how can this be?

THE NONTELEOLOGICAL VIEW OF NATURE IN MODERN SCIENCE

The Cartesian Reduction of Physics to Mathematics

Having thus laid out the seeming impossibility of doing so in the present day, let us now attempt the impossible and see whether a teleological view of nature might not be defended after all? I will start with the blunt question: why was it, and how did it come about that modern natural scientists—and with them, the rest of us ordinary mortals as well—should have been led to prefer a nonteleological to a teleological account of nature and of the natural world? Was it not because the testimony of experience and the evidence of observation spoke so unequivocally in favor of such a nonteleology and against anything like a teleology? Yet was it so really? Following the lead of many recent historians of science, it turns out that the evidence of experience could hardly have been the decisive factor in leading to a general acceptance, ever since the seventeenth century, of a nonteleological world-view over a teleological one.

For example, even if we manifestly oversimplify the account of the rise of modern science, it would surely not be incorrect to say that any such account owes much to the acuity and ingenuity of the great French philosopher, René Descartes. For it was largely because of him that a nonteleological way of conceiving nature came to displace the older teleological conception that had been predominant among physicists and philosophers of nature ever since Aristotle. Moreover, if we consider the factors that led Descartes to prefer a nonteleology to a teleology, I believe it would need to be recognized that Descartes, in a curious way, must have been influenced by Aristotle's earlier celebrated distinction between physics and mathematics. Not that Descartes made the Aristotelian distinction his own exactly; still he must have been thoroughly imbued with it. Otherwise, how could he have so successfully turned it to his own ends, and with an ingenuity that amounted to nothing if not genius?

For ourselves, accordingly, why may we not begin by reminding ourselves of how Aristotle sought to differentiate the subject matter of physics from that of mathematics.[6] To put it briefly, if a bit naively, it is well known that physics, as Aristotle conceived it, was concerned with ordinary objects or substances in the natural world—plants and animals; the sun, moon, and stars; the substances the ancients considered to be the elements, *viz.*, earth, air, fire, water, *et al.* Moreover, the hallmark of each of these physical or natural substances, including human beings, was that each had within itself what Aristotle called its own "intrinsic principle of motion and rest." Aristotle apparently meant that all of them have their own characteristic activities or modes of behavior. Thus a lion acts differently from a termite, or a cranberry bush from a human being, or water from fire. Moreover, these characteristic differences in the actions of different substances reflect the differences in their powers or capacities or capabilities. Thus the capabilities of a gazelle are patently different from those of a hippopotamus. Or again, the potentialities of coal are different from those of granite or wood.

Moreover, from all of this, one can begin to see what Aristotle's strategy must have been in the account he sought to give of nature in his *Physics*. For the world of nature for Aristotle is what we all recognize, from our everyday experience of it, to be the world round about us. It is a dynamic world, a world of change. As the Scholastics put it, the subject matter of physics is *ens mobile*, or objects or beings insofar as they are subject to change. But for an object to be thus subject to change, must it not be possessed of certain powers and potentialities, both a power to effect change and a power to be changed? And what is any such a power to be changed if not a potentiality inherent in an entity's very nature to become other and different from what it is? And what is a power to effect change if not what Aristotle termed an efficient cause or a moving cause? That is, any cause or causes that effect a change in another entity will be those causes that act upon the entity's potentiality, or potentialities, to be other and different, thereby causing it to become other and different, and so actualizing its relevant po-

6. Cf. Aristotle, *Metaphysica*, trans. W. D. Ross (Oxford, 1928), Books E, chap. 1, esp. 1025 b 18–1026a, 32.

tentialities. Indeed, Aristotle calls those potentialities that a substance has to be changed the material causes of the change. Moreover, since any potentiality is always a potentiality for, or with respect to, a certain specific actuality, what is such an actuality if not the final cause of that particular process of change? It is that toward which the change is directed and which, insofar as it represents what the substance in question might be or could be, insofar as it comes to be actualized, it is therefore that which constitutes a perfection or a fulfillment of that substance, and so what the substance is able to be, or should be, or ought to be, to the extent to which it attains its full actuality.

From all of this, of course, it is not hard to see how and why Aristotle's account of the natural world as being an account of things or substances that are subject to change cannot be other than teleological.[7] For how can any real change be other than ordered to a so-called final cause, inasmuch as anything that undergoes change can do so only in virtue of the potentialities that it has to be other and different, and inasmuch as each of these potentialities is determinate with respect to what the substance in question might be or could become—that is, with respect to the *telos* or endpoint toward which the actualization of any given potentiality might be said to be ordered or directed?

But now contrast this Aristotelian account of principles and causes in physics with the account which he gives of mathematics and mathematical objects. To point up this contrast, Aristotle first notes that although the objects of physics—substances in the physical world—are able to exist in themselves and in their own right, mathematical objects—say, geometrical objects like squares, circles, triangles, *et al.*—are unable to exist separately or in their own right. Thus a triangle can exist only as the triangular shape of something. Still, even though triangles or circles cannot exist separately, they can nonetheless be conceived separately. That is, to understand what a triangle is, or what the nature of triangularity involves, one does not have to think of such triangles as being the triangular shapes of physical substances in the natural world. Rather, one can consider triangles just as such; and when one does, one will of course find that each geometrical figure will have its own characteristic features or attributes: triangles will have theirs, and circles theirs, and rectangles theirs.

7. In this discussion of the so-called teleology of nature, we shall be concerned only with teleology as it pertains to the *natures* of things, not to teleology as it might pertain to *nature* as a whole.

Nevertheless, what is striking about the attributes or characteristics of such mathematical objects, in contrast to substances in the physical world, is that none of them is ever in any way subject to change. No circle or square or triangle, for example, ever is to be conceived as having a capacity to become other and different. There is no sense in which they can ever be thought to grow or develop. They cannot even change in size, for if you double the area of a rectangle, you get a different figure and not the identical rectangle twice as big. Nor, of course, is there any locomotion in the world of geometrical objects and certainly no generation and corruption. Rather, each geometrical figure is eternally and immutably the same, without difference and without change.

And now note the consequence of this ever-unchanging character of mathematical objects. For not being subject to change, the nature of a triangle, for example, will not admit of what Aristotle called material or final causes or of efficient or moving causes. There will be no final cause because, not being subject to change, there will not be in a triangle any end or *telos* that any change in or of the triangle could be said to be ordered toward or directed toward. Nor will there be any material cause since a triangle will have no potentiality or capacity to become other or different in any way. (Aristotle does ascribe "intelligible matter" to mathematical objects—but that is a different story, and not one that would be of any relevance to our present purpose.) And, of course, there being no potentiality or capacity in a triangle to become other and different, there is no way that any efficient or moving cause could ever act upon it so as to make it other or different. In short, as Aristotle notes, in the case of mathematical objects, all causes are reduced to the formal cause alone—that is, to the cause in virtue of which an entity is just the kind of entity that it is, and not another.

With this, will not my readers begin to complain, "Buy why, pray tell, do we have to submit to all of this antiquated and outworn business of Aristotle's pet way of differentiating physics from mathematics?" The answer is that, as we all know, there emerged in the seventeenth century a very smart Frenchman, one René Descartes by name. And what did Descartes do but simply collapse Aristotle's account of physics and of physical nature into the Aristotelian account of mathematics and mathematical objects alone. I may be oversimplifying the picture here; and yet is it not true that Descartes, seemingly just by fiat, decreed that physical objects or physical substances (in Aristotle's sense) were reducible to mathematical objects? Nor is that all, for this same Cartesian decree would seem to have been accepted by the then emerging community of the more up-to-date scientists in the seventeenth century, with the result that the almost complete mathematizing of physical nature that became the hallmark of the so-called scientific revolution in the seventeenth century has continued to be the dominant characteristic of just about all of the so-called sciences of nature right down to our own day.

Nor should it be surprising that our scientists still continue to insist that no so-called final causes—that is, no ends or purposes—are to be found anywhere in the whole of nature. And if no natural ends or purposes, then no natural teleology; and if no natural teleology, then no natural goods or values anywhere in the whole of nature; and if no goods or values that one might be able to understand, and thus identify with, in terms of the natural ends and perfections of the various natural substances, then there is no way one can possibly speak of what human beings ought to be, or have a veritable moral obligation to try to be or become, in accordance with the requirements of their own human nature. In other words, from this scientific perspective, there is no way morals and ethics can be based on any facts of nature. Nor would there seem to be any way, as a remedy for the desperate plight of contemporary ethics, we would seem ever again able to return to the "way of Aristotle," as MacIntyre has called it.[8] For as I noted earlier, it is the imposing figure of modern natural science that seems to debar us from taking that way.

All the same, why do we need any longer to be held so completely in thrall to this still dominant scientific outlook and attitude? Indeed, can it rightly be said that scientists are even in any position to tell us that nature is not, and cannot be, teleological, or that nature cannot possibly provide any basis for ethics? The more one reflects upon the origins of the modern scientists' anti-teleological stance, the more it begins to appear that the stance was almost a dogmatic one, not strictly based on evidence, at least not on any patently empirical evidence. Thus from the account that I have already given, it would seem that it was Descartes' seemingly high-handed and almost arbitrary reduction of physical objects to mathematical objects that is the source of that "absolute wall of separation" between fact and value that scientists nowadays seem unquestioningly to accept.

8. See Chapter II, note 1.

Yet how was Descartes able to bring off his mathematization of physics so effectively? For surely, it was hardly on the basis of observation and empirical evidence that he was able to say that physical objects could be reduced to mathematical objects. Instead, if our experience teaches us anything about the world of physical nature, it is that the objects of nature are undeniably subject to change. Yet by the logic of Descartes' effort to mathematize the entire physical world, one finds oneself constrained to deny that real change can ever take place in nature. Given the mathematized picture of nature that Descartes projected, there could not possibly be anywhere in nature any material causes or final causes or efficient causes that might make such changes possible. Instead, all there are in nature are successions of events, for which there can be no proper causal explanations except ones such as Descartes put forward, when he suggested that any given overall geometrical pattern or configuration of nature at any one given moment of time would then need to be thought of as being succeeded in the next moment by a slightly different pattern or configuration. And what explanation does Descartes give for such a succession of different geometrical world-configurations? Presumably, Descartes' only answer was that God miraculously recreates the world at every successive instant in time.[9] But now I ask, how rational an explanation is that? Is it any wonder that when Hume in the eighteenth century sought a rational explanation of what he called "necessary connection," it was impossible for him to find one? No, if rather than the stark geometrical methods of Descartes, it is experience and empirical observation that we are to go by in the account that we give of nature and the natural world, then it would surely be Aristotle who would show himself to be the true empiricist, and not Descartes.

Modern Scientific Theories and Hypotheses
Are Radically Underdetermined by Experience

Nevertheless, let us look beyond Descartes and consider the spectacle of modern natural science generally. For may not one say that not just the Cartesian view of nature but doubtless the entire nonteleolog-

---

9. For a vivid and spirited account of the character and import of Cartesianism in science and philosophy, the summary presentation by Etienne Gilson has never been surpassed. See his *The Unity of Philosophical Experience* (New York, 1937), pt. II, 125–220.

ical outlook upon nature as a whole that we have seen to be characteristic of modern science would seem scarcely to be based on any direct
evidence of experience? And here I appeal to the testimony that has
recently been emerging from all of those new and exciting discussions
of the philosophy of science—or perhaps more accurately, discussions
in the logic of science—that have become a feature of present-day philosophy.

This is neither the time nor the place, nor can I give more than a
cursory account of what seems to have been going on. Why not begin
our story with Sir Karl Popper and his celebrated emphasis upon, and
treatment of, what he felicitously termed the *hypothetico-deductive method*
of science? For Popper considered this to be the method of modern science—in fact, the method that might be said to incorporate the "logic
of scientific discovery." Nor even among the more recent authorities
within the field of the philosophy of science would there appear to be
any who would deviate very far from the Popperian position in this respect, in thinking the hallmark of modern science to be its reliance upon
the hypothetico-deductive method. Moreover, what is distinctive about
this hypothetico-deductive method as Popper elaborates it is that it is
not to be thought of as a method that relies primarily upon empirical
observation or induction from experience. No, Popper says, the great
overarching hypotheses and theories of science—as propounded by the
great scientific geniuses such as Kepler, Galileo, Newton, Einstein, *et
al.*—are not based on experience. What, then, are they based on? Popper says that they are not based on evidence in the strict sense at all,
either inductive or deductive. Instead, all of the great scientific theories and hypotheses in the history of modern science, Popper contends, have been initially nothing but sheer inventions in the minds of
the scientists, or free creations of the mind, much like the creations of
great artists, poets, or musicians. Indeed, the very last thing that one
can think of such hypotheses and theories as being is in any way derived from observation or from experience of the world.

Nor is it to be denied that what Popper thus insists upon turns out
to be eminently plausible, as soon as it is considered against the background of that older tradition in the philosophy of science, *viz.*, the tradition of logical positivism or logical empiricism that immediately preceded the advent of Popper upon the scene. For on the older positivistic
view, it was largely taken for granted that scientific knowledge was basically an affair of empirical observation, followed by inductive gener-

alization. Event *a*, for example, was observed to precede event *b*, not once but many times and under varying circumstances; and from there one went on to conclude, by inductive inference, that *a* necessarily precedes *b*, or is the cause of *b*. In other words, scientific procedures were to be thought of as fitting entirely into the traditional setting of so-called Humean empiricism: the first stage was the establishing through observation and experiment of what Hume called "constant conjunctions" in nature; and the second stage was that of an induction or generalization from experience to a "necessary connection," or to what has sometimes been called a "nomic universal"—for which, of course, it was admitted there could presumably be no proper logical warrant.

Not only was such an empirical procedure in science not able to come up with any genuine logical warrant for the inductions involved, but also the procedure itself seemed not to square with what the great figures in the history of science would always seem to have done in their own practice. Certain low-level scientific laws might be said to have been arrived at by a process of induction—"Water boils at 100° C," or "Silver melts at 960.5°," or "Acid turns blue litmus paper red." Nevertheless, it begins to appear silly to suppose that the great overarching hypotheses and theories of science that have been propounded by the great figures in the history of science were derived through procedures that could be described as inductive in any strict sense.

Thus take Kepler's celebrated hypothesis of the elliptical orbits of the planets. Could Kepler be said to have arrived at this theory by any process of induction, as though from having observed a number of planets to move in elliptical orbits, he then generalized that all of the planets must therefore move in elliptical, rather than circular, orbits? Such an idea is patently ridiculous. In fact, the great Danish astronomer who was a contemporary of Kepler's, Tycho Brahe, who was far more familiar with the observational data than Kepler ever was, never saw in the data any evidence that he could consider as being decisive that the planets moved in anything but circular orbits. Tycho Brahe remained a Ptolemaic astronomer to his dying day.

Or what about Newton? How did he establish his first law of motion? Was it by observing any number of physical bodies that were not acted upon by any external forces yet continued indefinitely in motion or at rest; and from this observation generalizing that all bodies not acted upon by an external force must continue indefinitely in motion or at rest? Of course not, for the idea of such a procedure in Newton's case is absurd.[10]

Moreover, what we thus recognize as being characteristic of the use of the hypothetico-deductive method in science—that in its initial stages it is, as the current saying goes, radically and completely "underdetermined" by experience—does this not remind one of our earlier discussion of Descartes and of his seemingly high-handed reduction of the physical properties of natural bodies to mere geometrical properties? For what was Descartes' empirical evidence for such a reduction?[11] Presumably, there was none, the reduction being carried out, not on the basis of any evidence but only in virtue of a dogmatic Cartesian decree.

Empirical Tests for Scientific Theories

Of course, it is true—and this is an integral part of Popper's account of the use of the hypothetico-deductive method in science—that no sooner is an explanatory hypothesis in science devised and invented by the great scientific genius than at once that theory or hypothesis is recognized as having all sorts of deducible consequences, which could well turn out to be observable consequences as well. Thus if the planets do move in elliptical rather than in circular orbits, this would surely make a difference so far as the observable positions of the various planets at various times are concerned. In addition, if one is ever to know whether a proposed explanatory hypothesis about possible occurrences or happenings of events in nature does indeed offer a fruitful explanation of what goes on in nature, as opposed to being a wild guess that has little or no relevance to the facts, it certainly will be necessary to put that hypothesis to some sort of test of experience.

Indeed, by the very logic of the situation, this testing can be done in either of two ways. Either one can test the hypothesis by showing that

10. Newton contended that he never invented or devised hypotheses, although when it is considered what Newton understood by a hypothesis, I do not believe either that Newton's own pronouncement must be qualified or rejected or that my use of Newton as an example needs to be seriously altered.

11. This notion of the "underdetermination of a theory by empirical data" has become current in contemporary philosophy of science largely, no doubt, as a result of Quine's influence. See Mary Hesse, *Revolutions and Reconstructions in the Philosophy of Science* (Bloomington, 1980), esp. viii.

the predicted consequences actually do occur, which, as we know, is called trying to *verify* the hypothesis; or one can produce evidence to show that some or all of the predicted consequences do not in fact occur, which is called *falsifying* the hypothesis. Unfortunately, both of these methods have, as a result of recent investigations in the logic of science, been shown to have not just palpable weaknesses but insuperable weaknesses as well. Thus Popper himself pointed out that the attempt to prove a hypothesis by verifying it commits the simple and elementary logical fallacy of affirming the consequent. Thus the mere fact that the predicted consequences of, say, Einstein's hypothesis do in fact occur no more proves the truth of that hypothesis than it might be supposed that I could prove myself to be a true genius merely on the grounds that any and every genius is bound to act oddly at times, and I certainly do act oddly, not just some of the time but perhaps even all of the time.

And so because hypotheses cannot be established by a process of supposedly verifying them, Popper proposed that practicing scientists should follow a method of ever trying to falsify, or knock out, theories or hypotheses that had earlier been propounded by great scientific geniuses and innovators. Thus if certain of the predicted consequences of Kepler's or Newton's or Einstein's theories or hypotheses should be found upon investigation not to occur, that certainly would serve to upset any such hypothesis as was thus in question. And indeed, this proposed procedure for scientific investigation, of ever trying to falsify any or all of the regnant hypotheses, is certainly an impeccable procedure logically. To be sure, such a reliance by scientists upon a procedure of falsification of hypotheses would have as its consequence that, considered as a cognitive enterprise, so-called scientific investigations could never even in principle inform us as to what is the case with respect to nature and the natural world; they could only inform us of what is not the case. But at least, this would be something. Besides, if science were to be regarded as ever proceeding through repeated efforts at falsifying hypotheses in the light of the data, one could then no longer say that science was completely "underdetermined" by experience.

But even this solution will not do. For upon further reflection it turns out that science may not even rely upon a process of falsification as a sufficient means of ensuring that science will have at least some base in experience and in empirical observation, even if only an indirect one. For in subsequent developments in the history and logic of science since

Popper's heyday—and much to the embarrassment of Popper—a number of thinkers, most notably Thomas Kuhn perhaps, have astutely pointed out that the method of falsification of hypotheses is in its way no more satisfactory or reliable for scientists to follow than is the method of verification. For although it is true that logically there is nothing amiss with trying to falsify a hypothesis, practically it turns out that there never can be a properly definitive falsification of a hypothesis. And the reason is that the great overarching scientific hypotheses and theories that we are talking about are not just explanations of data, they are actually ways of seeing the data, in the sense that, so far from the theories having to conform to the data, it is rather the data that come to take on the color of, and thus to be found to conform to, and thereby to confirm, the theories. To draw on still a rather crude analogy, we all know that when we put on jaundiced glasses everything that we see is bound to appear yellow: the objects that we see through our glasses are not really yellow, and yet there is no way that they will appear as anything other than yellow as long as we keep on the glasses. In other words, so far from the data of observation being able to falsify the theory in terms of which we come to see and to apprehend these data, it is rather that the data will appear the way they do because of the theory through which we view them. And what does this mean but that there can never be any proper or definitive falsification of scientific theory and that, simply because if the data take on the character and color that the theory assigns to them and are then seen through the eyes of the theory, they will invariably confirm the theory and never show themselves as being at variance with it. Little wonder that, though Tycho Brahe presumably observed the same astronomical data as Kepler, he nevertheless did not see them in the way Kepler did; to him they only confirmed the Ptolemaic scheme, whereas to Kepler they disconfirmed it.

Alas, though, consider the consequences of this turn of things: if no scientific theory or hypothesis can ever ultimately be either definitively confirmed or disconfirmed, either verified or falsified, by the facts or by the data of experience, then it is hard to see how any one scientific theory or hypothesis can be any better as an account of nature than any other. True, one theory might enable us to gain a better control over nature in terms of technology. And yet this is a far cry from saying that the one theory provides a truer or more accurate description of the way the nature of things really is in itself. In fact, the eminent contemporary Harvard philosopher W. V. Quine, I suspect rather puckishly, raises the question as to whether he might be better advised to believe in a world of physical objects, whose behavior is controlled by the laws of modern physics, or to believe in the world of Homer, where physical events and happenings were controlled by the Homeric gods. To such a question Quine answers:

> As an empiricist I continue to think of the conceptual scheme of science as a tool, ultimately, for predicting future experience in the light of past experience. Physical objects are conceptually imported into the situation as convenient intermediaries—not by definition in terms of experience, but simply as irreducible posits comparable, epistemologically, to the gods of Homer. For my part I do, qua lay physicist, believe in physical objects and not in Homer's gods; and I consider it a scientific error to believe otherwise. But in point of epistemological footing the physical objects and the gods differ only in degree and not in kind. Both sorts of entities enter our conception only as cultural posits. The myth of physical objects is epistemologically superior to most in that it has proved more efficacious than other myths as a device for working a manageable structure into the flux of experience.[12]

Might the Hypothetico-Deductive Method Serve as a Means of Defending Even Natural Law?

If the most up-to-the-minute scientific account of events in the physical world and of the laws that govern them cannot in principle claim to be one whit superior to an account of the happenings of the physical world through intervention by the gods of Homer, then how can it be claimed that the nonteleological account of nature of the modern scientist is in any way superior to the teleological account that was given by Aristotle? Or to put it otherwise, why not say that the physics or metaphysics of a natural teleology has just as much going for it as has the nonteleology of modern science?

If the answers to these questions should be in the affirmative, we would seem to be in a fair way toward surviving our own day of reckoning, which I earlier announced had now come upon us, and which we could no longer postpone having to face up to. For why need we

12. Willard Van Orman Quine, *From a Logical Point of View: Logico-Philosophical Essays* (Cambridge, Mass., 1953), 44.

worry any more about the apparent dual fact (1) that a natural-law ethic cannot but presuppose a teleology in nature, and yet (2) that such a natural teleology cannot be other than radically at variance with the nonteleological account of nature that is given by science? It would seem that we could now reply by merely noting that, given the implications of the modern scientist's reliance upon the hypothetico-deductive method, it turns out that a mechanical and nonteleological view of nature, which is taken as basic in science, can claim not the slightest evidential superiority over the older Aristotelian teleological account. And yet who is there among us who, from childhood, has not been indoctrinated with the prejudice that this older teleological account was displaced and was forever superseded, once modern science had made its advent upon the scene in the seventeenth century?

But now, if we take our cue from Thomas Kuhn's analysis of what he calls the "structure of scientific revolutions," we should be able to say that when in the seventeenth century the scientists nearly all tended to forsake the older Aristotelian teleological account of nature in favor of the newer nonteleological account that was proposed by someone like Descartes, so far from this representing anything that could properly be called a scientific advance, it actually represented what Kuhn would call a "scientific revolution." After all, as Kuhn would construe them, scientific revolutions are not brought on as a result of the uncovering of new evidence either in confirmation of a new scientific theory or world-view or in disconfirmation of an older theory. Rather, it is as though scientists had tired of working with their older paradigm, which had heretofore governed their investigations, and had come to embrace a new paradigm, for scarcely any other reason than the sense of relief, to say nothing of the zest and exaltation, that come with doing something new and different.

Accordingly, with respect to our own situation, in which we are now called upon to infuse new funds into our defense of natural law to make good on our borrowed capital, why do we not take Kuhn's analysis of the structure of scientific revolutions at face value? We would then need to make no bones of the fact that any natural-law ethic must necessarily presuppose a natural teleology; and a natural teleology, in turn, is not reconcilable with the nonteleological outlook of the modern scientists. But why concern ourselves over that, for when we go back and reconsider the circumstances of the transition in the seventeenth century from a teleological world-view to a nonteleological one, we can assure ourselves that such a transition was not a reasoned one, or one based on evidence, so much as it was a scientific revolution in the Kuhnian sense.

Accordingly, could we not now propose a reverse transition, or, if you will, a counterrevolution, to take place at the end of the twentieth century, which would in a measure undo what was done in the seventeenth-century revolution? After all, if such a counter scientific revolution is necessary to salvage ethics in our own day, why not proclaim this counterrevolution, particularly if it has to be admitted that, as judged by the terms of the hypothetico-deductive method, there do not seem to be—and indeed there could not be—any good and sufficient scientific reasons against it?

"Oh, but this will never do," you will say. And indeed, I would be the first to agree. For just how, in my attempted defense of natural law, could I ever suppose that I had bettered my position if it now turns out that, by using the resources of the hypothetico-deductive method, it is possible to take heart somewhat at the negative reassurance that my natural-law view may at least be no worse off than any other view? Besides, there is the further consideration that seems to be almost the obverse of the first. For what profit comes from knowing that my view is in no worse evidential straits than any other view, no matter how prestigious that other view may be, if by the same token it becomes equally apparent that my view is no better off than any other, no matter how farfetched that other view may be?

Besides, there is perhaps still a further adverse consideration that may be raised against my implied argument for a natural teleology in terms of the hypothetico-deductive method. It should not be forgotten that although Quine, for example, may not think that the "myth of physical objects" has any better "epistemological footing" than does the myth of the Homeric gods, he at the same time has no hesitation in opting for the myth of physical objects and in counseling others to do so as well.

Moreover, the moral of such a counsel, at least so far as Quine is concerned, is that if one myth is superior to another on the basis of pragmatic considerations, then one need no longer bother one's head about any superiority or inferiority in terms of those more traditional, and presumably old-fashioned, concerns having to do with what Quine calls the "epistemological footing" of the new theory. For if the new theory has pragmatic considerations going for it, such as those having to do with advances in technology or with our greater control over the events in nature, there could be little argument that the nonteleological account of nature that is favored by the scientists (and by Quine as well) is far superior to any account involving any old-fashioned Aristotelian teleology. For certainly even in my wildest dreams I would never claim that Aristotle's teleological account of nature could ever be made to pay off in greater technological productivity than does the nonteleology of the modern scientists!

A Basic Difference in Method between Science and Philosophy

Perhaps, though, the problem is not a question of the disabilities that might be said to attach to the use of the hypothetico-deductive method as a means of defending an Aristotelian teleology and philosophy of nature. For in addition, it could prove to be wrongheaded for me, or for anyone else, to try to carry over a method of investigation that has proved itself in science into the domain of philosophy. For the objectives of philosophical knowledge could be radically different from those of scientific knowledge; and to mix up the two might only make for a "confusion worse confounded."

Moreover, anticipating what the differences in objective between a philosophical knowledge and a scientific knowledge of nature might turn out to be, let us begin with the following suggestion: although a philosophical knowledge of nature and the natural world aims at an account of nature or the world as it really is, for a scientific knowledge of nature such a realism is largely irrelevant, if not misleading. In other words, from the point of view of science and of scientific method generally—at least in terms of the hypothetico-deductive method—it makes no difference what the world of nature, or the things of nature, are really like so long as the account of nature which the scientist gives is found to pay off pragmatically—that is, in affording us a control over nature.

The Analogy between the Hypothetico-deductive Method as Used in Science and Kant's Proposed Transcendental Method for Philosophy

Accordingly, to confirm this contention as to the basic difference in method and in objective between science and philosophy, let us consider a number of apparently significant implications of the use of the hypothetico-deductive method in science, which many contemporary philosophers of science seem to have been hesitant to recognize. Thus it would seem that one could surely say with confidence that as soon as one reflects upon the matter a bit, it suddenly becomes apparent that the hypothetico-deductive method, as it has come to be used in science, is thoroughly Kantian in its import and implications. I would go even further and insist that the hypothetico-deductive method is but another manifestation, albeit in a new and different guise, of that celebrated transcendental turn in philosophy of which Kant was the author and to which so many philosophers since Kant have found themselves to be strangely drawn, not to say even addicted.

Thus why not just briefly recall the First Critique? Having become skeptical that as human knowers we could ever come to know nature and reality as they really are in themselves, Kant conceived of his project as being largely one of persuading us to be content with a knowledge only of the way things appear to us to be (when seen through the medium of the Pure Forms of Intuition and of the Understanding) and thus not of things as they really are in themselves. Kant would have us be satisfied with a knowledge of mere appearances (*phenomena*) and not any knowledge of reality (*noumena*).

Equally important are the characteristic Kantian reassurances that are held out to us if we accept that shift in perspective with respect to human knowledge that Kant would have us adopt. For what does Kant's Copernican Revolution in philosophy in the main vouchsafe to us if not that, being ever frustrated in our longtime human efforts to bring our theories and ideas into conformity with objects (that is, with reality or with objects as they really are), we can now obviate this frustration by occupying ourselves henceforth with the far more hopeful and fruitful business of bringing objects into conformity with our theories and ideas.[13]

And is not this essentially the very program that is put forward by the advocates of the hypothetico-deductive method? Thus as we saw earlier, the hypotheses and theories that we human beings (and especially the scientists) advance to gain what they call an understanding of

13. Immanuel Kant, *Critique of Pure Reason*, trans. Norman Kemp Smith (London, 1929), Preface to 2nd ed., esp. B XVI–XVIII.

nature, as well as a certain control over nature, are not put forward with either empirical or demonstrative evidence in their support. As Popper says, they are simply dreamed up, or made up out of whole cloth, like so many inventions of the mind. And do we not find somewhat the same thing with Kant? For where do the Kantian Categories come from, in terms of which the whole of our experience is supposedly ordered and shaped and molded? They certainly do not come from facts. Rather, they represent the equipment, or the machinery of the mind, in terms of which everything that the mind comes to know is ordered and structured and even in a way fabricated according to the scheme of the Categories. In other words, the Categories, so far from being derived from our experience of the facts, are rather the conditions under which the facts of our experience come to have the character they have.

Besides, may we not also recall how, on the account I have already given of scientific hypotheses—at least as such hypotheses are construed within the context of the hypothetico-deductive method—that the same hypotheses are not subject to decisive verifications or falsifications in experience? And is this not again somewhat in like case with Kant? For within the Kantian framework, it makes no sense to talk about the possibility of either verifying or falsifying the Categories. Instead, to borrow the felicitous phrase that G. J. Warnock hit upon some years back (albeit he employed it in a somewhat different connection): Kant's Categories represent only our human "way of seeing" the facts and not in any sense any new discovery of what the facts might be in themselves. (Warnock's wording suggests a contrast between "new ways of seeing the facts," as opposed to "seeing new facts."[14]) Surely, though, this sounds very like what we hear the partisans of the hypothetico-deductive method saying all of the time: the great overarching hypotheses that the scientific genius puts forward are not to be reckoned as discoveries or disclosures of what experience reveals to be so in the facts; rather, they represent only our own constructions that we have placed upon the facts, which accordingly result in the facts coming to be seen in such various new ways as our different hypotheses will determine.

True, Kant thought of his Categories as deducible (by virtue of the "Metaphysical Deduction") from the Table of Judgments in logic. And therefore, for Kant the Categories were like "the law of the Medes and

14. G. J. Warnock, *English Philosophy Since 1900* (London, 1958), 136–37.

Persians that altereth not." But for our latter-day advocates of the hypothetico-deductive method, although one might think of the major theories and hypotheses of science as being like so many surrogate Kantian Categories, they are categories that we human beings can change or alter practically at will. In fact, if we take seriously what Kuhn says about the structure of scientific revolutions, any change of paradigms, or any shift in our categorical scheme or in our world-views can be effected largely at will. This is indeed why Kuhn calls such categorical shifts "revolutions," which is to say that they are not logical progressions based on facts or evidence.

And while we are pushing the analogy between the hypothetico-deductive method, as applied to modern science, and Kant's proposed transcendental method in philosophy, why could we not go even further and insist upon an analogy between Kant's transcendental deduction of his categories and the pragmatic justification that Quine and others would appear to want to invoke in support of modern scientific theories and hypotheses. For much as Kant insisted that without the use of the Categories, which he held to be the categorial equipment of the human mind, there would not be any world, or even any experience, for human beings, it being thus in a sense we ourselves who create and construct the objects of our human experience, so also the contemporary partisans of the use of the hypothetico-deductive method as regards modern science would say that our only justification for accepting such hypotheses as the scientists have propounded is that these hypotheses enable us to introduce certain patterns of order into the data of our experience so that we may thereby gain a more sure control over nature in the manner of modern technology. In other words, neither for Kant nor for the modern proponents of the hypothetico-deductive method are our human world-views or theories of nature literally true, in the sense that they represent the way things really are in themselves, or in nature, or in reality. It is rather that we hold them to be true for no other reason than that they pay off—that is, either they enable us to introduce a certain intelligible order into what otherwise would be the "booming, buzzing confusion" of our unstructured experience (so the Kantians); or they at least assure us of a possible technological control over the so-called forces of nature (so the latter-day proponents of the hypothetico-deductive method).

In neither case, however—either of Kant's transcendental deduction or of the pragmatic justification of modern scientific theories—may

239

one say that the theories or the laws of nature that thus come to be "deduced" or "justified" can claim to disclose the way things really are in themselves or purport to represent what nature is really like independently of us. Quite the contrary; given any variant on a Kantian transcendentalism, the world of nature that emerges for us within the context of this transcendental turn in philosophy is precluded from being the world as it really is in itself. Rather, it is only the world as it appears to be, or a result of the ordering principles and frameworks that we impose upon it and import into it. In this sense, the world as it is for us is the world as we human knowers make it to be—even as we create it for ourselves—inasmuch as we have fashioned it according to our own categories and our own theories and our own world-views.

Transcendentalism Will Never Do in Philosophy

And now what may be the implications of this approximation of the hypothetico-deductive method in science to the Kantian transcendental method in philosophy, that Kant would recommend for human knowledge generally? Why could we not simply say that although the use of a transcendental method (for example, the hypothetico-deductive method) may be just fine for science, it will not do in philosophy? True, Kant would never admit of such an excepting of philosophical knowledge from the scope of his transcendental method. But *pace* Kant, I think that it can and must be so excepted.

First, though, let us consider why a reliance upon a transcendental method of knowledge such as is manifest in the hypothetico-deductive method of the scientists is in all ways appropriate for natural science. And to this end, why not recall once more the criteria of truth in science, as represented by Quine? Are they any more than merely pragmatic criteria? Thus Quine insists that there are, in the final analysis, no other reasons for our accepting any scientific theory or hypothesis save that it gets results; and by results, Quine might be taken to mean that it pays off in the practical consequences that the theory or the hypothesis has with respect to our greater human mastery or control over nature. But if this is what counts as truth in science, why need the scientist worry about the truth of his theories in any traditional sense—as, for example, whether they are able to get at the reality behind the appearances? No, all that matters is whether a scientific theory works, not whether it is true or whether it tells us the way the things of nature really are in themselves.

Contrast the philosopher, though. With him it would seem that it would need to be almost the opposite of what it is with the scientist. For it can never be claimed that philosophy pays off in terms of technology; instead, the aim of philosophy can only be to know the nature of things or to come to know the truth about nature and reality as they are in themselves. Thus in my attempted defense of a natural-law ethic, I have repeatedly insisted in any number of different contexts that ethics must be based on fact, that *moral* "oughts" need to be shown to have their foundation in *natural* "oughts," and that our human obligations and responsibilities demand verification in terms of the realities of nature and our characteristic human situation within nature. In short, with respect to moral philosophy, as contrasted with natural science, one cannot rest content with what merely appears to be so. Indeed, if you tell a person that his obligations are apparent and not real, it is hardly to be expected that he will take such obligations seriously if he thinks he can get away with doing otherwise.

Nor is that all, for in the course of my earlier argument I repeatedly had occasion to see how, in many cases of contemporary ethical theory—for example, in so-called ethical teleology and ethical deontology—the effort was made to find what might be called mere surrogate facts that could do duty for the real facts of nature, as if the former might be able to prove a sufficient foundation for ethics, without our having to worry about the latter. But no, such a move never worked: the surrogate facts were unable to do duty for real facts of nature. In other words, ethics can rest on nothing else than natural laws; nor is it ever possible to know what such laws of nature really are, unless one can muster up a physics or a natural philosophy that is able to disclose what the nature of things is, really and in itself. And to this end a reliance upon the hypothetico-deductive method of the modern scientist will never do. For being implicated as it is with Kant's transcendentalism, such a method is in principle incapable of ever establishing what the laws and facts of nature really are in themselves.

And now finally there is still another consideration that I adverted to somewhat earlier and that would seem to indicate decisively that if philosophy allows itself to make anything like a Kantian transcendental turn, it must inevitably follow that any attempt to find a proper justification for morals and ethics will thereby become hopelessly compromised.

True, at first sight and perhaps on a more superficial level, anyone who might wish to find support for a natural-law ethics, for example, might be tempted to argue that it might be possible to treat a natural teleology (such as might be needed to defend a natural-law ethics) like a hypothesis, or another way of looking at the world, alternative to the way the modern scientist tends to look at it. Therefore, it would seem that one would need only to invoke the hypothetico-deductive method as an instrument in support of a view of nature and the natural world quite different from the fashionable scientific view. Indeed, since no hypothesis or world-view conceived in such a context would need admit to being any worse off, or to have any less evidence going for it, than any other and competing world-view, why would this not enable us to look at the world through the spectacles of a natural teleology, rather than through those of a Cartesian mechanism or antiteleology?

But if a would-be defender of natural law were to avail himself of such a device, he would in effect be consigning himself to living in a fool's paradise. For no sooner would he avail himself of the hypothetico-deductive method than he would soon find himself maneuvered out of "the way of Aristotle" and headed right down "the way of Nietzsche" instead—and that would be nothing less than "the primrose way to everlasting bonfire." I have already indicated the disaster that this way to Nietzsche could lead to.[15] But let us again recount the steps toward that disaster. For surely, the way of Nietzsche—at least as a number of recent philosophers would conceive it to be—is a way that would seem to rely upon the hypothetico-deductive method. And what else must the use of such a method in such a context imply unless it is that there cannot possibly be any decisive objective evidence in support of any one such hypothesis as against any other?

What, then, will determine our choice of, say, any one basic hypothesis over another? Will it be anything other than such chance values as we happen to have, which will accordingly lead us to prefer one hypothesis over another? But is this not tantamount to saying that our choice of hypothesis will reflect our own will to power—that is, our will to make our own particular values prevail, "our" values here meaning

15. See Chapter II, notes 1 and 2.

such arbitrarily chosen values as those simply of ourselves, or of our own particular in-group, our class, our culture, or whatever?

In other words, the way the world is—at least on this Nietzschean variant on a Kantian transcendentalism—will be a world that is cut entirely to the specifications that he whose will to power has become dominant will prescribe for everyone else and thus will presumably be able to brainwash everyone else into accepting. In other words, where else does the way of Nietzsche lead if not into the nightmare of a *1984*, where nothing will ever be the way it really is but only the way Big Brother or the Party says it is to be?

Two Final Difficulties

Need I say more by way of stressing that although a Kantian transcendental turn may well be a turn that contemporary scientists will and do choose to make—nor is there any reason why, *qua* scientists, they should not make such a choice with impunity, so long as they do not become imperialistic about it—it is not a turn that philosophers ought to allow themselves to indulge in. For philosophy, it would seem, cannot but remain committed to an unequivocal realism, not just in matters of ethics but in matters of physics and metaphysics as well. In fact, if, as so many contemporary philosophers of science would appear to imply, the proper method of science is the hypothetico-deductive method, and if, as I have been insisting, the hypothetico-deductive method inevitably commits its users to a Kantian transcendentalism, then where else can we turn if not to philosophy, supposing that what we are looking for is a knowledge of nature and of the things of nature as they really are, and not merely of such things as they are made to appear to be in view of the hypotheses and categories and theories in terms of which we human beings structure our experience? For if we cannot rely upon philosophy to provide us with a knowledge of being and of reality and of the way the world really is, then, as I have argued repeatedly, we will really be undone, so far as ethics is concerned. For there can be no knowledge of ethics without a knowledge of nature; and without a knowledge of ethics, all our human institutions of law and politics will be no more than "a tale told by an idiot, full of sound and fury, signifying nothing."

Unhappily, though, I can imagine everyone responding to this idea with skepticism if not with derision. For how can anyone claim that there is a legitimate philosophical knowledge that is a proper knowledge in its own right and is completely independent of science, being beholden to science in no way, either in fact or in principle? Nor is that all. For even if the independence and autonomy and reliability of a distinctively philosophical knowledge could ever be established, would it not have to be admitted that it could not help coming into conflict with a scientific knowledge? After all, consider my oft-repeated example: the world as seen from the standpoint of science is a mechanistic and non-teleological universe, whereas as seen from the standpoint of philosophy that same world is reckoned to be permeated with teleology. And how, pray tell, can such conflicting views ever be reconciled with one another, save in terms of some untenable doctrine of "two truths"?

An Illustration of How Natural Philosophy Might Yield a Partial Knowledge of Nature

Why do we not simply turn to Aristotle for examples of how philosophy can provide us with a genuine, if limited, knowledge of nature, and a knowledge of nature that does not rely upon the hypothetico-deductive method? Thus in the *Physics* does not Aristotle adduce both evidence and argument in support of the fact that substances in the natural world are subject to change, that they do indeed undergo change upon occasion, and that when they change, what is involved is always and necessarily a change *of* something, *from* its having been something, *to* its being something else? Clearly also, for anything thus to undergo change and to become other and different from what it was—be it in quantity, quality, place, or even substance—it must have had what can only be called a capacity or a natural potentiality thus to become other and different. Without such a potentiality, the object could not change; it could not become other and different. And of course, too, such potentialities as substances in the natural world do in fact have will naturally be ordered to their appropriate actualities, as if in each case such an actuality were what the substance in question might be, or could be, and in this sense could even be said to be ordered to being as its final cause.

But note when Aristotle argues in this way, and thus lays out these obvious considerations, he is not propounding a hypothesis in explanation of his observations. Rather, he is simply describing or reporting

244

what does take place and what the factors—the principles and the causes—are in the changes that occur in the natural world. So far from dreaming up or inventing any hypothesis as to the necessary principles that enable change to take place—matter, form, and privation—he simply describes the factors that are evident in the facts of change and that upon reflection appear to be necessary factors or principles in all change.

Nor is it any less so as regards the so-called causes of change. For these are not put forth as if they were so many explanatory hypotheses, which, so far from being evident directly in the facts, have to be first invented, or fabricated, and then imported into the facts or read into them from the outside. And no more can there be any attempt to verify or falsify hypotheses for which originally there was no direct evidence. Instead, the empiricism of Aristotelian physics and metaphysics is of a kind that cannot be fitted into the scheme or framework of any hypothetico-deductive method.

Yes, even from this simple and seemingly all-too-elementary example of the Aristotelian account of the principles and causes of change in the natural world, why may we not definitely conclude that philosophy has nothing to do with and should have nothing to do with a hypothetico-deductive method? Although such a method may be entirely proper for the natural sciences, it is neither appropriate nor does it belong in philosophy. And once the hypothetico-deductive method thus comes to be extruded from philosophy "root and branch," then philosophy can claim to be free from the characteristic disability that inevitably accompanies the use of that method: the disability of being a knowledge that is only of appearances and not of reality.

In other words, if the scientists choose to make what I have called the transcendental turn, fine. Yes, if they want to insist that, rather than their theories and hypotheses having to conform to the way things and objects are in the natural world, it is rather that the things and objects of the natural world, at least as the scientists conceive them to be, have to conform to the specifications devised by the scientist and then simply read onto the facts—if such is the game that contemporary scientists want to play, so be it.[16] For why should the scientists not furnish

16. I do not mean to imply that no scientists or philosophers of science fail to attribute a realism to the enterprise of science, contrasted with the Kantian transcendentalism that seems to be entailed by a reliance upon the hypothetico-deduc-

their own house and keep it according to their own tastes? Nor am I suggesting that by conceiving of their scientific knowledge in the way they do, the scientists are in any way unjustified in boasting of their results. For the triumphs of modern technology are certainly to be ungrudgingly attributed to the achievements of modern science.

All the same, however the scientists may choose to furnish their own house, let them not presume to furnish the philosophers' house as well according to their own designs and specifications. For the method of philosophy cannot properly be a hypothetico-deductive method; nor is the knowledge of philosophy a function of Kantian transcendentalism. No, philosophical knowledge is an empirical and a realistic knowledge; and in terms of the brief examples I have drawn from Aristotelian physics, we can perhaps see how it is possible through philosophy, although not through science, that one can come to recognize that teleology is nothing if not a fact of nature. In addition, on the basis of such a fact of nature, one can also come to understand how a natural-law ethic is at once possible and justifiable in terms of such a natural teleology as is an inescapable fact of our natural world.

Granted that such a knowledge of nature as philosophy can thus afford is not, and can never be, even a particularly detailed knowledge, much less an exhaustive one. Nor is it such a knowledge as ever pays off in terms of technology. No, in all of these ways, philosophy must be said to offer but a comparatively slight knowledge of nature, involving little more than the most basic and general principles and causes. Nor do I propose here to try to explain why such a philosophical knowledge of nature is thus both limited and restricted. And yet that it is a legitimate and even a demonstrable knowledge as far as it goes; that it is a realistic knowledge in the sense that it discloses the way the world of nature really is or the way the things of nature really behave; and

---

tive method. Rom Harré and Edward Madden in their book *Causal Powers* (Oxford, 1975), or Father William Wallace in his book, *Causality and Scientific Explanation* (2 vols., Ann Arbor, 1974), insist that modern natural science is to be interpreted realistically. Nevertheless, this would seem not to be the prevailing view among modern philosophers of science. Instead, the fashion seems to be to go along with such authorities as Mary Hesse, who, in her *Revolutions and Reconstructions in the Philosophy of Science*, acknowledges that current scientific practice has discarded both the traditional scientific empiricism and the traditional scientific realism that were for so long held to be the hallmarks of modern natural science.

finally, that it is a knowledge that owes nothing to modern natural science or to the hypothetico-deductive method—these contentions I would reiterate, and with some confidence that I have cited convincing evidence in their support.

Is There a Conflict or Incompatibility between a Scientific Knowledge of Nature and a Philosophical Knowledge of Nature?

And now, will I be accused of a blatant, not to say an obnoxious, obscurantism? Thus I have presumably admitted that the knowledge that science attains through the use of the hypothetico-deductive method is an entirely legitimate type of knowledge. But I have also insisted that there can be, and is, a no less legitimate knowledge of nature that comes through philosophy and that such a philosophical knowledge owes little or nothing to the findings of modern science. But is it not patent and obvious that these two different forms of knowledge must often conflict? Indeed, have I not recognized that nature as the scientist describes it is nonteleological, whereas philosophy establishes that the changes that take place in nature both can be and are teleological? How, though, are such conflicts between these two different forms of knowledge to be reconciled with one another? Worse yet, would it not seem that I have argued that when the philosophical thesis of a natural teleology conflicts with the scientific thesis of a nonteleology, it is the latter that must give way before the former and yet that we must cling to the thesis of a natural teleology in order thereby to salvage a natural-law ethics. And what is that if not obscurantism?

But this reproach must surely be based upon a misunderstanding. For have I not been ever careful to point out that a scientific knowledge, being based on the hypothetico-deductive method, is a knowledge only of appearances, and hence not of nature as it really is in itself? In contrast, a philosophical knowledge, involving a straightforward empirical realism and avoiding reliance upon the hypothetico-deductive method, is nothing if not a knowledge of nature as it really is. But how, then, and why, need there be any incompatibility between these two?

True, modern science proclaims that there is no teleology and therefore no basis or foundation for morality anywhere in nature. And yet such a proclamation on the part of the scientist must be regarded as a proclamation in the form only of a hypothesis, which the scientist cannot pretend is an account of the way nature really is in itself. In short, it is a proclamation of the way the scientist chooses to look at nature and this for no other purpose or end than the purely pragmatic one of gaining a certain control over nature. But for the scientist to assert that that is the way nature really is would violate the precise constraints and constrictions that the use of the hypothetico-deductive method places upon its users—in this case the scientists.

Instead, if the scientist wants to know the way nature really is in itself, whether it is teleological or nonteleological, he must turn philosopher; and as a philosopher—at least as an Aristotelian philosopher—he must come to see in the light of the evidence of his everyday common-sense observations and reflections that nature is teleological. True, this philosophical knowledge that the philosopher—or the scientist qua philosopher—thereby comes to have of reality and the natural world in which he finds himself, although admittedly very limited and not a knowledge sufficient for anything like putting a man on the moon, is at the same time an entirely bona fide knowledge of what the world is really like and of what the true character of nature is. Nor is that all, for there is no denying that this same knowledge of nature which our philosopher may thus claim to have, *qua* philosopher, will be a knowledge of the very foundations in nature that underpin all our natural rights, our natural responsibilities, and our natural moral obligations as human beings.

And with that, is not the feared conflict between science and philosophy, or between nature conceived as nonteleological and nature conceived as teleological, successfully obviated? For what possible conflict or incompatibility need there be between knowing things on one level as they are in themselves and as our common sense experience reveals them to be, and knowing them on another level only as they are made to appear to be, as a result of our imposing upon the data our own classifications and ordering schemes, not for the purpose of knowing the truth about things but only of knowing how best to manipulate them to our own ends and to our own advantage?

Here there is no problem of "two truths." For what lent a real bite, if we might so term it, to that problem when it plagued the Latin Averroists, was that it was then apparently being claimed that there were two conflicting testimonies as to the character of one and the same world or reality, the one being a testimony based on revelation and the other based on natural knowledge.[17] And such truths, involving contradictory statements about one and the same thing, would scarcely seem reconcilable.

But by the account I am proposing, in which science and philosophy are of a different character, each with its own proper object, this conflict would not seem to exist. True, science proceeds by its method—call it the hypothetico-deductive method—and philosophy proceeds by its method—call it the method of a common-sense realism and empiricism. And the reality that is talked about in the two disciplines might seem in a sense to be the same, that of nature and the natural world. In another sense, though, what is discoursed about in science is not, or should not be, the same as what is discoursed about in philosophy: for in the one case it is nature only as it appears to be and as it is constructed and decked out and made to appear for purposes of the scientist's and the technologist's prediction and control; but in the other case, it is nature as it really is in itself. It is objective reality, in other words, and not reality as it is relative to the scientist's particular purpose and interests. But with such qualifications, why need the respective pronouncements about nature of a natural science and a natural philosophy be incompatible or irreconcilable, for it is not nature in the same sense that is being talked about?

With that, what more may I say in defense of natural law? This time the answer happily is, "Nothing—or at least not now."

17. For an account of this issue of "two truths," as it might be thought to have presented itself in the Middle Ages, see Etienne Gilson, *Reason and Revelation in the Middle Ages* (New York, 1938).

SELECTED BIBLIOGRAPHY

CLASSICAL TREATMENTS OF NATURAL LAW

Aquinas, St. Thomas. *Summa Theologiae*, esp. I–II, Qus. 90–100 (any edition).
Aristotle. *The Nicomachean Ethics* (any edition); *The Politics* (any edition).
Hooker, Richard. *The Laws of Ecclesiastical Polity*, esp. Bk. I (any edition).

BACKGROUND BOOKS IN MODERN MORAL, LEGAL, AND POLITICAL PHILOSOPHY

Hobbes, Thomas. *Leviathan* (any edition).
Locke, John. *Second Treatise of Government* (any edition).
Kant, Immanuel. *Foundations of the Metaphysics of Morals* (any edition).
———. *Critique of Practical Reason* (any edition).
Mill, John Stuart. *Utilitarianism* (any edition).

RECENT DISCUSSIONS OF NATURAL LAW

Crowe, Michael Bertram. *The Changing Profile of Natural Law*. The Hague, 1977.
Finnis, John. *Natural Law and Natural Rights*. Oxford, 1980.
Grisez, Germain. "The First Principle of Practical Reason: A Commentary on the *Summa Theologiae*, 1–2, Question 94, Article 2." *Natural Law Forum*, X (1965), 168–201. Unfortunately, Volume I of Grisez's mammoth and magisterial work, *The Way of Lord Jesus* (Chicago, 1983), came to hand too late for consideration in this book.
Strauss, Leo. *Natural Right and History*. Chicago, 1953.
Wild, John. *Plato's Modern Enemies and the Theory of Natural Law*. Chicago, 1953.

CURRENT DISCUSSIONS OF LEGAL AND POLITICAL PHILOSOPHY

Ackerman, Bruce A. *Social Justice in the Liberal State*. New Haven, 1980.
Dworkin, Ronald. *Taking Rights Seriously*. Cambridge, Mass., 1977.
Hart, H. L. A. *The Concept of Law*. Oxford, 1961.

Jenkins, Iredell. *Social Order and the Limits of Law: A Theoretical Essay*. Princeton, 1980.
Nozick, Robert. *Anarchy, State, and Utopia*. New York, 1974.
Rawls, John. *A Theory of Justice*. Cambridge, Mass., 1971.

CONTEMPORARY BOOKS IN ETHICS

Bourke, Vernon J. *Ethics: A Textbook in Moral Philosophy*. New York, 1958.
Donagan, Alan. *The Theory of Morality*. Chicago, 1977.
Finnis, John. *Fundamentals of Ethics*. Washington, D.C., 1983.
Frankena, William. *Ethics*. 2nd ed. Englewood Cliffs, N.J., 1973.
Gewirth, Alan. *Reason and Morality*. Chicago, 1978.
Hare, R. M. *The Language of Morals*. Oxford, 1952.
Harman, Gilbert. *The Nature of Morality: An Introduction to Ethics*. New York, 1977.
McInerney, Ralph. *Ethica Thomistica: The Moral Philosophy of Thomas Aquinas*. Washington, D.C., 1982.
MacIntyre, Alasdair. *After Virtue: A Study in Moral Theory*. Notre Dame, Ind., 1981.
Mackie, J. L. *Ethics: Inventing Right and Wrong*. Harmondsworth, 1977.
Porreco, Rocco, ed. *The Georgetown Symposium on Ethics: Essays in Honor of Henry Babcock Veatch*. Lanham, Md., 1984.
Robins, Michael H. *Promising, Intending, and Moral Autonomy*. Cambridge, 1984.
Veatch, Henry B. *For an Ontology of Morals: A Critique of Contemporary Ethical Theory*. Evanston, 1971.
Williams, Bernard. *Morality: An Introduction to Ethics*. New York, 1972.

BOOKS OF A MORE OR LESS LIBERTARIAN INSPIRATION

Den Uyl, Douglas, and Douglas Rasmussen, eds. *The Philosophic Thought of Ayn Rand*. Urbana, 1984.
Machan, Tibor. *Human Rights and Human Liberties: A Radical Reconstruction of the American Political Tradition*. Chicago, 1975.
———, ed. *The Libertarian Reader*. Totowa, N.J., 1982.
Norton, David L. *Personal Destinies: A Philosophy of Ethical Individualism*. Princeton, 1976.
Paul, Jeffrey, ed. *Reading Nozick: Essays on Anarchy, State, and Utopia*. Totowa, N.J., 1981.
Rothbard, Murray M. *The Ethics of Liberty*. Atlantic Highlands, N.J., 1982.

RECENT DISCUSSIONS OF ISSUES IN THE LOGIC AND PHILOSOPHY OF SCIENCE

Brown, Harold. *Perception, Theory and Commitment: The New Philosophy of Science*. Chicago, 1979.

Duhem, Pierre. *The Aim and Structure of Physical Theory.* Translated by Philip Wiener. Princeton, 1954.

Hanson, Norwood Russell. *Patterns of Discovery: An Enquiry into the Conceptual Foundations of Science.* Cambridge, 1958.

Harré, Rom, and Edward H. Madden. *Causal Powers: A Theory of Natural Necessity.* Oxford, 1975.

Hesse, Mary. *Revolutions and Reconstructions in the Philosophy of Science.* Bloomington, 1980.

Kuhn, Thomas S. *The Structure of Scientific Revolutions.* 2nd ed. Chicago, 1970.

Popper, Karl R. *Conjectures and Refutations: The Growth of Scientific Knowledge.* New York, 1962.

———. *The Logic of Scientific Discovery.* New York, 1961.

Quine, Willard Van Orman. *From a Logical Point of View: Logico-Philosophical Essays.* Cambridge, Mass., 1953.

———. *Word and Object.* New York, 1960.

Wallace, William A. *Causality and Scientific Explanation.* 2 vols. Ann Arbor, 1972–74.

———. *From a Realist Point of View: Essays on the Philosophy of Science.* Washington, D.C., 1979.

INDEX

Ackerman, Bruce A., 5, 157
Actuality: concept of, 69
Alcibiades, 74, 76
Analytical Philosophy: failure of, 49
Anarchism: and recognition of rights, 202
Aquinas, St. Thomas: and concept of freedom, 107; ethics of, 25, 26; on friendship, 131n; on law, 54–55, 59, 113–14, 115, 135, 210; on practical reason, 70, 70n; on relation between desire and moral obligation, 19; on the good, 69, 70; mentioned, 20n, 54, 69n, 102, 103, 104, 137, 154, 173, 221
Aristotle: concept of happiness of, 79, 151–52; concept of natural law of, 49, 53–55; concept of natural justice of, 2; critics of, 104–105; on creativity in human life, 106; on distinctions between nature and art, 65; on distinction between potentiality and actuality, 69; on freedom, 106, 107, 147, 176; on friendship, 131; on knowledge, 74n, 214n; on morality, 83, 109; on political nature of man, 116, 119, 125, 134; on proper human action, 77–78, 81, 82, 110, 122; teleology of, 101, 236; view of nature of, 56, 222–25, 234; mentioned, 50, 63, 91, 92, 98, 102, 104, 123, 150, 154, 163n, 184, 189, 210, 227, 233, 242, 244, 246, 248
—works of: *Nicomachean Ethics*, 77–78, 102, 110; *Physics*, 223, 244–45; *Politics*, 116, 147, 176

Art: and morality, 105, 108–109; and nature, 63–67; of living, 74n, 82–84, 123
Austen, Jane, 73, 87, 90, 91, 111, 112, 204
Authority: role of, in pursuit of common good, 138–39

Behavior: as determined by law of nature, 60–61
Bentham, Jeremy, 3, 155
Bible, 17–18, 50, 83, 132, 172, 187, 188
Blackstone, William, 3, 158–59, 199, 203
Brahe, Tycho, 229, 232
Bush, Douglas, 111

Charity: obligation to perform, 187, 188, 189; vs. rights, 195
Children: rights of, 195–96, 198
Commandments, Ten, 17
Common good: and individual rights, 156–57, 197–212 *passim*; and *polis*, 125–26, 127, 148, 185; and welfare state, 186; components of, 120; differentiated from Utilitarianism, 154–56; obligation of community to work for, 188; obligation of individuals to work for, 206–207; reasons for pursuit of, 149, 150; role of, in individual *telos*, 120–22, 126–27, 128, 129, 130, 133–34, 150, 151, 153
Constitution, U.S., 1, 2, 3, 7, 11, 38, 39
Constructivist fallacy, 137
Contract, social, 4, 9–11, 18–19, 32, 36–37

255